'If you feel like you have lost your sparkle then this wonderful, exuberant book is here to help. Underpinned by sound scientific understanding it is jam-packed with all the tools you need to shine brightly and live your best, most colourful life.'
Becky Goddard-Hill, psychotherapist and author of Be Happy, Be You

'Tanith Carey has the rare ability to make psychology, biochemistry and neuroscience not only accessible but also vastly entertaining and intellectually stimulating. I devoured this book in one greedy sitting.'
Jane Alexander, journalist and author of The Energy Secret *and* Ancient Wisdom for Modern Living

'At last. A scientific explanation of feeling "meh". This book is unique. Brilliantly researched and written.'
Alice Smellie, menopause campaigner and author of Cracking the Menopause

'Tanith has a unique way of communicating scientific jargon with ease, simplicity, and clarity. *Feeling "Blah"?* is a must read!'
Professor Hana Burianová, professor of neuroscience, department of psychology, Bournemouth University

'The book is evidence based, gives a name to how people feel and then offers options for change. No "motherhood and apple pie" here but sound well researched techniques that have been evaluated and offered for consideration.'
Averil Leimon, author, executive coach, and leadership psychologist at White Water Group

'As this is the first book for the general reader on anhedonia, I love that it also has practical elements full of useful guidance for those who are in this state of mind.'
Lohani Noor, psychotherapist

'Often women in menopause do feel "blah" and don't understand that fluctuating and the eventual flat-lining of hormones can play a huge part. It's fabulous to see Tanith addressing this. I loved it.'
Christien Bird MSc, women's health physiotherapist and co-founder of Menopause Movement

'A clear and compelling overview of anhedonia that will be a Godsend to those who have it. I highly recommend it!'
Jackie Kelm, author of Appreciative Living *and creator of the Anhedonia Support Program at www.AnhedoniaSupport.com*

'The best way to deal with a problem is to look at it and to understand it from many different perspectives. Tanith has risen to the task.'
Deanne Jade, psychologist, founder and principal, National Centre for Eating Disorders

FEELING 'BLAH'?

Why Anhedonia Has Left You Joyless
and How to Recapture Life's Highs

by Tanith Carey

WELBECK
BALANCE

Published in 2023 by Welbeck Balance
An imprint of Welbeck Trigger Ltd
Part of Welbeck Publishing Group
Offices in: London – 20 Mortimer Street, London W1T 3JW &
Sydney – 205 Commonwealth Street, Surry Hills 2010
www.welbeckpublishing.com

A CIP catalogue record for this book is available from the British Library.

ISBN
978-1-80129-237-5

Typeset by Lapiz Digital Services
Printed in Great Britain by CPI Group (UK) Ltd, Croydon CRO 4YY

10 9 8 7 6 5 4 3 2 1

FSC
www.fsc.org

MIX
Paper | Supporting
responsible forestry
FSC® C171272

Contents

Introduction   vii

Part One: What is Anhedonia and Why Does it Happen?

1. What Does Anhedonia Look Like?   3
2. Blame Your Ancestors: Why our Stone Age Brains
    Make it Hard to be Happy   13
3. How the Modern World Makes Joy More Elusive   35
4. How Your Childhood May be Standing in the
    Way of Experiencing Joy Today   49

Part Two: What Anhedonia Means for You

5. Physical Reasons for Feeling "Blah"   71
6. What's Happening in Your Brain?   108
7. How Anhedonia Can Affect Different Pleasures   128

**Part Three: How to Feel Fully Alive Again: Solutions
                to Feeling "Blah"**

8. Getting Back on the Same Side as our Brains   149
9. Does Happiness Happen to You – or Do You
    Make It?   158
10. How to Get Going Again   168
11. How to Harness Your Happiness Chemicals   198
12. How to Create a Lifestyle That Beats "Blah"   219

Conclusion   260
Acknowledgements   265
Further Reading and Support   268
Reference Sources   270

About the Author

Tanith Carey is an award-winning writer and author of 12 books on psychology, parenting and social history which have been published in over 35 languages. Her pieces are published in newspapers and magazines across the world, ranging from the *Daily Telegraph* and *The Sunday Times* to *The Spectator* and the *Sydney Morning Herald*. As a speaker, Tanith has addressed audiences on platforms ranging from BBC Radio 4 to The Cheltenham Science Festival and the Child Mind Institute in Palo Alto, California. Tanith also holds a Certificate in Therapeutic Skills and Studies.

Introduction

How much do you like your life? To what extent are you enjoying and to what extent are you enduring it? Do you feel fully alive, or do you feel you are just going through the motions?

If you are reading this book because you were drawn to the word "blah" on the cover, you probably don't feel depressed (or you'd be reading a book with that on the front.) This feels different. Maybe it's more that when you are at social events you are supposed to enjoy, everyone else appears to be having a better time than you. Or perhaps you feel strangely uncomfortable when others seem to be having fun and that nagging feeling that your life should "feel" better than it does just won't go away.

Does the world no longer seem to be in glorious technicolour and more in a palette of muted greys? Instead of being in sharp focus, does it appear as if you are standing on the other side of frosted glass?

If you recognize any of these feelings and struggle to remember the last time you let go, or laughed – really laughed, until your sides ached – then I get it.

Because until I worked out what this feeling was, I was the same as you.

My own feeling of "blah"

For a long time, I didn't know there was a name for these feelings, or rather lack of them, either. The closest words were half-hearted monosyllables like "blah" and "meh". Then I got a phone call which made me think that surely there must be a better description for this non-state of being. The moment when this dawned on me a few years ago is going to sound insufferably smug, but bear with me and hold your judgement because that's precisely the point.

After months of research for a book I'd always wanted to write, honing the pitch and going to various meetings, I got a call from my agent. Good news, she announced. A major publisher (my biggest to date) had said they wanted the book and were offering a generous five-figure sum. As she delivered the news I'd been hoping for, I heard myself making all the right noises.

"Brilliant … fantastic … amazing!" Yet far from feeling the surge of joy I was expecting, it felt like these words were coming from some disembodied version of myself.

Actually, I felt nothing much at all.

When I finished the call, I knew I should have felt elated. Instead, I felt flat. This didn't make sense. After all, I wasn't depressed. I was a get-up-and-go, get-sh*t-done career woman, with a lovely husband, two healthy, happy children and I'd just ticked off another life goal. Yet, far from feeling happiness course through me, the only sensations I felt were mild panic that I'd just landed myself a giant task for my to-do list and a dollop of guilt that I didn't feel more grateful. As I set off to pick up my daughters from school, all I could think about was: "Tanith, what the hell is wrong with you?"

After that day, I started to notice this strange disconnect more and more. I felt indifferent at parties and social events. While everyone around me looked like they were having a great time, I felt I had to put on a mask. I had always loved Christmas, but at times even raising some yuletide cheer felt like a charade.

In the middle of this, I unwittingly described anhedonia in a cri-de-cœur I wrote for *The Times* describing the pressures of modern working motherhood. Throughout, I scattered words like "numb", "zombie" and "blur", not realizing there was a name for what they all added up to.

The fact I wasn't enjoying my life defied logic. After all, I'd played the game well. I was racing through the checklist of a "successful" life. I had all the things that were supposed to add up to one thing: happiness. Still there was something tugging at my sleeve, holding me back from enjoying it.

I could see how great my life looked. But rather than being "in" it, I was like an observer looking onto it. In this state, feeling bad came much more naturally than feeling good. When things went well, I'd barely get a flicker of satisfaction; when they didn't, I'd fall into a slough of despond. Had I graphed my mood, my downs would have been ravines, while my ups would have been molehills.

Pleasures that were once comforting now felt more elusive. When I put on my favourite songs, the chills no longer came. My Instagram looked like an enviable patchwork quilt of lovely experiences. In truth, trips abroad no longer felt like adventures. Even when I went somewhere new and exotic, I found it impossible to immerse myself fully in the experience. I remembered how when I was younger, travelling felt exhilarating.

Now it felt like a feat of organization before I went and daunting piles of extra work when I got back for daring to take time off. But what right did I have to complain?

Every day, my newsfeed was filled with the sight of other people dealing with tragedies or living with war, and famine or ill health. All my human needs for food, security, job satisfaction and love were being met – and then some. But when you have everything, where do you go to find the missing piece?

Shouldn't I just count my blessings and stop being such a miserable cow? Despite telling myself to get a grip, the question still niggled at me. Surely, I couldn't be the only person in this position who felt like this?

Finding a name for it

As an author and a journalist, I have always written about what I need to learn. My job is to be curious and look for answers. So, putting my guilt to one side, late one night in bed, after another day of wondering what was wrong with me, I went in search of an explanation. With my oblivious husband sleeping next to me, it felt like the ultimate shameful secret to be Googling "Why aren't I enjoying my life?"

I'd like to say there was a more exciting story behind how I found the answer. In 0.63 seconds, the offer of 6,770,000,000 results flashed up on my screen. One of the first headlines that jumped out at me was: "Don't enjoy anything anymore? There's a name for that." The piece was by a psychologist who called this state of existence "anhedonia". So, there was a word for it.

I read on to find that anhedonia was the opposite of hedonism, or pleasure, and defined as "losing the ability to get pleasure from things you used to enjoy". But although it is often a symptom of major depressive disorder, I discovered you didn't need to be depressed to feel anhedonic. You could be ticking along, getting on with life, appearing just fine to everyone else, with everything you need, except the mental bandwidth to enjoy it.

After taking this in, my immediate question was: "Why have I never heard this word before?"

We hear so much about modern life's most pernicious disease, depression, at one end of the mental health spectrum, and happiness at the other. Why do we hear nothing about the grey space in between – even though it's the area where so many of us live our lives?

> *My biggest problem with feeling this way is that I feel*
> *like I can't connect with other people the way I used to.*
> *My friends talk about their problems, but I don't have the*
> *emotional energy to empathize with them and wish they'd*
> *stop moaning. To be honest, I don't really care anymore.*
>
> Louise, 46

How anhedonia went mainstream

Now I knew it had a name, anhedonia went on my list of issues I needed to write about.

In the meantime, I felt increasingly irritated at how it seemed to follow me everywhere: to parties, concerts and days out, which never seemed to move me out of robot mode.

And then came Covid. If there was anything that was supposed to make us appreciate our lives, lockdown was surely it. For more than a year, we were deprived of many of the things that were supposed to make us happy: socializing, live music, haircuts and holidays. For months we sat on our sofas imagining how brilliant it would be when it was all over.

It was only when we started to get back to the life we'd been looking forward to, that some people noticed that rather than wanting to make up for lost time, they felt JOMO (the joy of missing out) rather than FOMO (the fear of missing out). Some of us felt so "blah" about our old lives, we were in no hurry to get back to them.

On the other side of the Atlantic, in Spring 2021, organizational psychologist Adam Grant wrote in *The New York Times* about a growing cohort who were not depressed, but who were not thriving either. He looped it back to "languishing", a term first coined by the American psychologist Corey Keyes in 2002, who defined it as "the void between depression and flourishing – the absence of wellbeing".

Grant framed it for the new generation: "You don't have symptoms of mental illness but you're not the picture of mental health either." He went on: "It appears to be more common than major depression – and in some ways it may be a bigger risk factor for mental illness."

Clearly people recognized the description of the feeling as it was the newspaper's most shared article of the year.

All this pointed to the possibility that even before the extraordinary interruption of the pandemic, a lot of us hadn't been enjoying our lives as much as we might have hoped.

Hardly surprisingly, I noticed it too. When I saw friends and family again for the first time after lockdown and expected the tears to flow, I felt nothing much, except it was "quite nice" to see them.

So, in August 2021, as the UK was coming out of lockdown, I emailed the commissioning editor of a glossy supplement to suggest that a piece about anhedonia might resonate with a lot of people stuck in the grey zone. The next day – lightning speed in magazine terms – I got an email back saying: "Yes, please. So many readers are going to relate to this."

I know my feelings are in there somewhere but it's like I can't access them. I can still cry but I don't feel chills or extremes. I'd just like to get "me" back.

Atul, 44

Everything feels the same. Logically, I can look up at the sky and see it's beautiful, but it doesn't mean anything. I think about my emotions but I don't feel them.

Joel, 32

Anhedonia: A quick history

Now that my research was underway, I discovered anhedonia is on a spectrum and comes in many forms. Taken from the Greek for "without pleasure", it was first coined by French philosopher and psychologist Théodule-Armand Ribot in his book *The Psychology of Sentiments* in 1896. A few years later American psychologist William James warmed to the theme, describing it in his 1902 scientific paper as "passive joylessness and dreariness, discouragement, dejection, lack of taste and zest ... incapacity for joyous feelings ...

loss of appetite for all life's values." By 1922, the American psychiatrist Abraham Myerson devoted an entire lecture to the subject at the annual meeting of the American Psychiatric Association.

But after the initial flurry of interest, anhedonia wasn't talked about until it made a return, perhaps not coincidentally, as post-war affluence started taking off in the late 1950s. In clinical papers, it was the word professionals used to describe how people with Parkinson's disease, schizophrenia and addiction – all conditions in which the dopamine system is disrupted – could lose all interest in life. It became notorious as the symptom which made these conditions so difficult to treat because patients lost hope in helping themselves. It was depicted as an intractable iceberg which couldn't be melted by drugs or therapy – and it was even perceived as a character flaw.

But then along came a scientific invention – the MRI scanner – which managed to look inside the brain to see how pleasure was formed and why some people didn't experience as much as others. It helped break anhedonia down into its component parts and bring a more nuanced perspective. Clinicians began to realize it could come in many shades and strengths. Researchers started finding so many flavours, some suggested it would be more accurate to refer to it in the plural, as "the anhedonias".

Despite a growing number of papers and research over the following decades, many recognizing that anhedonia needed to be studied in its own right, the rest of us had never heard of it.

How widespread could "blah" be?

So, how many of us are living in a state of "blah"? Figures are not easy to come by, partly because anhedonia can be described in different ways. As we've heard, it was psychologist Corey Keyes who first recognized that just because you don't feel bad doesn't mean you feel good. In his first studies on "languishing" in the early 2000s, it was estimated that 12.1 per cent of US adults were affected by it.

Two decades later, using the same criteria, an IPSOS US Mental Health report found that 21 per cent were in the same mental space. In a breakdown of age, it was found that millennials (age 26 plus) were most likely to be languishing at 30 per cent. Next were Gen Z (up to age 25) at 26 per cent, Gen X (age 42 plus) at 21 per cent and, lastly, baby boomers (age 57 plus) at 14 per cent.

Surveys of workforce wellbeing found even higher rates. A 2021 survey for Better Up, a leadership coaching company (who admittedly might be biased in saying employees need help to flourish), found 55 per cent in this lacklustre space, compared to 35 per cent who were thriving and a lucky 5 per cent who were "super functional". This chimed with Gallup research that found that 62–68 per cent of US employees were not engaged at work and Deloitte's finding that 46 per cent also lacked motivation.

Eddie Medina, who commissioned the Better Up survey, said people who are languishing "Struggle to stay focussed, to find meaning and, for many, to find optimism and hope for the future … When people are languishing, the normal stressors of life and work pile up and hit them harder – everything else feels like a struggle. Major transitions and life changes can amplify the effect."

In a separate snapshot in the UK in June 2021, when workers were asked about their sense of purpose and direction, 42 per cent said the pandemic had left them feeling "aimless".

> *At work, people would chat to me and crack jokes, but I felt like an outsider looking in. I found I couldn't relate to people because I was so numb. I found it hard to feel compassion. I acted like I cared because I knew it was what I was supposed to do. But really, everything washed over me.*
>
> Joe, 28

Hidden costs

Does apathy really matter if it's not a mental illness? Yes, it does. Anhedonia may keep a low profile, but that doesn't mean it's not taking a toll. It can be much more than feeling a bit flat. In our current healthcare system, we tend to intervene when people's health has broken down, a tendency Corey Keyes called: "Parking ambulances at the bottom of the cliff."

Far from just being a state of "blah", anhedonia can be a precursor to depression, a red flag that the brain's reward system is no longer working as well as it should. Left unchecked, anhedonia can become the purgatory before depression sets in. Tackling it is preventative.

Research has found that the people most likely to develop major depression and anxiety disorders in the next ten years are not the ones with obvious symptoms today. They are the people who lack positive mental health *now*.

When depression hits, antidepressants like SSRIs are usually the first choice of treatment, but while they are often effective at blunting pain, they can blunt joy too. If left to spin downwards for too long into depression, anhedonia is the symptom of depression which lingers the longest and makes it the most difficult to treat.

Anhedonia can also be an early warning sign of the final stages of burnout. One more stressor and it can make a cup that is already full to the brim, run over. It can dim our experience of the world. Sex, our senses of smell and taste, our love of music, socializing – and life in general – can all be dialled down by anhedonia.

The alternative: flourishing

For a moment, let's look at how different life looks at the other end of the spectrum.

It's not just a pleasanter place to be. Studies have found when you psychologically flourish, you feel less helpless, your life goals are clearer, you're more engaged with others and you are more resilient. There are physical benefits, too, like better heart health and a reduced risk of chronic disease.

Advances in healthcare are extending our physical lives. Don't we need to make sure that we stay mentally and physically well, so we can make the most of this longevity? Should we really be prepared to accept life without joy as the status quo?

Why you may not have heard this word before

If it's so pervasive, why has anhedonia stayed out of public view for so long? Probably because feeling "meh" is almost invisible. It's not the jazz hands of joy or curl-up-into-a-ball style depression. When it comes in its milder and most everyday form, many of us blame ourselves, thinking that the novelty of life has just worn off or we should count our blessings.

Feeling "blah" doesn't demand attention. We are socialized to ignore it, born into cultures where, when asked how we are, we typically say: "Fine", even though that itself is a "meh" abbreviation for what we're really feeling. Give a more downbeat answer, without very good reason, and it sounds monumentally moan-y. We soon get the message that the correct answer is to politely gloss over the fact that life doesn't feel all that great. Plus, most of the time, we are too busy to check in with ourselves and haven't had the word to describe this in-between state anyway.

As "blah" has become normal, it's easy to assume that it's the price we pay for keeping our lives on track in a stressful society.

First World Problem?

Another reason we don't talk about anhedonia is because it feels like a First World problem. It can feel shameful to admit that having a decent home and enough money doesn't make us happy. Should we really be worrying about not enjoying life when there's so much suffering elsewhere on the planet? When we hear about severe mental health issues, like the rise in suicide and self-harm, saying we don't feel as good as we'd like to sounds like the least of our problems.

What we are missing here is that life the way we live in First World societies is what often helps to produce this state of "meh" in the first place.

It's true that if you have the cash and education to sit down and read this book in a safe, secure environment, you're likely to be getting all your material needs met, thanks to where you live. You are also part of a generation who have come to enjoy the sort of affluence once only enjoyed by royalty. Yet becoming better off over the last half century has done little for our mental wellbeing.

Yes, we live in a world in which it has never been easier to get our basic material needs met, but there's been a biological pay-back. As we shall hear, the constant dopamine hits of a convenience society have helped throw off our brain's reward systems – where good feelings are made. Instead of everything feeling good, as it's designed to, nothing does. There's a growing consensus that modern life has made dopamine addicts of all of us, blunting our sensitivity to pleasure and letting stress hormones prevail.

Biological reasons

While it affects all genders and ages, anhedonia can often hit women particularly hard. One reason may be because hormonal changes over the course of their menstrual cycle can affect how well the body makes serotonin, a chemical messenger in our brains and bodies, that is important for mood. Then when menopause hits, the drop-off of oestrogen and other hormones can have a domino effect on feel-good chemicals like dopamine, and oxytocin too.

Though it's more gradual, men's moods are also affected by a drop-off in their main sex hormone, testosterone, which over time can rob them of their verve and enjoyment of life.

For both genders, modern diets also play a role in maintaining a hopeful, optimistic frame of mind. We are finally starting to understand the critical link between what we eat and how we feel. For most of history, we tended to believe moods are made in the mind. Now we know that what we eat also makes a big difference to the production of mood-maintaining serotonin. A Western diet, heavy in sugar, preservatives, red and processed meats, and refined carbs, has also been found to trigger gut inflammation. The problem is that the gut is also where huge amounts of this serotonin is made. What's more, inflammation that affects the gut can also reach the brain. There it dials down production of still more feel-good chemicals and stops them circulating as smoothly. It's going to be more difficult to feel positive and optimistic about life if your diet means you are not producing a balance of feel-good chemicals, and then the inflammation it triggers gets in the way of them flowing freely.

A legacy of Covid

When it comes to feeling joy, modern life has recently been throwing even more curve balls at us. When the Covid-19 virus hit, it wasn't just the disruption, uncertainty and forced seclusion of lockdown which made us feel "blah".

Quite soon into the pandemic, scientists observed that cytokines – the immune system cells which our bodies release to fight the virus – could also over-react and affect the brain too. If this knock-on effect reached the brain, often it could hit the reward circuits and interfere with the synthesis and release of dopamine.

Even after the virus was destroyed by our immune system, this was one of symptoms that could hang around. A study in the journal *Nature Medicine* published in July 2022 – well over two and a half years after the start of the pandemic – named anhedonia as one of the persistent Long Covid symptoms people were still living with.

This domino effect is not limited to Covid. More and more, we are recognizing that any illness that causes inflammation can have the same impact. While the virus has abated for now, there are other diseases of the 21st century which show no sign of going anywhere, and which can also trigger anhedonia.

Take obesity and type 2 diabetes, the twin scourges of modern human health. Both are also linked to inflammation in the brain which specifically hits the reward circuits.

This creates a vicious circle. Could it be that anhedonia is the missing link which helps explain why the people who most need to make diet changes and take exercise often feel too hopeless to do so? Is the real problem that they are being exhorted to make lifestyle shifts, precisely when their conditions have silently robbed their brains of the motivation?

This has huge repercussions. Anhedonia may be a key reason why public health campaigns to combat both obesity and type 2 diabetes tend to barely make a dent in the figures – and the numbers of cases continues to rise across the world.

After I got Covid, I felt lacklustre for a long time, like I had been drained. I couldn't get excited about anything. I wasn't sure if it was me or the state of the country! I am a keen baker, and I couldn't even think what recipes I wanted to make.

Sarah, 50

Time to bring it into the open

It's not often we hear about a new word in mental health. This book is the first attempt to bring anhedonia into the open and add it to our emotional vocabulary; to shine a light on this state of grey for the general audience and examine it as a standalone issue, as many researchers are now trying to do.

It's a synthesis of hundreds of research studies, carried out by armies of brilliant scientists, which deserve a wider airing so we can benefit from their findings. Above all, it's the first acknowledgement of the people left wandering in the middle ground. If so many people are unable to live their lives to the full, it is a terrible waste. Life is too short to be lived on furlough. Furthermore, what does it mean for the planet if millions of people aren't living up to their potential? Where are we heading if so many are just spinning on their wheels?

Naming it is a first step in bringing this nebulous state into focus. Having more granular ways to describe how we feel can save people from slipping into more serious, difficult-to-shift states. A wide range of studies show that people who can differentiate between nuances of emotions are less likely to be overwhelmed by them and better able to regulate how they feel.

If we don't know what this feeling is, too many people will spend their lives feeling neither good nor bad, but just not very much at all.

Lightbulb moment

On a personal note, I hope when you heard the explanation of the word "anhedonia" you felt better understood, as I did. For many of the people I interviewed for this book, knowing that anhedonia had a name was a lightbulb moment, as it had been for me. While some people I mentioned it to genuinely looked baffled (because they were living their lives to the full, and good luck to them), I saw other people's eyes light up before they told me they couldn't wait to hear more.

A couple of my social media posts asking people about their feelings of "blah" quickly attracted nearly 100 replies. Many people confided they thought this was just what their life had become. Menopausal women were particularly keen to talk about it, many sharing their secret fears that they might never feel good again. Overworked 20- and 30-somethings, trying to juggle stressful careers and side hustles, said they assumed "blah" was just the way their lives were. Strung-out parents confided they were too tired to ever enjoy their children. Middle-aged men confided they'd had turned into the "grumpy gits" they'd sworn they'd never become.

The words and phrases people used to describe how they felt ranged from "stuck" to "on autopilot", "unplugged", "cold inside" and my personal favourite: "not burnt out, but definitely well toasted".

When I go out, I come back and think: Well, that was a waste of time and money!

Jorge, 37

What this book will do

In the pages ahead, I will be presenting the research on anhedonia in an accessible, easy-to-read way, before laying out the evidence-based strategies you can use to address it. By travelling back to our earliest origins and then travelling forward to look at the present-day causes, I will join the dots on the aspects of your mental state you may not have realized were connected. You will see how the modern world has taken advantage of our basic reward circuits and overloaded them so much they have gone "offline". I will examine how the "too much to do", always-on culture has allowed stress hormones like cortisol to drown out feelings of joy, love and calm. To do this, I have interviewed some of the world's leading neuroscientists to help you see how pleasure is formed in the brain – and why you possibly have stopped feeling it.

At the same time, I am also aware that the self-help genre has become synonymous with toxic positivity and hucksterism. Once the novelty of the positivity psychology movement wore off, a certain weariness set in. But this book isn't about Pollyanna-ish cheerleading. You already know you're supposed to "live, laugh, love", "shoot for the moon" and "dance like no one is watching" etc...

You will be provided with a run-through of the latest research across psychiatry, psychology, endocrinology and nutrition, woven together with the voices of those who have experienced anhedonia in its many forms. Although modern life challenges our ability to enjoy life, the good news is we are now entering a fresh, and uniquely helpful phase in brain science. We have more reasons than ever to be optimistic.

You don't need to be a neuroscientist to understand the basics of how your brain makes your mood. The upside is that if you are still functioning well – and your anhedonia is more of a quiet, guilty secret you are carrying with you – you probably don't need therapy. Understanding more about how your brain creates joy, what might be standing in its way and finding out how to allow those feelings to flow again will help.

The aim of this book is not to move you magically from "blah" to bliss. It's to help you feel a wider range of emotions so you can engage with the world around you and start to live a full life again. By the end, instead of asking yourself "What's wrong with me that I don't feel happy?" you will be asking some different questions: "What happened to me that I can't enjoy my life?" and "What am I going to do to change that?"

How this book works

The book is divided into three parts:

In Part One, I look at what anhedonia looks like, as well as its various causes and some of the social changes which are driving it. I will explain how, once the human race's initial battle for survival was won, our quest for pleasure was turned against us and how this has biologically affected our ability to feel good.

In Part Two, I will break down anhedonia into its different types and look at how it can dull the senses. By being aware of the physiological reasons for feeling "blah", you will start to shed some of the shame and frustration with yourself, and with those who tell you to "cheer up" or suggest you're "just depressed", when you know that's not it. By looking at what we now know about how the brain's reward circuits are activated, I hope you will be able to metaphorically visualize what's happening inside your mind. With this understanding, I hope you will see the importance of feeding your brain better experiences and discover that your emotions are more in your control than you realize.

In the final part, I will take a comprehensive look at what you can do to specifically address "blah" so that you can rediscover joy and pleasure in the things you once loved. Everyone develops anhedonia a bit differently. There isn't a one-size-fits-all solution, but there are lots of small, practical things you can do which will add up to more than a sum of their parts. I won't insult your intelligence by repeating the same solutions you've heard before on diet, exercise, gratitude and mindfulness, but I will share the latest evidence to spell out *why* these tools can be more powerful than any antidepressant ever invented. With this knowledge, you will be able to make informed decisions that are right for you.

A time to have fun?

With so many global challenges, you might be asking yourself if this is really the moment to be focussing on enjoying yourself. If anything, I'd say this is *exactly* the time. Too many of us are starting to feel so overwhelmed by life, folding our cards and deciding we don't want to play. To move forward as a planet, more of us need to be flourishing, not just surviving.

Feeling just OK is not making the most of your life. Just because you're not depressed doesn't mean you should be grateful and accept feeling "fine". We need to show the future generations how to enjoy life. As we have got better off in material terms, we seem to get less happy. Until we start to work out how to make more of our time on the planet, depression will continue to rise.

Our relationships are transactions. Emotions are contagious. If we address our feelings of "blah" about life, it will also make for happier homes. Sensitive to mood from birth, children and young people tend to interpret our low moods as a rejection, a sign that we are somehow not happy with them either. Partners who think they have failed us if we don't like our lives also feel blamed and become detached.

Yes, it feels like we are living in chaotic times. Living the best life we can not only spreads to lovers, family and friends, but also into the world beyond. Whether we have children or not, it's time to step back think about the emotional legacy we leave behind. What better contribution could we make than role-modelling a joyful, meaningful life?

PART ONE

What is Anhedonia and why does it happen?

1

What Does Anhedonia Look Like?

Now that I knew the word for anhedonia, I set out to explore the different ways it could surface in people's lives. As I was to discover, it can come in many shades and flavours. At the start of this process, one of the most vivid, and perhaps useful descriptions that stuck in my mind came during an early conversation I had with psychotherapist Lohani Noor.

"Remember the moment when Dorothy's world turns from black and white to technicolour in the Wizard of Oz?", Lohani asked me. "Then imagine it happening in reverse."

"It's like the film," she explained. "But the other way around. I recognize anhedonia when it walks into my therapy room, and it can be easily confused with depression.

"But there is a distinct nuance in the flavour of anhedonia. While it may well lead to depression – it's not depression ... It can make someone who is suffering with it feel like they are left stranded in a dinghy in the middle of the ocean, drifting further away from the bright lights of joy and laughter."

I also approached Canadian psychologist Dr Rami Nader who was one of the first to discuss anhedonia as a standalone state on his YouTube channel. His descriptions highlight the sense of loss than can come with it. He notes that you are most likely to notice it first when it dims your love of the activities you used to enjoy the most.

"Say, you used to really enjoy hiking, but now it just feels like a chore. Or when you're painting you feel no sense of engagement or creativity. It's just paint on a canvas. Or perhaps you used to love eating out with friends but now the food just doesn't taste like anything, and the music is just too loud. It can feel like 'What's the point of it?' You may find you have no drive to do any of these things. There's the loss of pleasure in the activity itself but also there's also a loss of desire to do it again, so you stop engaging."

For this reason, Dr Nader also likens anhedonia to "quicksand". "The more you lose interest or pleasure in the activities you once liked, the worse it gets."

Or it can be the feelings of overwhelm when your mind and body are so overwhelmed by stress hormones, it feels like it's closing down. Psychotherapist Phillip Hodson believes anhedonia can also be a defence against the stress of modern life and its many demands: "Emotional sterility is the price we pay."

It can also be the voice that tells you to dismiss the small moments of joy, or tells you, "Well, I didn't feel any better after that, so what's the point?" If we stop looking forward to things, it can start a vortex which fools us into believing nothing will make us feel better.

Feeling more bad than good

Whatever form it comes in, feeling "blah" doesn't necessarily mean you are depressed. If you have standalone anhedonia, you may not be happy, but you may not miserable either. But you have probably lost delight in the little things. There's a good chance that often you don't really want to get out of bed in the morning, but you still do anyway. Anhedonia can make you feel like the balance in your brain has tipped – and boredom, apathy and weariness are drowning out your enjoyment of the good things in life.

As we will hear, there are three parts to anhedonia:
1. You have stopped looking forward to activities.
2. While you are doing them, you don't enjoy them anymore.
3. Afterwards you tend to have a negative memory of them, so you don't want to do them again.

No one enjoys life all the time, but if that spiral continues downwards, and you've noticed you can't think of anything that makes you feel good anymore, it's time to take action. The good news is that if you are not clinically depressed, you won't need to address negative feelings first, like guilt and shame. These are two of the hallmarks of depression which often need to be tackled with the help of therapy.

To tackle standalone anhedonia, you will need to concentrate on getting all three of these components of your reward system back online. As we will hear, one of the key ways to do this is a technique called Behavioural Activation Therapy, focussing on really noticing the positives of an experience, so it starts to be coded in your brain as fun again.

> *As you get older, and you're out, your mind thinks: "Well, this is good. But is there a pile of washing that needs to be done?" Life gradually gets in the way, and you stop living in the moment the way you used to. There's something carefree about being younger that just sort of ebbs away.*
>
> Nina, 42

Think you may be depressed?

We've already talked about some of the differences between anhedonia and depression, but what if you *are* depressed? If you have at least five of the symptoms below nearly every day for two weeks, then you may have Major Depressive Disorder, also known as clinical depression. Take note of the symptoms, but don't leap to conclusions. Instead, see a medical professional as soon as you can for a proper diagnosis.

- Feelings of low self-esteem, or excessive guilt
- Significant unintentional weight gain or loss or loss of appetite
- Loss of pleasure of all – or nearly all – activities you used to enjoy
- Insomnia or more need to sleep
- Depressed mood like feeling empty, sad or constantly irritable
- Tiredness or loss of energy

How bad is your "blah"?

So if you don't meet the criteria for depression, it's time to pin down what your "blah" feels like, so you can start to tackle it. Look at the following statements to see how many resonate with you:

- When asked how I am, I often struggle to articulate it.
- I can't easily remember a time recently when I really enjoyed myself.
- I often feel I have to fake having fun.
- Most mornings, I don't want to get out from under the duvet.
- If I start to feel I might be enjoying myself, I worry that something bad will happen.
- I don't enjoy my favourite food or music as much as I used to.
- Sex seems a bit pointless.
- I struggle to remember the last time I really laughed.
- If I feel about to have fun, a voice pops up in my head saying: "I'm too old for this" or "This feels uncomfortable".
- When other people rave about things, I often find it hard to join them there or see what they are appreciating.
- I feel I'm holding myself back or distancing myself during emotional moments.
- I feel irritated by other people around me being too lively and having fun.
- I can't remember the last time I took part in a hobby or pastime I enjoy.

- I find it difficult to empathize when people tell me they are going through a tough time.
- I am always planning my escape and thinking about the life I really want to live.

Circle the ones what apply to you. As you read the book, you will now be able to home in on the different sections that will help.

I have had depression in the past but anhedonia is different. In depression, I don't want to do anything at all. When I have anhedonia, I do go out but I don't get the same buzz.

Nat, 41

Tracking your anhedonia

Like any mental state, anhedonia is on a spectrum. Like a dimmer switch, it can dull your capacity to experience joy just a little, or a great deal. As you tackle it, the light may turn up imperceptibly so it's hard to notice the difference. If you've been in a state of anhedonia for a while, it can also take a bit of time to notice how your emotional colour palette, just like the one on the cover of this book, is changing.

We are used to measuring our heart rate and weight as a way of tracking our physical health. Even though mental health is the one of the greatest health challenges the world faces, we tend not to track our minds in the same way. Tracking your anhedonia requires doing daily check-ins with yourself. Monitoring your mood will help you to keep an eye on the ups and downs and, by checking in on yourself daily, you will give your brain a better chance of helping itself. The other benefit is that if you have told people you are tackling anhedonia, a visual representation will communicate how you feel to others.

If you've ever gone back and re-read an old diary, you will see that we are generally not good at remembering our changing mental states accurately unless we record them. This need only take a couple minutes every day at most, but try to do it at roughly the same time. That way you can start to build a picture of the direction in which your mood is heading. The end of the day is probably the best time because you are likely to be in a calmer place to look back and reflect. As it becomes a habit, you may want to start drilling down and unpacking the reasons you feel certain emotions. Writing a short explanatory note next to your daily mood will help you see cause and effect.

Different methods suit different people. Apart from the obvious choice of getting a mood tracking app, easy and free options include:

- Using a note document on your phone, pick a daily emoji to sum up your mood or simply write a number from one to ten.
- Draw a line graph. On the bottom horizontal line, mark out the days of the month. On the vertical axis, mark from one to ten. Every day, put a dot to show where your overall mood is. Then start to join the dots for a representation of how your mood is changing.

- Get a piece of squared paper. Every day colour in a single square with the colour of the mood you are feeling. Greys, dark blues and blacks can represent "blah'" days, while pinks, yellow or oranges can represent brighter days. A mood mandala in which you colour in sections of a circle clockwise every day to depict how you feel is another good option.

It doesn't matter how you do it, as long as you do it regularly. These "micro-introspections" should be simple. Don't let the fact it could be as simple as noting down a number from one to ten in your diary deceive you. This awareness could be the difference between letting your emotions control you and getting mastery over them.

Starting point

Finally, let's establish a firm baseline going forward. Circle the numbers below, with 1 being strongly disagree and 5 being strongly agree, then come back to it fortnightly as you take steps to shift your mood.

- I feel chills when I hear music I like – 1 2 3 4 5
- I feel able to let go enjoying myself in social situations – 1 2 3 4 5
- I really enjoy my food – 1 2 3 4 5
- I wake up most mornings feeling ready to face the day – 1 2 3 4 5
- I am making plans for the future – 1 2 3 4 5
- I laughed at something I found funny in the last week – 1 2 3 4 5

If you scored between 6 and 15, now is the time to find out why your emotions and enjoyment of life seem to be flatlining.

If you scored between 15 and 20, you seem to be ticking along in the medium range, but could the dimmer switch be turned up on some areas of your life?

If you scored between 20 and 30, you seem to be flourishing and making the most of your life.

Tracking your progress

So, as you move through this book, how will know how to spot the signs that your anhedonia is lifting? First, don't chase joy manically. Instead, let it creep up on you slowly. Don't we all know that person who once couldn't run for a bus and now runs marathons? Week in week out, by using their body in a new way, they gradually got fitter. Think of enjoying your life again as training yourself too, only this is your brain. You will also need to keep showing up, but gradually it will get easier, take less effort and become second nature.

Look out for small wins. Let them happen in the moment, but record them at the end of the day. Train yourself to notice them so you know you are heading in the right general direction, even though life will inevitably put obstacles in your way.

Here are some signs to look out for that are you are starting to move out of anhedonia:

- You hold your gaze longer when you see things you like.
- You catch yourself smiling.
- You start planning things and enjoy looking forward to them.

- When you are enjoying yourself, you do it for the fun of it, not because you want to picture it and share it or build your "brand" on social media.
- Hearing music you like makes you want to sing along or dance.
- You don't notice the passing of time when you are enjoying yourself, or feel you should be doing something else.
- You go back to hobbies you'd stopped doing.
- You cry more often because it feels like your emotions have become unblocked.

In other words, as your anhedonia lifts you will stop feeling less like a spectator and more like a participant in your life. You will laugh more easily too. Not tense, uptight titters but body-shaking laughs that last longer than you expect or can control. Reading this book will also encourage those moments and allow you to hold onto them longer.

But in case it sounds like there's much to be done, take heart. The very fact that you now know there's a word for anhedonia is an important step forward.

You may be impatient for ideas to start to lift you out of "blah", which are in the third and final part of the book. But the fact is that, as you read and understand what this feeling is, you are already changing and finding your way out of "blah".

2

Blame Your Ancestors: Why our Stone Age Brains Make it Hard to be Happy

For the ultimate edition of *Who Do You Think You Are?* I'd like to take you on a trip back through your family tree. A very long way back – about 5,000 generations to the days of the earliest Homo sapiens. Though humans were still relatively insignificant at the start of the Ice Age, now is an interesting time to pay a visit. About 100,000 years ago, they were well on their way to becoming the most dominant species on the planet.

By this point, there is a family resemblance too. Our forebears are now looking less like apes, and more like we do now. Your ancestors had smaller, less pointy teeth, flatter brows and less hairy bodies. Imagine a tribe of them waking up together under shelters, possibly made of wooden branches, covered with animal skins. Though it may have been a long time ago, it's safe to guess that the moment their eyes opened, for most of them, their first thought was: "Where are we going to find breakfast?"

Before we look at how your ancestors got their first bite to eat that morning, let's go back even further in time. Although the race was not yet won, the species we came from – Homo sapiens – was still on the right track for leaving all the other competing species of early humankind, including the Neanderthals and the Denisovans, behind.

Like them, they were also making the most of their ability to walk on two legs, developed five million years before. This gave them the freedom to use tools to manipulate the environment, whether by building shelters, making clothes or finding food. Their brains were evolving accordingly now that they were developing new motor skills. In particular, the upper cortical layer was getting larger and more complex. Yet the brains of their cousins, the Neanderthals, whom they might have bumped into from time to time, were still bigger overall.

But your relatives didn't win the race because of their brain size or complexity. They won it because it contained a little more of a chemical that drove them to explore and adapt to a challenging environment. And it's this extra ingredient which still plays a critical role in how we think and how much we enjoy our lives today.

The "more more more" molecule

All animals have a central pleasure circuit in their brains. When this "lights" up, it stimulates them to seek out the basic requirements for survival and to continue their species – food and sex. Dopamine has long been known as the molecule of pleasure, but more recently it's been found to be more about get-up-and-go. Research is finding that a key reason early humans may have prevailed was that they had more of this evolutionary rocket fuel.

It's believed that only one in two million neurons in the brain make dopamine – a key part of our mesolimbic reward pathway (see page 106). That doesn't sound much, but over the millennia, human brains have evolved to produce *three times* the amount, compared with other apes, despite sharing 99 per cent of their DNA.

Considering we have little more than fragments from early humans, how can we possibly know how much dopamine was circulating in their brains? The answer is that anthropologists can work backwards by looking at the neurotransmitter levels of humans compared with other primates. This extra amount meant that your ancestors wouldn't have been satisfied just to breakfast on the not-too-tasty leaves and tubers they found near their shelter, even though these were also a part of their diet. Dopamine, the chemical of craving, will have supercharged them enough to organize the members of the tribe into scavenging or hunting parties to find something tastier and more nutritious. This "molecule of more" is probably what gave our ancestors the drive they needed to leave Africa, where Homo sapiens originated, and go on to conquer the rest of the world.

Getting the balance right

Dopamine is powerful stuff. For the Homo sapiens' brain to evolve into the finely tuned survival machine it became, it also had to be measured about how much it released. (Too much dopamine, for example, circulating in the brain is believed to be a contributory factor in schizophrenia.) So that morning, as your ancestors sought out a breakfast, their dopamine levels would have risen as they got hungrier and thirstier and closer to their goal. Dopamine was the magic ingredient which helped give them the drive and energy to keep searching for more nutritious foods.

Rather than just settle for nearby fruit, seeds and nuts, which could be gathered in the surrounding areas, it might have sent some tribe members in search of a beehive from which to get honey. It would have sent others into the branches of nearby trees to find eggs or to follow the footprints of predators to find a recent kill, from which they could scavenge meat and bones. But dopamine's effect is also deliberately short-lived. Once your ancestors had eaten and drunk that morning, the extra spurt of dopamine – along with the release of feel-good opioids – which they got as a reward did not last very long. As soon as they took their first mouthfuls, those levels quickly dropped and even dipped below baseline. After all, unless those dopamine levels fell back down again, where would they have found the necessary motivation to go and seek out lunch?

An overload of dopamine

Fast forward about a thousand centuries. If you have the time and money to be sitting down to read this book, it's likely you have a roof over your head, with a kitchen containing enough food for your next meal. Even if your fridge holds little more than a jar of out-of-date pasta sauce and a shrivelled carrot, you probably have a supermarket close by. If you don't fancy cooking, you could order whatever dish you dream of to be delivered to your home in the next hour.

While your ancestors spent about 80 per cent of their lives foraging for food, you don't even need to move from your sofa. You could simply call across to your digital assistant to order it for you. Unlike 95 per cent of humans in history, who spent most of their lives simply seeking enough food to survive, everything you need comes to you. (You could argue that you must earn the money to buy that food. But even if you did nothing, we mostly live in societies where your basic needs would still be met so you wouldn't starve. No such safety net existed for our ancestors and at some points during the Ice Age, their numbers dwindled to alarmingly low levels.)

Apart from some slight changes due to genetic selection over the years, you basically have the same brain as your ancient family members, powered by the same reward system. Yet, the environment modern humans live in has changed beyond recognition. Our modern economies are built entirely around products and services designed to give you what you want, when you want it, in return for almost no effort. Furthermore, our reward circuits are now inundated with many more sources of pleasure.

As well as our primal needs for food and sex, our dopamine pathway is also activated by the endless novelty. Social media likes, binge-watchable TV, video gaming, drugs, foods high in sugar, fat and salt, alcohol and internet shopping. The list goes on. But there's a downside to an economy built on dopamine.

There's a big difference between getting a few dopamine hits every day after a considerable amount of effort, as your ancestors did, and getting thousands of hits a day in return for doing not much. Our brains were designed to get measured releases of dopamine to motivate us to meet our basic needs. Since convenience became our currency, every product and service we use is designed to keep dopamine coming in deluges, a state which has been described as "limbic capitalism". When everything is provided for you, it's not surprising that this very primal pleasure system gets overloaded – and metaphorically "short-circuits".

If you keep the hits coming, the dopamine levels in your brain never get a chance to return to normal, as they did for your ancestors. Over time, your reward system becomes less sensitive, more blunted. Gradually, the neurons lose their dopamine receptors, so it no longer circulates as easily. The result is that it can get harder to hit the highs, and feel excitement or real pleasure. And still that stimulation keeps coming. Broadband speeds get faster, music becomes easier to stream, drugs get more potent, porn gets more accessible and extreme.

Too much pleasure and we tip the balance into a dopamine-deficient state. Our baseline for pleasure can keep dropping. When everything is designed to be pleasurable, nothing feels good.

Too much of a good thing

Yet, like addicts, we may keep seeking the things that give us easy "hits", past the point where it feels good. As director of Stanford Addiction Medicine, psychiatrist Dr Anna Lembke has long studied the effect of the modern world on the brain's reward system. She explains: "Imagine our brains contain a balance – a scale with a fulcrum in the centre. When nothing is in the balance, it's level. When we experience pleasure, dopamine is released in our reward pathway and the balance tips to the side of pleasure. The more our balance tips, the faster it tips, the more pleasure we feel. But here's the important thing about the balance: it wants to remain level in equilibrium. It does not want to be tipped for very long to one side or another. The cost is an after-reaction that is opposite in value to the stimulus. Or, as the old saying goes, 'What goes up must come down'."

As Professor Lembke points out, we've all experienced craving – whether it's reaching for another piece of chocolate or binge-watching a boxset. "It's natural to want to recreate those good feelings rather than let them fade away. The simple solution is to keep eating, playing, or watching or reading. But with repeated exposure to the same or similar stimulus, the initial deviation to the side of pleasure gets weaker and shorter and the after-response to the side of pain gets stronger and longer, a process scientists call neuroadaptation. That is, with repetition our gremlins get bigger, faster and more numerous, and we need more of our drug of choice to get the same effect."

"With prolonged use," says Professor Lembke, "the pleasure-pain balance eventually gets weighted on the side of pain. Our hedonic pleasure set point changes as our capacity to experience pleasure goes down and our vulnerability to pain goes up. The paradox is that hedonism, the pursuit of pleasure for its own sake, leads to anhedonia which is the inability to enjoy pleasure of any kind."

No wonder then, that despite all its luxuries and comforts, modern life doesn't make us as happy as we might expect. This finely calibrated reward system has been turned against itself. It's this mismatch, which explains more broadly, some of your "blah" feelings.

Your worrying brain

Let's revisit your ancient relatives a bit later that day, off on foot looking for their next meal.

We tend to imagine so-called "cave" people from this era chasing down woolly mammoths, but in this period of prehistory, humans were just as likely to be hunted as be the hunters.

Still a long way down the pecking order, they were mainly scavengers, picking the bones out of carcasses which powerful carnivores, like big cats, had left behind. That meant that the danger from lingering predators, who wanted to make them the next meal, was never far away.

Threats came from every direction too. Talon marks on Ice Age skeletons show that human children could be carried off by birds of prey, bears, hyenas, wolves, wildcats and crocodiles, many of which were bigger than they are today. If humans were to survive these threats, they had to learn to foresee danger.

But imagining the future takes a lot of mental work. In time, these acute demands led to humankind developing a thick neo-cortex – the folded, outer layers of the brain, which are involved in higher thought processes such as imagining and strategizing.

Over the generations, natural selection meant that the humans who anticipated danger and where to find food next were the ones who survived to live another day and passed on their genes. Over time, this part of our brain became proportionately larger and more complex than any other species, tripling in size. And, as we shall hear, even though the threats have passed and there is usually food in the fridge, our brains are just as busy as ever.

Still on high alert

Sitting in the comfort of your own home, you no longer need to scan the horizon for threat. Even if you step outside your front door, your risk of meeting a violent death is miniscule.

However, stress triggers the same physiological response in your body, whether you are being chased by a predator or getting an email about your work deadline. It activates the same impulse to run away. Your pituitary and adrenal glands still pump out stress hormones, like cortisol and adrenaline. Your breathing speeds up. Your heart beats faster.

One of the main barriers to enjoying modern life is that, despite all its comfort and conveniences, we are anxious about something, pretty much all the time, leaving many of us afflicted with chronic stress. Although we tend to believe that worrying helps us head off a threat, a range of studies has found that between 80 and 90 per cent of what we worry about simply never happens – except in our minds.

Yet our imagination is so powerful that our brain has trouble telling the difference between reality and projection. Even though we are at no actual risk, our bodies respond with the same flight-fright-or-freeze reaction and release of the stress hormone cortisol.

Stress vs Joy

So how does stress contribute to anhedonia? The stress and pleasure systems are closely aligned. Both are mediated by the brain's early warning system, the amygdala. Dopamine and our main stress hormone cortisol both motivate but pull in different directions. Dopamine makes you want to run toward what makes you feel good. Cortisol makes you try to run away and avoid what makes you feel bad. However, it's cortisol that prevails. It inhibits the release of dopamine and blunts reward sensitivity. Furthermore, as a neurotransmitter which acts on nerve impulses in the brain, dopamine spikes very quickly in the brain. In a matter of moments, it subsides.

Cortisol, on the other hand, is a hormone which spreads more slowly throughout the body in the bloodstream. It hangs around in the body for nearly an hour after it is triggered. This is to make sure we're still ready to run if that predator is still lurking in the bushes. In terms of survival, this makes perfect sense. If your ancestors spent their time gazing at the horizon enjoying sunsets, instead of checking the environment for enemies, none of them would have stayed alive very long.

Basically, we still have the same brains. Given the cortisol-raising nature of modern society, no wonder we don't always find it easy to relax and enjoy ourselves.

Pecking orders

Having survived another day wandering the savannah, your ancestors would have gathered with the fellow members of their tribe, underneath their latest make-shift shelter, or perhaps in a rocky recess, safe from attack. It's hard to know at this point in human history whether humankind had harnessed fire well enough for us to imagine them sitting around a campfire. There are no traces in the archaeological record of the embers, or the conversations they had. At this stage, however, it's likely that any chat would have been rather rudimentary.

However early humans communicated, whether with hand gestures, body postures, facial expressions or various noises, bonding was critical to human success. While analysis of Neanderthal campsites shows our cousins didn't seem to be able to live within groups of more than 20 to 30, by this point early Homo sapiens were living in collectives of 50 or more. The larger the group, the more mouths there were to feed and the more organized the tribe needed to be. They had to learn to share resources, information and skills, and work better as a team.

This extra work had an upside. Over time, these intellectual requirements led to the development of our brain's more complex prefrontal cortex. Without it, we would never have evolved the sophisticated language that has powered our progress ever since.

As surprising as it sometimes seems today, these language skills have allowed humans to develop into a particularly co-operative and friendly species, compared with the rest of the animal kingdom.

Serotonin and status

Just as those extra doses of dopamine were the magic ingredient that helped humankind leave Africa to explore the rest of the planet, there was an extra dose of yet another feel-good chemical circulating in your ancestor's brain. Professor Mary Ann Raghanti is a biological anthropologist at Kent State University. Her research has looked at the differences in the chemical cocktails in the human brain compared to other primates, such as gorillas and chimpanzees. As well as having more dopamine in our reward circuits, we also have raised levels of serotonin, which acts as both a hormone and a neurotransmitter. Humans also have less acetylcholine, a neurochemical linked to dominant and territorial behaviour, than gorillas or chimpanzees. All this appears to make us more socially intelligent, less aggressive and better at adapting. The combination "is a key difference that sets apart humans from all other species," Dr Raghanti says. "Over evolutionary time you begin to get a feedback loop – it feels good to co-operate and affiliate."

But there was a flip side to having more serotonin. Your ancestors would have cared a lot about what their peers thought. This was much more than a popularity contest. Each tribe member's relationships and place in the pecking order were essential to their survival. Your relative's status in the tribe would have determined how much food they got access to, which mate they could choose, and the quality of the genes they could pass on. Any member who was cut loose from the group would have faced certain death alone in the wilderness. It's hard to know what moved someone up the pecking order, but athletic prowess, symmetrical features, food-gathering skills and fertility might have been some of the early markers of "success". Within the tribe, your ancestors also knew their roles. One member might have been known for being the best spear-thrower, another may have stood out for making the finest flint tools, or for being the quickest at skinning animal carcasses.

Our brains weren't just evolving to reward us with a little hit of serotonin when we felt bonded to other members of our tribe. They also rewarded us with a spurt when we got a little bit of status too.

For no less than two million years, our species lived as hunter-gatherers like this. Then around 15,000 to 10,000 years ago, we learnt how to herd livestock and grow plants and started to settle into farming communities. For centuries after, most humans continued to live in small- and medium-sized villages, then, starting in Britain in the middle of the 18th century, came the Industrial Revolution. Steadily and significantly, the human population started to rise. Villages became towns. Towns became cities. Cities became metropolises. As more material goods started to become available, the more we amassed and the more these markers for success became obvious. On top of that, there was more competition for status.

A population explosion

In 1804, the world's population was one billion. By the 1920s it had doubled. Since 1960, the global population has risen another billion every 12 or so years. So, what has it got to do with experiencing anhedonia? The simple answer is that we live in a modern world which challenges our brain chemistry and doesn't make it easy to enjoy life.

Firstly, we stopped living in tribes in which we knew the people around us. Today, you could see more humans in an hour than your ancestors would have seen in their entire lifetimes. Television and social media mean the number of other people we are exposed to has exploded, but almost all of them will be complete strangers.

Take the challenge of finding a mate. For millennia, you were unlikely to have had contact with more than a handful of potential partners your whole life and there was a good chance some of those were your relatives (obviously this was far from ideal, genetically). At the other end of the spectrum, we now willingly commodify ourselves and allow ourselves to be rated or dismissed with a cursory swipe by thousands of strangers on dating sites. This isn't good for how we feel about ourselves or the brain chemicals that we release in response to social rewards.

It's just one of the ways we pay a high price. People using dating sites like Tinder have been found to have lower self-esteem and more body image issues than people who don't use them.

In short, your brain was designed to worry about what the other 50 members in your tribe thought of you, not 50,000 strangers you've never met.

Gaining possessions
Our forebears were nomads who would have viewed any possessions, apart from basic tools and coverings, as a burden. They wanted nothing that was surplus to their needs. Then when humans discovered agriculture, they started to settle. Now they lived in just one place, they started to amass objects that were

useful to them. Gradually, the importance of different members of the tribe was signalled by the value of these possessions.

Fast forward to the second half of the 20th century. By now we owned more possessions than we could ever need or use. So, for a while, we competed about how *much* we had, and how much our possessions were worth, believing that would make us happy. Soon that didn't work either, because as living standards rose, affluence became normal. Even if the price tags varied if you looked closely, many people could afford gadgets, big TVs, designer clothes, cars and the rest.

So to hold up our serotonin levels and deflect the stress of feeling ourselves slipping down the pecking order, humankind invented a new realm in which to win status: social media.

In the same way that money has become a way to signify status, so have followings on these public platforms. The problem is that over time, this virtual competition can start to affect our happiness levels too. If everywhere we look we see others with more fame or followers, we still get a hit of cortisol as real as if a tribe-mate pushed us out of the way to grab the juiciest bone from a carcass.

Judge or be judged

Trying to keep up is a zero-sum game. So, to release a little serotonin to feel better, we resort to judging others. It might work in the moment we smirk at a workmate's attempt to become a fashion influencer or laugh at a friend's humblebragging holiday photo, but there is a payback. The downside of judging others is that we know we are being judged in return, making us feel more stressed and worried about keeping up.

When we step out of a precious experience, not just to take picture of it but to capture it for the evaluation, and hopefully envy, of others, we also stop experiencing it for ourselves.

When your more analytical cerebral cortex keeps whispering: "Do I look OK in this picture?" or "I need my peers to know my life is successful too", it stops good feelings in their tracks.

Now that that message is that you must be on social media to exist, these feelings can be hard to avoid, and can be a bigger drain on our day-to-day headspace than we realize.

Nearly five billion of the world's population are on some form of social network, whether it's Twitter, Facebook, LinkedIn, YouTube, Snapchat, Instagram, Pinterest, TikTok, Telegram, Douyin, QQ … the list goes on. In 2022, the average amount of time internet users spent on social media per day was two hours and 27 minutes, the highest figure ever recorded.

The things we choose to compete in might vary across different fields: how we look, how fit and fashionable we are, how popular or successful in business we are, how cute our children look, or our political virtuousness.

Research has found that 10 per cent of our daily thoughts involve making a comparison of some kind. In short, our nervous system is under attack from these ego assaults and it rarely gets a chance to recover.

How the cuddle hormone changed our history

There is one more feel-good hormone that's also affected by modern life. Oxytocin is both a hormone and a neurotransmitter which helps us to feel love and trust for others. From conception, it's essential to maintain social bonds, keep parents loving their children, partners loving each other and to bind groups of people together so they co-operate. Just like dopamine and serotonin, we had more of it than our old rivals the Neanderthals.

To see how important oxytocin is to group harmony, let's look at two of our closest living relatives, who share 98.7 per cent of our DNA – bonobos and chimpanzees. While bonobos live in the tropical rainforests of Central Africa, where food is plentiful, over thousands of years chimps spread across the continent. To the naked eye, there's not much to distinguish them apart from the fact that bonobos tend to be slightly smaller and stockier.

Then researchers started to notice some major behavioural differences. Unlike chimps, who can be hostile and aggressive, bonobos have evolved to welcome strangers, share food, not kill each other and resolve conflict with shows of affection, like hugging, kissing, playing and sex. And there may be one telling reason.

In some fascinating new studies, researchers have found that humans and bonobos have brains with more oxytocin receptors, which may account for why they appear to show more empathy, are better at anticipating the thoughts of others, and pay more attention to faces and eyes. "They are also better at regulating [aggressive] impulses and better at avoiding anti-social behaviour," said lead author Professor James Rilling, who published the study in the journal Social Cognitive and Affective Neuroscience.

Go back a bit further and analysis of Neanderthal DNA suggests they had less oxytocin, leading to more male-on-male competition and possibly more infighting, which may have contributed to their extinction. This all sounds like great news for Homo sapiens, except that love and community are no longer the only ways we get oxytocin.

Though it will always be an essential ingredient in forging parent and child bonds, the modern world has also designed ways to mainline oxytocin without loving face-to-face interaction. Loving sex can trigger its release. But so can porn. This hormone of love is oddly indiscriminate. It can also "bind" someone's memories to the object which gave them sexual pleasure. This can also be a porn site, not a person. Online porn means oxytocin can be rapidly elicited multiple times a day, unlike meaningful sex which is harder to come by.

According to Gary Wilson, the late author of *Your Brain on Porn*, overuse of porn means your brain starts to work against you, so it becomes desensitized to reward. Even moderate use can lead to a loss of motivation and apathy. Studies at Germany's Max Planck Institute found that the higher and longer the porn use, the more reduction there was of the grey matter in the striatum part of the reward circuit, resulting in numbed responses.

Not just oxytocin is affected. It was also found that the brain reduced the number of dopamine receptors and released less dopamine.

The effects on our ability to feel enjoyment don't stop after the porn video has ended. It can make the rest of life feel more "blah" too. As eminent psychologist Philip Zimbardo has pointed out:

"Less grey matter in this region translates into a decline in dopamine signalling. The lead researcher [of this study] Simone Kuhn hypothesized that 'regular consumption of pornography more or less wears out your reward system'. This can be thought of as desensitization or a numbed pleasure response. This addiction-related brain change leaves the individual less sensitive to pleasure, and often manifests as the need for greater and greater stimulation to achieve the same buzz (tolerance)."

Since the Max Planck research, Zimbardo points out that still more brain studies have found desensitization in compulsive porn users. "While sensitization makes your brain hyperreactive to anything associated with your porn addiction, desensitization numbs you to everyday pleasures." Furthermore, our oxytocin supplies are not helped by the fact that, while we are technically more wired together than ever, we are more physically disconnected than at any time in history.

Loneliness is still registered in the human brain as a threat because, if isolated from the rest of their tribe, your ancestor would not have survived very long. Now everything can be delivered to our homes, and we message more on social networks than talk face-to-face, we do not get the same soothing oxytocin boost. Loneliness is as likely to hit a young person feeling isolated in their room at university and hearing other people having a good time outside, as a widower who hasn't left his home for days.

Of course, no one wants to be surrounded by other people all the time. How much time we want to spend with others varies according to our personalities and personal histories. But if there's a void between how much interaction and connection with other people you want and what you are getting, you will feel an oxytocin deficit – and your happy hormones will be taking yet another hit.

In my opinion, asking if porn blunts your enjoyment of life is like asking if alcohol gives you liver disease. It felt like I used up so much dopamine there was nothing left for anything else. I had to take a long break before I could feel pleasure from the ordinary things again.

Jayson, 43

Why the novelty of life wears off

As the planet became more inhospitable and food became harder to find during the Ice Age, it was essential your ancestors didn't stay in one place very long. Driven by dopamine, they had to stay on the move to discover new ways to feed their increasingly energy-hungry brains. As a result, love of novelty is built into our basic reward system.

Inside the mid-brain, there's a region called the ventral tegmental area (VTA), which is a key part of this circuit. For your distant relatives, this would have been lit up by the sight of a new tree bearing ripe fruit in the distance or the exciting discovery of a nest of eggs they could raid. But those rewards were hard-won.

The challenge is that, in modern life, our VTA gets almost constant hits from super-stimuli around us. It's why we can't stop checking our phones because there's always something new to see. It's also why checking one TV channel isn't enough; we have to flick through 80.

When your brain's "want" for something new is met, it moves on to desire something else. Over time, our over-exposure can create a world-weariness which is another hallmark of anhedonia.

As Professor Daniel Gilbert, author of *Stumbling on Happiness*, points out: "Wonderful things are especially wonderful the first time they happen, but their wonderfulness wanes with repetition."

Not for pleasure, but survival

By now, you might be getting the impression that the brain isn't an organ designed to make you enjoy life. You would be right. Its primary role is to keep you alive long enough to reproduce. The ancestors we met at the start of this chapter didn't have much time to get in a bad mood. If they got to the end of another day alive, uninjured, warm, not too hungry and safe amongst the tribe, that was a *really* good day. The first peals of laughter didn't evolve because an early group of humans were cracking jokes. They were likely to have evolved as a social bonding signal to communicate to the rest of the tribe: "Phew, we're safe now. The danger's gone."

Another legacy our Ice Age relatives left us with, which makes it harder for us to enjoy life, is an inbuilt negativity bias. If your ancestor was enjoying a walk through a forest, but then almost got attacked by a snake, it was more important to remember that narrow escape than the pleasant stroll that preceded it, to be on their guard next time. The result is that, as a protective mechanism, the human brain has evolved to remember more negative incidents than positive ones.

The amygdala is like a switchboard that decides what to do with the incoming messages into the brain. To err on the side of caution, it's biased toward identifying experiences as threatening to make sure we are ready to defend ourselves. In modern life, this is the reason criticisms stick in our minds like Velcro while compliments rarely have the same staying power.

It's estimated we have 60,000 to 70,000 thoughts a day, and between 70 to 80 per cent of those are negative. By mid-life, many of us have had enough memories of bad experiences to tip the balance toward viewing the world with some apprehension. This is not our fault, but we can do something about it. Being aware of this biological leaning is the first step.

Getting our brains back on side

All this may sound like bad news, but understanding that the brain was designed to keep you alive – and not be a pleasure generator – gives us a more realistic baseline to work with.

It's a reminder that happiness is never supposed to be a permanent state of mind, despite what the modern world – and companies who want to sell us things – tell us.

What seems like a scary realization should be counterbalanced by the fact that we are at the cusp of understanding the brain in a way we have never done before. Living in the 21st century doesn't mean moments of joy can't be achieved, but it may take a little more conscious work than we have been told to expect.

3

How the Modern World Makes Joy More Elusive

Given the world our brains were designed for, it's ironic we have been fooled into thinking that enjoying life all the time is a basic human right. This is, in fact, a rather modern concept. In the 6th century BC, Buddha was already advising against seeing happiness as a goal, pointing out that the more attached you got to the idea, the more likely you were to be disappointed.

On the other side of the world, the Greeks were among the first civilizations to have the luxury of stepping off the basic survival treadmill, due to a temperate climate and plenty of food. As they didn't have to worry so much about where the next meal was coming from, they had more time to think about the meaning of life. Within 300 years of Buddha, the philosopher Aristotle was also pointing out that chasing happiness for its own sake – or hedonism – wouldn't bring it either. He stressed that *being* good was more important than feeling good. Life, he advised, also needed meaning, and eudaemonia – a life well-lived – was a worthier goal. Christianity and Islam ran with this idea too and aimed to keep followers' minds focussed on the ecstasy in the afterlife, rather than the here-and-now.

The importance of pleasure did keep popping up in the 17th and 18th centuries, during the Enlightenment, in glamorous hedonistic hotspots like the courts of Louis XIV in France and Charles II in England. But this was more as a guilty pleasure, because debauchery was seen as the privilege of kings.

It took the establishment of the New World in the Americas to formally enshrine happiness as something everyone should feel entitled to enjoy throughout life. The right to "life, liberty, and the pursuit of happiness" in the 1776 constitution was recorded as a goal that anyone could attain.

It was in 1942 that American psychologist Abraham Maslow pointed out that happiness can only be achieved if basic needs like food, safety, rest, relationships and shelter are met first.

Now that these were being met more easily in industrialized societies, and particularly in the US which had rapidly become the most successful economy, happiness started to be seen as a commodity which could also be bought.

Striving for happiness

It didn't take long for the advertising industry to work out how to sell products on the promise of how happy they would make buyers feel. As television spread into homes in the 1950s, TV channels pumped out commercials featuring housewives beaming at the acquisition of washing machines, as if their happiness depended on it.

Over the next few decades, the idea that happiness should be a static state which we shouldn't have to deviate from, was reinforced by laugh tracks on sitcoms, and smiley faces on badges and T-shirts. As more people could afford a camera, the standard instruction when you posed for a photo was to smile and look like you were enjoying every moment.

Up until the 1970s, psychology and psychiatry had mainly been seen as sciences for people who were seriously mentally ill. Yet, as the pressure to "keep up" in competitive societies ramped up and communities became less close knit, depression rates started to rise over the next few decades, and most sharply in the most affluent societies, like the US. As religion became a less important part of people's lives, they no longer looked forward to happiness in the next life. They wanted it *now* and they looked to the growing number of psychologists to tell them why they didn't have it.

The more we gained materially, the more we believed we deserved emotionally. The convenience of the modern world started to fool us into thinking happiness-on-tap was our birthright when it was really originally designed by evolution as a motivator which repaid us only with fleeting moments of satisfaction. The more our sense of false entitlement rose, the more miserable it made us. We created a society in which we started to feel like there was something terribly wrong when reality did not meet our overly high expectations.

It was then that the world of psychology decided that something had to be done to help people close the gap. In 1998, psychologist Martin Seligman took to the stage in his inaugural speech as president of the American Psychological Association and announced that the profession needed to focus not just on what made people sad, but what made them happy too. Happiness, and how to find it, became a science in its own right.

When analysts noticed happy workers were more productive, it became seen as a commodity that had to be quantified because it was essential for growth. In 2012, the launch of the first World Happiness Report looked at how nations compared. From the beginning of the index, the happiest countries have consistently been the same: Finland, Denmark, Norway and the Netherlands.

So, what are the secrets of the world's happiest people? Although prosperity helped a bit, it wasn't everything as Germany, the US, Canada and UK came much further down the list. Instead common factors were found to include freedom, an honest corruption-free society, lasting relationships and strong social support, access to the outdoors and, tellingly, a better work-life balance. Yet, as we shall hear, even positive psychology couldn't overcome the fact that the model of human happiness, created by consumer-driven 20th-century standards, almost always hits an invisible glass ceiling.

> *At college, I used to laugh loads. Now I laugh,*
> *like, once a week.*
> Jamal, 29

The high cost of success?

In 1979, a new kind of self-help book hit the shelves. With giant flaming red letters, the title was a concept that the modern world was about to hear a lot more about: *Burnout: How to Beat The High Cost of Success*. The author, psychologist Dr Herbert J Freudenberger, introduced the idea of "the syndrome of the overachiever", calling it "a distressing symptom of modern life".

The checklist for burnout on the back cover of the book had a lot in common with anhedonia. It asked if you were once "zestful, hard-working and optimistic" but now "tired, disillusioned and frustrated". And whether you had to "force yourself to do even routine things". It talked about the "extinction of motivation or incentive".

Quizzes that popped up on the new topic over the next few years asked questions like: Is joy elusive? Can you laugh at yourself? Does sex seem more trouble than it's worth? Do you have very little to say to people?

Quickly the word burnout entered the mainstream. In 1991, an article in Florida's *Palm Beach Post* suggested parents, who were increasingly both working, might get burnout too. "It's not that they don't care about their children," said nanny Carole Wolter who was busy observing the trend. "But they are doing too much."

The era of the smartphone

Burnout was already on the rise, even in an era where once you left the office, you could switch off for the evening. Yet this was a still a full decade before email became commonplace, 20 years before faster WiFi, and a quarter of a century before the first smartphone.

Then, in 2007, Apple launched the iPhone, enabling you to do most of the tasks you did on a computer on the go. It was designed to be so indispensable you could never put it down, and before long cameras, maps, dating apps, diaries, stopwatches, exercise trackers and virtual wallets become wrapped into this single modern Swiss army knife. At first it felt like freedom to be able to get work calls and messages anywhere, but it turned out we would pay a high price for liberation.

It's not easy to enjoy the here and now when we are clutching an object which noisily demands so much attention. Phones bombard us from every direction – email, text messages, social media messaging, notifications and voicenotes. It's rare we don't check our phones and not find something cortisol-raising – whether it's news, or a reminder that someone, somewhere else is doing better. When we see an unknown number, or an email from our boss, we react as sharply as if we were being pursued by a predator. Yet, we feel compelled to keep checking our phones because it gives us an illusion of control and we kid ourselves that we can keep on top of the deluge.

Your smartphone is millions of times more powerful than the first computer that sent man into space. Processing power has gone up a trillion times since the 1960s. Yet the brains which are charged with working through this huge volume of data are the same ones we've always had.

With most behavioural addictions, the cure would usually be abstinence. But cold turkey is not easy to achieve with a tool that's purposely made to be essential. Once our smartphones became impossible to leave at home, there was no blissful bubble that couldn't be interrupted. "Always on" had become a way of life.

What happens to your brain in burnout?

Whenever you receive a stressful message, your amygdala – your brain's radar – sets off the alarm. Having registered that there's something to worry about, it sends a message to the hypothalamus, the "flight desk", which tells your body what to do next. Now it's all systems go in your autonomic nervous system. Your adrenal glands, which make the steroid hormones that help to control heart rate and blood pressure, start pumping out adrenaline. This release speeds up your heart and lungs to supply oxygen and blood to your muscles so that you can get ready to "run away". All this can happen before the more logical part of your brain has even been notified or had the chance to give a more considered response. If the brain is still not sure if the threat has gone away, it raises the alert still further by rallying the hormone system too. This time, it triggers the release of cortisol, which tells the body that you still need to be vigilant.

This system was designed to deal with short, sharp threats. It wasn't created to deal with a round-the-clock barrage of stressful inputs. Over time, cortisol creates wear-and-tear on the body and can even alter brain structure, shrinking the hippocampus and enlarging the amygdala, making it even more reactive. Chronic stress also thins the prefrontal cortex, which can help talk you down from a place of panic and put incoming stressors in perspective. All these effects are amplified and more likely to trigger burnout if these stressors feel relentless and out of your control.

Crucially, when cortisol is always raised, it dials down the other chemicals of pleasure. It also narrows your attention to the things you need to do to dig yourself out of the latest crisis, so you have little energy for anything else.

Amy Arnsten is a professor of neuroscience at Yale School of Medicine, who studies what happens in the brain in burnout.

"One of the most striking [changes] is thinning of the grey matter of the prefrontal cortex," she says. "It's a double whammy. At the same time as the prefrontal cortex is getting weaker and more primitive, the brain circuits that generate emotions like fear are getting stronger. You start seeing the world as harmful when it is not."

We also forget the brain has finite resources, so one of the coping mechanisms it adopts to save its energy is to go numb. Allostatic load is the term for the wear and tear on the body which builds up when you are repeatedly exposed to high stress – and when the demands on you exceed your ability to cope. It's the price the body and brain eventually pay for trying to keep going. It can cause changes in hormone profile and immune function and is closely related to depression – and anhedonia.

The effects of burnout

Naveed Ahmad, CEO of Flourish, an organization which aims to address why modern life is often characterized by feeling stressed and overwhelmed, recalls his own realization at the age of 28 of how burnout was blunting his ability to feel. In Switzerland for a high stakes meeting for the global food industry, two emails helped him see what his life had become. "They represented the two extremes of emotion I could have experienced at that point in my life," Naveed recalls. "The first was from my boss's boss congratulating me on a new promotion that I earned ahead of schedule. That should have been a moment of joy and satisfaction and excitement, but I didn't feel any of those things. The other email was from my girlfriend breaking up with me. Over email. Which, by itself, is bad enough. It's hard to even put into words how I should have been feeling at that moment. But, again, I didn't feel anything."

Naveed closed his laptop, collapsed on his hotel bed – in his suit – and fell fast asleep. "In the moment, I didn't really realize or feel anything. I was numb to the fact I was numb. All I knew was that something had to change – I couldn't keep living this way. It took me a while to regain feeling. I took time off from work, started going to psychotherapy, and began focusing on my health to start to feel better. It took several months."

Asked why he thinks burnout can cause emotional flatlining, Naveed says: "With the caveat that I'm not an expert on physiology, I think it's the body's way of coping with stress. At some point, when things get so bad, it's easier to not feel than to feel the challenging emotions. But doing this is really hard on the body – it takes a lot of energy to numb these feelings, which is why we become deeply fatigued and lose motivation."

In her research on burnout, Harvard-trained biologist Joan Borysenko, breaks down burnout into steps: "It starts with wanting to improve yourself through working like a maniac moving onto putting your own needs last, feeling miserable and not knowing why, becoming frustrated, aggressive, and cynical and into a state of 'why bother'– anhedonia – before Stage 12 – physical and mental collapse."

Describing her own journey, Dr Borysenko told how she used to fantasize about having a car accident, because it would give her the excuse to step off the treadmill for a few days without feeling guilty. She notes that burned-out people quickly lose their sense of humour, become whiny and cranky, and often depersonalize – and feel like they are viewing their own lives as a spectator rather than being active participants. They also experience emotional blunting, which is one of the most recognizable signs of anhedonia. "The chasm that separates you from life is so vast at this point that stimulation of any kind has to be especially intense to generate any feeling at all," Dr Borysenko explains. "Food that you once enjoyed may seem flat or uninteresting. A salad may feel too bland. Some people report seeking intensely sweet or salty food like bacon. Emotional exhaustion, hopeless indifference, apathy, and everything seeming meaningless are obvious overlaps. Cynicism about your work is also a hallmark. It's a coping mechanism which gives you an illusion of control and distance from a situation in which you feel otherwise powerless. Over time, it becomes the filter through which we can see our entire lives."

Fun has slipped a long way down my list of things
I have time for. Work and family commitments meant
it felt like a luxury.
Rob, 46

My own experience of burnout

Halfway through my career, I was a fully paid-up member of the burnout club. I was working in the office four hours before I checked into the hospital for a C-section for my second daughter. As an executive editor working on the re-launch of an American magazine, I had gone to the wire, hoping that my epic 40-page handover memo would buy me more time with my baby. Some hope.

A week later my boss rang to ask if I would mind working from home as the person lined up to cover for me had decided it wasn't the job for them after all. Of course, we could have done with the extra money. But the underlying fact was, that like so many of my generation, I had been conditioned to believe that if you worked and wanted to do well, you had to pay a high price.

It got to the point where a necessary visit to the doctor felt as self-indulgent as a week at the spa. Instead, I struggled to meet demands from my children and editors while my husband worked 14-hour days in the office. I began to realize that "having it all" had come to mean having to do absolutely everything, all at once.

I knew I didn't want to become one of those fabled mothers who read their children bedtime stories over Facetime. So, I thought the solution was working from home. Yet that seemed to expose the children to an even more harassed parent. I always seemed to receive the most stressful phone calls between school pick-up and bedtime when I'd hoped to be completely there for the girls. My least favourite memory of parenthood was feeling like my head was about to explode as Lily, then 5, lay prostrate on the floor as I tried to answer an urgent work query, screaming: "But you said you'd make cupcakes!" Back then, bosses and clients didn't worry about the domino effect of the tension levels in family homes. That was your problem. Not theirs.

Yet even though our working day is only our first shift, mothers are still exhorted to "lean in" in the workplace. The problem is that, as American writer Amy Westervelt has pointed out, many of us were leaning in so much, we were starting to fall flat on our faces. I had never heard of "anhedonia", but there were clues I was already in a zombie state. At Clio's fourth birthday party, I presented her birthday cake with great ceremony and then wondered why there was such an anti-climax. Everything was such a blur that I had completely forgotten to put on the candles. It never occurred to me that I could enjoy my daughter's birthday – or revel in the lovely moments of awe and sweetness that a small child's party brought with it. It had become just another stressful event to plan on my to-do list.

The overwhelm was stealing away what should have been my biggest joy – my children. The truth is that no matter how good our intentions, overwork and overwhelm make enjoying life very difficult. Stress is quite simply the greatest enemy of joy there is. Yet too often we stay in this zone because the Western world encourages us to live on autopilot. We are taught to tick boxes, but not to ask what's good for our wellbeing. My own clue that I was in burnout was that at end of another day juggling childcare and meeting deadlines and queries from numerous editors, I'd lie on the bed unable to speak or do anything but watch mindless TV that wouldn't tax my brain.

We all have our own personal experiences which can tip us into overwhelm and anhedonia.

Studies show that unlike depression, which is twice as prevalent in women than men, anhedonia appears to affect men and women equally. Social constraints, however, mean men may feel less able to express it.

Anhedonia can also surface at any age. It's just as likely to appear in the college student who realizes that the pressure they were under to get the exam grades they thought they needed to get a decent job isn't going to let up anytime soon, to the pensioner who realizes they have lost interest in their grandchildren.

What if it's mild depression?

Anhedonia is a well-known core symptom of depression, but, as we've heard, you don't have to be deeply depressed to experience it. While depression is a serious mental illness, which often incapacitates, dysthymia is a stealthier less obvious version that often gets overlooked – and often co-exists with anhedonia. You will still be able to function. You may never have had a major depressive episode. But dysthymia – also known as "smiling depression" – slips below the radar because you are still getting on with life, and it doesn't seem serious enough to be addressed.

But it can settle into a way of being, so it becomes impossible to imagine living any other way.

Just because dysthymia is lower grade depression – and you can keep going – doesn't mean it should be ignored. You may be keeping the plates spinning – just. But only because your fear of what would happen if they crashed to the ground is greater.

If you have consistently been unhappy for two years, along with at least two of the following symptoms, it's time to reassess. Over this period, have you persistently had:

- Lasting empty moods of sadness, emptiness, and hopelessness
- Trouble concentrating and making decisions

- Changes in sleeping patterns – like getting the 4am "panics"
- Feelings of irritability
- Being able to fake being fine in public, but finding it difficult not to feel down and be bad-tempered at home
- Poor appetite or over-eating
- Low self-esteem and high self-criticism
- Loss of interest in everyday activities and avoidance of social activities

Source: Mayo Clinic

Anhedonia and loss of enjoyment in life is just one symptom of dysthymia – and there may be a lot of overlap because they could be cross-pollinating each other. But if you recognize many of the symptoms above, find a qualified mental health professional to assess you. Persistent negative thoughts and raised cortisol create fertile soil for depression. In the same way as a cold can develop into pneumonia, dysthymia can develop into something more intractable.

Having this as your baseline means it can take just one major stressor – like a job loss, or a family difficulty – to tip you into a more serious state.

4

How Your Childhood May be Standing in the Way of Experiencing Joy Today

When I was age nine, I went to visit my father for the weekend. As my parents had separated once again, I was looking forward to seeing him back at our family home. I remember the sun streaming through the windows in the living room as I talked excitedly about the things I hoped we could do together that day. One idea was a visit to Hampton Court, a Tudor palace across the other side of the park from where we lived, and which I loved to visit. But today when I suggested it, my father's face darkened as he sat across from me. Out of nowhere, he snapped at me, saying no we couldn't. Didn't I know his business was failing and he had no money for the entrance fee? (A nominal amount then, compared to now.) No, I didn't.

I can still remember my terrible confusion, as he took his anger out on me. Even now, I can feel the sensation of the back of my bare legs sticking to the leather chair and my small voice assuring him we could just go to the nearby park instead, because that wouldn't cost anything. While my father was a mostly loving parent, it was not the only time when his reactions could be unpredictable. It taught me that it wasn't safe to feel happy – and, if I did, something or someone could snatch it away from me.

Beliefs about happiness

Not all feelings of "blah" relate to how our brains are designed or the stresses of modern-day life. Your capacity for joy may also be linked to your childhood. You may not even realize that just beneath your conscious awareness there are invisible obstacles getting in the way of your positive emotions. Indeed, research has found that for some people, happiness and joy doesn't feel pleasurable. It can also feel uncomfortable. Something happened to them in childhood that gave them the message it's not safe to look forward to things, they don't deserve to be happy or, if they do feel good, something will come along to ruin it.

Your childhood could have affected more than your beliefs about happiness. It may also have moulded the way your nervous system was wired. As a tiny baby, you arrived unfinished, defenceless and desperate to latch onto anything that made you feel safe. When you were held and soothed by your carers, hormones like oxytocin increased in your body given you feelings of contentment and safety.

If you felt alone, frightened or hungry, this soothing would also have reduced your cortisol levels again. If someone picked you up when you cried, you no longer felt overwhelmed. Oxytocin would also have quelled your levels of adrenaline and noradrenaline, bringing you back down to a place of calm. But if no one came to comfort you after your flight-fright-freeze response was triggered, it may have shaped how your nervous system responded. If it happened before you could talk, you may not have any memories of feeling abandoned, afraid or confused.

A wide range of research has found that a child's early experiences are critical in deciding how they release stress chemicals as they grow up. If you experienced things which swamped you while you were still learning to regulate your emotions, they may have influenced how your stress response was wired. Your body will have got used to pumping out high levels of hormones, like cortisol, adrenaline and noradrenaline, long after the traumatic situations have passed, even though you are now an adult in control of your life. Children who are not soothed when they experience prolonged or unpredictable stress can become hypervigilant. They grow into adults who feel unsafe and under attack, even when the initial stressor has passed. This means that even in adulthood, it's hard to stop scanning the environment and expecting bad things to happen at any moment. If you are always on guard, it makes it harder to relax and enjoy experiences.

I went to a therapist, and she said to try to feel emotions
in my body rather than try to immediate analyse them.
I realized that being distant and analytical had become
the way I had pushed my feelings down since childhood.
Davina, 45

Studies show there is also a negative knock-on effect on the feel-good chemicals serotonin and oxytocin into adulthood, which creates a higher likelihood of anhedonia. As psychiatrist and neuroscientist Bessel van der Kolk, author of *The Body Keeps the Score*, says: "Traumatized people have a tremendous problem experiencing pleasure and joy ... [They] tend to have bodies which are either too alert, responding to every breath and touch, or else too numb."

> *The message at home growing up was: "Your job is to work hard to make our family look good." I went along with it as a child because it was all I knew and fulfilled those expectations by becoming a lawyer. But the fact that even childhood felt like a job, meant I didn't know what fun felt like either.*
>
> Abhi, 53

A FEAR OF HAPPINESS

How many of these statements do you recognize from the "Fear of Happiness" scale (a measurement tool in psychology)?

- I worry that if I feel good, something bad could happen.
- Feeling good makes me feel uncomfortable.
- I find it difficult to trust positive feelings.
- Good feelings never last.
- When you are happy, you can never be sure something is not going to hit you out of the blue.

- If you feel good, you let your guard down.
- I don't let myself get too excited about positive things or achievements.
- I feel I don't deserve to be happy.
- I am frightened to let myself get too happy.

All my life I watched other people get excited about things and never felt the same. They'll say: "This is so fun" but I never really understood what the big deal was. I wondered if it was perhaps because we didn't have a lot of laughter around when I was growing up.

Jo, 34

Dissociation

Another reason you may struggle to enjoy yourself is because you dissociate from feelings of joy. In our childhood, we are, in effect, all hostages. We don't choose the families we are born into, and we rely on our parents and carers completely for every survival need. If we are not born into an emotionally healthy home, usually there is nowhere to escape to. If we saw things that scared us at an age before we were old enough to cope or process what was happening, we may have learnt to freeze and distance ourselves. This was a way to buffer ourselves from feelings we were not yet old enough to understand or put into perspective. Long after the shock has passed, this wiring can persist into adulthood, so our nervous system keeps reacting in the same way.

Although the process is not yet completely understood, one theory of dissociation is that when children are in the presence of a threat they are too young to handle, their nervous system responds by reducing the flow of blood to the prefrontal cortex. According to Dr Susan Overhauser, a clinical psychologist specializing in treating trauma, attachment and dissociation: "The amygdala lights up and fires warning signals. In response, the frontal lobes (the part of our brain which supports reasoning), go offline, unable to respond. Instead, blood flows to our limbs in the hope we can perhaps avert danger by fighting or fleeing. In this bodily state, perceptions of the world go directly into our body-mind, unfiltered by thinking."

Stressful, traumatic experiences may not be the only times when you distance yourself in adulthood. You may dissociate yourself at other times when you should feel good too.

At first when I realized that I could dissociate from stressful situations, it felt like a superpower. Then I realized it was a defence I had developed in childhood to protect myself when I saw adults in my family acting in scary ways. But I wasn't just distancing from stressful situations. I was also distancing myself from happy ones.

Maya, 46

My own dissociation

In my teens I was aware that I became strangely distanced in stressful situations, like moments of family conflict, as if I was viewing the experience from the other end of a tunnel. From the outside, this made me look calm and in control, but in fact I wasn't feeling any emotion. At the time, I thought it was a strength. Then I started to notice there was a flipside. This distancing feeling happened at moments when I should have been happy too.

The most striking example was at my wedding. I was 33, so my childhood was a long way behind me. While I could see tears of happiness in my husband Anthony's eyes as we stood in front of the altar, I noticed I wasn't present enough in my own body to experience the joy of the occasion. Although I wanted to feel the elation, I felt like I wasn't completely there.

My wedding day moment stuck in my mind for a long time. It really bothered me. After all, how was I ever going to find my way out of anhedonia if I couldn't enjoy what should have been one of the happiest days of my life?

Nervous system wiring

During therapy in the years that followed, I mentioned this wedding day experience to counsellors but got no clear explanations. Then during a conversation with anhedonia expert Jackie Kelm, as part of the research for this book, she suggested a newer approach which looks at how our nervous systems are wired. This had helped hundreds of people she had counselled with anhedonia to understand why they were never fully present during joyful moments.

Although we have long tended to rely on talking therapies to address difficult childhoods, the body is not just a stick to carry the brain around on. Both are part of the same system. As our bodies are being wired during infancy and toddlerhood, we may not even remember the traumatic moments which led to our nervous system adapting to try and cope. Irene Lyon, one of the world's leading experts on somatic therapy and the nervous system, which looks at this connection, says: "People don't have to have been abused in childhood to have hypervigilance or dissociation. They could have witnessed something out of their control, not received comfort afterwards, or had their feelings ignored, dismissed or denied. It could be that your Mum and Dad hated each other and argued a lot. Or they were super busy with their work and they paid very little attention to your feelings or needs. Usually children don't run away from less-than-ideal conditions because deep down they know they wouldn't survive on their own. So they cope by taking themselves out of their bodies. People who dissociate will say things like: 'I saw myself from above, I floated up'. They may even feel a sense of lightness. They lose their grounding in the here and now. At the time, it felt like a superpower that can help us, but dissociation persists when we don't need it anymore. It can show up as not feeling joy in joyful situations too."

SIMPLE WAYS TO COME BACK FROM DISSOCIATION

At times of dissociation, somatic therapists recommend techniques to bring yourself back into your body. These will also help when you realize that at moments that should feel good, you feel like an outsider looking on. Although they are many approaches, commonly used basic techniques include:

- Breathing slowly and noticing your breath.
- Becoming aware of the sounds around you.
- Touching something with an unusual texture.
- Smelling something with a strong smell.
- Tasting something and noticing the flavours.

Childhood messages and thinking patterns

During your childhood, you may have received other messages which have made it harder to feel joy now. If you grew up in a home where adults did not behave in predictable ways, where the atmosphere could become threatening at any moment or where grown-ups didn't follow through on promises, you may have fallen into a pattern of becoming cynical or pessimistic to try to protect yourself from disappointment. To protect yourself, you may have decided to believe it's never safe to let your guard down, "let go" or make yourself vulnerable by really *feeling* an emotion.

As a child, I would get told "Boys don't cry" and "Not to turn the taps on," if I was upset. To cope as a child, I learned it was best to numb what I felt. I learnt that only superficial, acceptable feelings were allowed and that included never getting too excited about anything either.

Robin, 58

For a long time from my late thirties onwards, I didn't feel anything. Then last year, I started to see a therapist and we talked about my childhood. I started to see the connection between my past and my present. As the youngest of four, I felt I had to fit in. To be accepted, my response was to become a people-pleaser who pushed down my own needs – and that meant not doing the activities that made me feel good. I went along with what my family wanted. With my therapist's help, I went back into my past to question my core beliefs about happiness, so I could become aware of them and change them.

Ingrid, 52

You may also have developed a pattern of thinking that it's not safe to look forward to events.

Thoughts like: "Don't bother getting your hopes up" may run through your head. As we shall hear, by never positively anticipating events, you sabotage your brain's own reward system.

Your defences may even seem to have become a personality trait, when really your cynicism is an attempt to protect yourself from disappointment.

We had pretty much no good times together as a family growing up because my parents divorced when I was 11. When I was about 35, on holiday, I remember sitting by a pool and watching a family of five – two parents and their tweens and teens – having a great time in the water. They were really laughing, playing games and fooling around. I just couldn't understand it. I actually felt irritated. Then I realized I'd never seen a family have real fun together before. When I realized it brought up such strong feelings, I knew I had to work out why.

Liz, 39

Childhood stress

A range of studies have found early childhood stress changes how the reward circuit develops, dulling its response even to good experiences. Brain scans by psychologists at Duke University in the USA found greater levels of cumulative stress during childhood and adolescence predicted lower activity in a key part of the reward circuit, the ventral striatum. In other words, people with these types of childhoods may not get as much pleasure from positive experiences. Early stress, specifically between Nursery and Year Three, was most strongly associated with muted responses to rewards when children grew up.

Children who were neglected and abused have also been found to have a narrower range of both negative and positive emotions. Those who had been abused were more likely to feel numbed. Researchers believe they may also have developed a pattern of negative moods which took up too much of their mental energy to be happy. Nervous system expert Irene Lyon says that at least half of people seeking help to deal with the after-effects of a traumatic childhood talk about feelings of emotional flatlining. "They say: 'I don't feel anything, I never cry. I can't remember the last time I was looking forward to something.' People will get injured and keep going because it can dull physical pain as well."

I tried to work out why I felt so much on the edge in social situations and at work. And with therapy, I realized this is how I had felt growing up in my family – never good enough and like an outsider. I had to go back and imagine giving myself the comfort and love I wish my parents had given me as a child. It wasn't easy but re-parenting myself was a start.

Polly, 51

Looking at your childhood

If you had a childhood with few happy memories, it may have lowered your expectations of how much you should enjoy your life. You may simply not know how happiness feels – or have lost hope of finding it.

If your parents were emotionally absent, put their own needs first again, or acted like they didn't want you around, subconsciously you may feel you are not likeable to others. If your carers were too distracted or stressed to play with you or smile at you, you may have processed this lack of responsiveness as a rejection. The outcome is that you never completely let go and enjoy yourself at social occasions.

If you got the message that you were not good enough, or weren't living up to their expectations, you may also have developed people-pleasing as a strategy, and always prioritize other people's enjoyment over your own.

Or maybe you are from a family where carefree fun was frowned on. Was a family member depressed or ill? Was there an unspoken rule that you shouldn't go against that? Or did you get the message early on that you had to forego fun to work hard and succeed at school?

It may mean that you feel uncomfortable when feelings of happiness or joy start to creep up on you. You suppress them because you don't know how to experience them. You may also have visceral bodily reactions, like sweaty palms or discomfort in your chest, which you cannot explain.

Or if you grew up in a chaotic home, that may have come to feel like the norm. You may have become so used to drama – and the adrenaline and cortisol that swirled around you – that you feel bored and numb if you don't see it in your adult life too.

I grew up in a very disrupted, unhappy household.
My saving grace was that I was good at schoolwork,

*so when things were tough at home, I threw myself
at that. It meant that workaholism became my coping
mechanism. It was when I got to about 50 and looked
back that I realized I'd worked so hard, I'd never allowed
myself time to have fun.*

Zoe, 55

As psychiatrist Paul Gilbert has described it: "It is not uncommon for some people to fear that if they are happy about something, it will be taken away." One theory is that the fear of having happiness taken away – known as "cherophobia" – is so great that people who experience it won't risk it. They might feel guilty or worry it will lead to something bad happening.

To explore how your own personal beliefs about happiness were formed during childhood, consider some of these questions. As these delve deep into your past, consider consulting a trained therapist.

- Did your parents have a happy partnership for most of your childhood?
- Did your parents enjoy spending time with you?
- Did you often go away for family holidays or breaks?
- Did you have as many opportunities to play and have fun in childhood as you wanted?
- Did you regularly laugh with your parents?
- Did you have funny, shared family jokes and stories (that don't typecast or make fun of family members)?

- Did you feel important in your family, growing up?
- Did you feel your parents treated all the children in your family uniquely and fairly?
- Did you feel you had an extended family who also cared and comforted you if you needed it?
- Did your parents seem to enjoy life?
- Did you feel loved unconditionally?
- If you were in trouble, did you feel you could confide in a parent or family member who made you feel better?
- Did you feel that all your feelings were "allowed"?

There is no such thing as a perfect family. But if you give more "no" than "yes" answers, it might be worth thinking more deeply with the help of a professional – about how your childhood might have had a knock-on effect on your capacity to feel joy now and how it might link to anhedonia.

> *If I start to relax into enjoying myself, I seem to pull myself up short. It's like there's a bad fairy whispering in my ear: "Have a good time now but there'll be a price to pay later".*
> Shaheen, 25

If you feel you didn't have the happy childhood you might have hoped for, the first step is to build an awareness of how the invisible strings of the past are still pulling on your adult self. The truth is this is not a quick process. It can be painful to imagine yourself as a small, helpless child. It may take some years of cycling through grief, anger and denial. It may help to go back and "re-parent" yourself, possibly with the help of a therapist. Return to the times when you felt alone, confused or rejected as a child and imagine giving yourself the hugs of comfort you would have liked to have had then. Release yourself from blaming yourself for things in your childhood that were not your fault. Ask yourself too how patterns you have struggled to break, like workaholism, might relate to your childhood coping mechanisms.

You may have to go through a process of grieving for your childhood. But at the end of any process like this, there is acceptance.

As part of this we may have to come to terms with fact much as we might like to, we can never redo our childhoods. The good news, and the first step, is to recognize you are no longer a powerless child ruled by the grown-ups who raised you. This may sound obvious, but in fact it's a huge step forward. First you may have to grieve the fact that the adults who you feel failed you are unlikely to change.

"People refuse to change because they want a redo on their childhood," says psychotherapist Lori Gottlieb, author of *Maybe You Should Talk* and presenter of the *Dear Therapists* podcasts. "Unconsciously what they are saying is: 'I won't change until you treat me the way I wanted to be treated when I was eight.' But that's not going to happen. So many people are waiting for their parents to change as adults. They are still waiting. They are saying: 'When you change, Mum or Dad, I will feel better, and I will be able to be the adult I was meant to be. But it doesn't work like that. Your partner will not redo your childhood for you, your job will not redo your childhood. Nothing will redo what happened. But you get to choose how you live your life now. Do you want to live it as the child who may be trapped in some ways? Or do you want to live it as the adult who is, in fact, free?"

I was 60 before I organized a birthday party for myself because, having been sent off to boarding school at the age of nine, I didn't trust anyone to turn up. After all, if your own parents didn't want you, why would anyone else want to be around you?

Henrietta, 68

Awareness is always the first step in the right direction. When you next have feelings of discomfort, stop to notice them, recognize where they come from and remind yourself that you're safe now. Even if your childhood wasn't full of fun and laughter, there is no invisible force that should be allowed to stop you enjoying your life now. It will take practice but conscious awareness of where that feeling is forming in your body is the first and most important step. Be curious when you notice this feeling so you can start to view it from a distance, rather than keeping it lodged inside you. When you are observing it, you are no longer being overwhelmed by it. That feeling is not right or wrong. It is not your fault. View it as a pathway built when you were a child. Somatic expert Irene Lyon says: "Everyone has the capacity to heal their nervous system. It's not just about feeling happy, it's about feeling *all* your emotions. You may have to work through the grief and anger first and get used to the feeling of knowing how to process joy. It's true that you can't change your childhood, but you can start to make sense of what happened in your childhood. There's always hope and the capacity to change."

> *Even though I was lucky enough to break the cycle of my parents' unhappy marriage, I noticed that when I was with my husband and children having fun, I felt a sensation of discomfort, like a tangle of negativity in my upper chest. When I tapped into it, I realized that I feared that if I gave in to good feelings, I'd somehow be letting my guard down and I'd have to pay for it. Somehow, the idea that I didn't deserve to be happy had become deeply lodged in my psyche, like a splinter I couldn't dislodge. It took me a session with a somatic therapist to realize this discomfort felt like a black knot in my upper chest and throat. Now I felt I could notice it, I felt more in control of it, and more able bring myself back to the present to remind myself that I was safe. As the therapist told me afterwards: "You know rationally that you have got a family that cares about you, and you should be able to enjoy it. Your body hasn't got the message."*
>
> Sabi, 45

EXPRESSIVE WRITING

If you want to go a little deeper into some of the feelings that are standing in the way of enjoying your life, try free writing. For example, you might want to go back to some of the moments when you felt happiness was not an option for you. The aim is to download the thought that has been circulating in your head onto paper, without self-criticism, judgement or rumination. If it's pushing you too far, stop. Try again another day until you can process the experience. You may feel angry or upset to start with, but you could soon feel a sense of relief.

Cognitive Behavioural Therapist Navit Schechter says: "Expressive writing can be used to work through stressful or traumatic events you've experienced. It can help you to process your emotions and experiences, making it easier for you to make sense of them and store them alongside other memories so that you can move on from them. It has been found to be really beneficial for people who tend to already manage emotions by expressing how they feel. If you feel drawn to trying uninterrupted expressive writing, then it's best to find a quiet and relaxing spot where you won't be disturbed. Bring to mind a stressful or traumatic experience that you've had in the past; it doesn't necessarily need to be the most traumatic experience you've had but whatever comes up for you. Allow yourself to bring pen to paper and write down whatever surfaces. If you don't know where to start, you can ask yourself "How am I feeling now thinking about this?" and continue asking yourself questions about what's happened to make you feel that way and how it's affected you since. Don't worry about spelling or grammar or whether it makes sense. Just write freely and continuously to get your experience out of you and onto paper. It's suggested that you write for between 15–20 minutes and on 3–5 consecutive days. You can write about the same, or different, experiences each day. Make sure that when you've finished writing you take a moment for yourself to unwind before getting on with your day. If you're worried that someone will read what you've written and that this gets in the way for you writing freely and openly, you can find somewhere safe to store it or even burn it safely if this feels helpful for you. Make sure to reach out to friends, family or a professional if these feelings feel too difficult for you or if you're experiencing any symptoms of PTSD. On the other hand, you may find that it feels liberating and a relief to unburden yourself of memories and feelings that had been held inside you."

All in all, free writing sounds deceptively simple, but studies show there are a wide range of benefits including physical ones, such as better immune function, fewer doctor appointments, improved memory and fewer symptoms of anxiety and depression.

Part One summary

By now, I hope you understand some of the sources of your anhedonia. Some of these will lie in pre-history. Some in your personal history.

There is no doubt a gap has opened up between what the brain was evolved for and the demands placed on it by modern lifestyles. But our growing understanding of how the brain's reward system works, its effects on our emotions, and what can make it falter (which I explore in the next part of the book) means we can now bridge the void into which you may have fallen.

PART TWO

What Anhedonia Means
for You

5

Physical Reasons for Feeling "Blah"

Anhedonia is not all the mind. Ask those deep in anhedonia when they first noticed the symptoms, and a good number will report it began after a bout of ill-health. Some will name viral infections like Covid-19. Or autoimmune illnesses like rheumatoid arthritis and lupus or parasitic infections such as Lyme disease. Some will say they developed it quite soon after having to take large doses of antibiotics. Others will mention lifestyle diseases like type 2 diabetes and obesity. As we shall hear, there could be a good reason for this.

Take a dive into the research into diseases which cause a strong auto-immune responses and inflammation, and you will find a growing number of studies listing anhedonia among the symptoms.

At this point you might be thinking, "Of course it's hard to enjoy life when you're not feeling your best and you can't enjoy the activities you used to." But the link is more specific.

Inflammation has a targeted effect on the brain's reward and motivation systems. When inflammation reaches the brain it interrupts the synthesis of feel-good chemicals and how well they circulate. The different regions in the reward circuit don't communicate as well. Inflammation reduces the flow of feel-good neurotransmitters like serotonin and dopamine between the neurons. This is something we need to talk about more.

When the brain's reward system breaks down, we lose the motivation to take the steps we need to improve our health – whether it's taking exercise or eating the more nourishing, less inflammatory foods we will talk about later in the book. It may mean we don't bother to take the medications or get the help we need.

In other words, until we recognise and tackle anhedonia, we can lose the will to fight back. And when the damage done to the brain's reward systems is part of some of the most prevalent lifestyle diseases in the world, it's time to start viewing anhedonia as a serious impediment to the world becoming a healthier place.

Take obesity. According to the World Health Organization, global rates have tripled since 1975. More than 1.9 billion adults are overweight and 650 million are obese. Most of the world's population live in countries where being overweight or obese kills more people than being underweight. To try and turn back the tide, governments all over the world mount public health campaigns to get their citizens active and all too often are left wondering why nothing much changes. In all this, we forget that excess body fat is also inflammatory – and therefore strikes at the very reward circuitry that overweight and obese people need to make lifestyle changes.

As Professor Edward Bullimore, a neuropsychiatrist at the University of Cambridge, points out his book *The Inflamed Mind*: "About 60 per cent of the cells in adipose [fat] tissue are macrophages, the Robocops of the immune system, and one of the principal sources of inflammatory cytokines. Overweight or obese people, with a higher body mass index, will generally have higher blood levels of cytokines and C Reactive-Protein (markers for inflammation in the blood) than slimmer people.

"The same vicious circle is found in a related global health epidemic, type 2 diabetes. As well as the vascular damage diabetes does, when the body can't regulate blood sugar levels, it also sparks inflammation in the brain. Some of the latest research into type 2 diabetes has found that it is 'significantly associated' with 'the anhedonic subtype of major depression'."

Once we recognize the loss of motivation – anhedonia's hallmark – as a distinct symptom of several illnesses, we can start to weaken its grip. Naming anhedonia can put us in a frame of mind which allows us to help ourselves.

Take a health inventory

Think back over the last few years. Did you notice a shift in mood or your enjoyment of life after you developed an illness?

Consider your treatments and medication too. While they may have helped beat the original illness, anhedonia may be the lingering hangover. For instance, some antidepressant medications like SSRIs can blunt feelings. But by reducing the intensity of sadness, they can reduce the intensity of happiness too.

Chronic pain also interrupts the reward system, possibly because rising stress levels dampen down the flow of feel-good neurotransmitters like dopamine – and obviously it's hard to have fun when your body hurts. If this is you, what kind of pain relief have you been taking? Some also contain ingredients, like acetaminophen, that make emotions flatline. If you see a possible connection, talk to the professionals who prescribed them to you. If you still take them, a change of dose or a different drug could be the answer.

Another possible trigger could be taking a large amounts of antibiotics. These may have been needed at the time to overcome a serious infection. But to beat it, they may have wiped out some of the microbiome in your gut that you need to make serotonin and dopamine. As we will hear, this may have thrown this forest of bacteria, which helps you digest food, out of balance, allowing your gut lining to become inflamed. Switching to foods and supplements which will help them grow back will help get happiness chemicals flowing again.

Consider whether any ongoing illness you may be living with – and which causes inflammation in the body – whether it's rheumatoid arthritis, lupus, coeliac disease, either type of diabetes, hypertension, or inflammatory bowel disease – may also be affecting your brain's reward system. Talk to your doctors about the lifestyle changes (some of which we will go on to discuss in Part Three) that could help reduce inflammation in your brain too.

Whatever the weather, it felt like the sky was grey. After 20 years of marriage, I know you don't have the same

excitement about your partner, but when I went through
menopause I didn't feel anything much at all towards
my husband, expect occasional feelings of irritation.
Even moments of loveliness with my pets or my children
didn't move me like they should have done.

Ruth, 55

Our changing bodies and mood

Our enjoyment of life is directed by chemical messengers which are in a constant state of flux over our lifetimes. Our stage of life, gender, diet and sleep patterns can all affect the interaction of our neurotransmitters and hormones. To understand why you might be feeling "blah", it also helps to understand how our normal bodily processes affect their ebb and flow.

Menopause

There is a multi-tasking chemical so powerful that in a woman's body it can help her sleep, concentrate, boost her orgasms and improve her mood. Then from around the mid-40s, the tap for this hormone gradually turns off. That substance is oestrogen.

For a long time, we tended to think that when a woman went through menopause the main effects were the end of periods and vaginal dryness, peppered with a few hot flushes.

While women have long sensed how the rise and fall of oestrogen can affect their mood over the course of their monthly menstrual cycle, it wasn't until the early 1990s that brain-scanning techniques revealed how much of an effect this key hormone has on the female brain.

Since I started getting into menopause, my emotions feel blunted. I get cross easily, but hardly ever laugh so there's no flipside. I'm not depressed but it does feel like I am going through the motions. It's like being lost in a mist of 'meh-ness'.

Eve, 49

The effects of reduced oestrogen

Far from just ruling the ovaries, many areas of the brain are packed with oestrogen receptors. They include the regions in the reward circuit, like the amygdala, and the hippocampus.

As women stop ovulating – and producing oestrogen – studies show this has a knock-on effect on the feel-good chemicals, dopamine and serotonin.

Oestrogen has also been found to stimulate dopamine receptors. So, falling levels mean that less dopamine is released into the reward system. One study by Yale University found that without oestrogen, more than 30 per cent of dopamine neurons disappeared in major areas that produce the chemical messenger. The fall-off also appears to affect the working of the brain's pleasure centre, the nucleus accumbens.

In rat studies, University of Missouri researchers found a link between a decline in ovarian hormones and changes in this pleasure centre. Furthermore, studies have also found higher levels of an enzyme called Monoamine Oxidase A during menopause. This breaks down serotonin and dopamine, meaning there's less of these feel-good chemicals circulating.

You're at that place in your life where on paper, you have got where you want jobwise. You've got through the early years with the kids and the house and the partner and the dog. Everything should be perfect. But it's not.

Jacqui, 51

To find out how oestrogen and the loss of other sex hormones affected the female brain, neuroscientist Professor Lisa Mosconi scanned more than 160 women between the ages of 40 and 65 who were approaching or going through menopause. She and her team looked at their brain structure, blood flow to the brain and its energy use. They did the same tests again two years later and compared them to the brains of men of the same age – and found a 30 per cent drop in brain energy levels pre- and post-menopause in the female group. "We associate menopause with the ovaries. But the symptoms don't start in the ovaries. They start in the brain," says Professor Mosconi. "What we found in women and not in men is that the brain changes quite a lot." Hormones like oestrogen are not only involved in reproduction, but also in brain function. "The transition of menopause really leads to a whole remodelling. Our brains and ovaries are part of the neuroendocrine system. As part of the system, the brain talks to the ovaries and the ovaries talk back to the brain every day of our lives as women. Oestrogen really is key for energy production in the brain. At the cellular level, oestrogen literally pushes neurons to burn glucose to make energy."

According to Professor Mosconi: "If your oestrogen is high, your brain energy is high. When your oestrogen declines, your neurons start slowing down and age faster. We should look at the brain as something that is as impacted by menopause at least as much as your ovaries are."

While this seems to massively stack the odds against women in the mid-life years, the good news is there are plenty of ways to address this. This new awareness of the effect of menopause on the brain is why the issue of hormone therapies, and other lifestyle changes, has now become such a hot topic. It's become clear that rather than putting up with it, or not talking about it, women want to make sure they keep enjoying life to the full.

As I entered my late 40s. I was surprised my husband didn't divorce me because I just didn't know how to feel fun anymore. I worried about getting older, stressed about how I was losing my looks and lost the confidence I'd acquired in my 30s. I guessed it was hormonal when I started getting incredibly annoyed by things which once wouldn't have bothered me. I'd wake up and the second I opened my eyes, it was like cortisol was already coursing through me. I knew something inside me had shifted.

Indira, 52

Crucially for mood, oestrogen also buffers the effects of the stress hormone cortisol. When it starts falling away, and cortisol starts to get the upper hand, it helps explains why some women feel more anxious and panicky about small things that never bothered them before. Because oestrogen is also important in helping different regions of the brain "talk" to each other, a fall-off in oestrogen can also make you feel ditzy, forgetful and stupid at a time of life when you should rightfully be feeling capable and knowledgeable.

Nor is oestrogen the only player. Other hormones and neurotransmitters also stop working in harmony. Levels of progesterone, a hormone which is a natural calmer, testosterone, which gives a sense of confidence, and GABA, a moderating neurotransmitter, also drop off.

Throw in the decline in the bonding hormone oxytocin, too, and there's a chance you may be feeling more impatient and snappier. As it's the hormone that bonds us to our partners and kids, it's not surprising if plunging levels mean make you feel less patient than you used to.

Oxytocin also moderates the impact of cortisol, tipping the balance even more in favour of the stress hormone.

Because of this perfect storm – some might say whirlwind – it's hardly surprising that the majority of women say they feel more bothered by small things that didn't affect them before. The loss of this cushioning effect during menopause can spell a shift from a "I can handle this" mentality to "This all feels a bit much".

Menopause campaigner and writer Alice Smellie, co-author of *Cracking the Menopause* with Mariella Frostrup, says: "We've long known hormones impact on mood at this time of life, but there's been little interest in talking about the subject in any serious way. Historically, it has been discussed mostly in terms of how women were insane and/or irritable. And, of course, there has always been the – deeply unfunny – joke about women going through 'the change' and being grumpy and volatile."

But, as Alice points out, the changes to our brain and body chemistry are anything but funny. "We have oestrogen receptors all around our bodies, including our brains, and it's now recognized that the brain undergoes changes during the menopausal years. There are over 50 symptoms, including changes in mood, such as irritability, anger, and a feeling of not being oneself, as well as 'brain fog'. It's often during perimenopause that women first report mood changes – feeling anxious, stressed or low for no reason. It's very hard to work out how many women are affected by mood changes during this time. Studies suggest it's around one in four, but I'd honestly – from personal experience – suggest that it could be higher. Don't forget that perimenopause and menopause also occur at a time of life when there are many other life stresses, such as busy careers, ageing parents and teenagers. Having interviewed literally hundreds of women about the subject, it's clear that frequently a lack of knowledge and education about menopause means that women may not realize that their low mood could be linked to hormones too. This and anxiety are symptoms that many of the woman to whom I spoke mentioned."

> *I felt so "meh" going through the menopause*
> *I pretended to be a robot just to get through it.*
> *No one had a clue!*
> Melanie, 50

Family overload

These menopausal changes are compounded by the fact that women often feel pulled in many different directions. The number of women in work has hit a record high at more than 75 per cent in the UK. It doesn't take long for motherhood to turn into a cortisol-inducing dash between work and childcare or school.

> *I loved being a mum when my kids were little. But as they got older and so did I, I found myself losing patience with their endless demands and self-centredness. To be honest, there were times when I couldn't wait for them to leave home, so I could get on with enjoying my life again.*
>
> Karen, 55

As lawyer Eve Rodsky points out in her book *Fair Play*: "Women are supposed to work like they don't have kids and parent like they don't work. While men's time is treated as diamond, women's time is treated like sand of which there is an unlimited resource. Women don't want to have to keep micromanaging, being the planners, asking others in the family to do the things they should already be doing just to get things done."

Psychotherapist Nancy Colier describes how the question that most often brings women to tears in the therapy room is: "Who's taking care of you?" "After the tears, the response that comes is usually a simple 'No one'," says Nancy, author of *The Emotionally Exhausted Woman*. "We spend our lives taking care of everyone's needs, playing our roles as caretakers of the world, being good girls, and working on self-improvement, but often at the expense of our own needs being met."

Sometimes I feel so overloaded, I'd just like to quietly
disappear in a puff of smoke.
Paula, 52

A Mumsnet thread called: "Am I unreasonable to just pack my bags and f*** off and leave everyone to it?" crystallizes the feelings for many women who feel too overwhelmed to enjoy their lives – and who fantasize about being free of demands. A flurry of replies like "I might do the same," "If you let me tag along, I'll bring cake" and "We could do a Thelma and Louise-type thing, coast-to-coast" showed how much it touched a nerve. As one mother summed it up: "I want someone to wait on me for a change, anticipating my needs and not questioning my every move". But perhaps the most succinct comment was: "I've Googled my symptoms and I just need everyone to f**k off."

I kept telling myself I had to keep all the plates spinning.
As a working mother trying to keep up our income, I
told myself I could keep pushing on through. I didn't
feel like I had a choice. Eventually it was like my brain
zoned out to save energy. At the end of some days,
I could barely have a conversation with my husband
because I felt so stressed, let alone have a laugh or a
joke with him. It was so burntout it was like my brain
shut down to save energy.
Allison, 49

The stress of being emotional shock-absorbers

Yet, despite the increased career workload, it is females who still tend to be the emotional shock absorbers in their families. When you add in the hormone shifts and sleeplessness that can start in the mid-40s, life can definitely lose its lustre and you have a powerful recipe for low mood.

As children get older and into the teen years, the demands don't dissipate. If anything, the problems scale up with the size of the children, especially as more young people are struggling with mental health issues. As the most common age to have a baby in the UK is the early 30s, the timing means many women are going through the start of the hormonal upheavals of peri-menopause quite soon into their parenting. When their children are hitting puberty, they are more likely to be hitting menopause proper – and parenting teens is harder than ever. Smartphones undermine parents' authority and make young people harder to get to bed, get up in the mornings and more irritable themselves. On top of that, research shows the task of setting limits for teens already falls more to mothers than fathers – and teens, particularly girls, tend to be more antagonistic toward mothers.

It's said you can only ever be as happy as your saddest child. Now our kids get so depressed, we parents can never enjoy our lives either. It's like today's teens now want you to suffer with them and offload all their pain onto you. I honestly think having a child with a serious physical illness would be easier.

Emily, 53

All too often, we fall into the trap of becoming like a concierge and PA service to our children, rather than letting them organize their own lives, at a time when our own physiological changes mean we feel drained of energy. As oestrogen and progesterone stop buffering the effects of cortisol, the inevitable teenage rudeness and self-centeredness that comes as they seek independence becomes harder to bear.

Bear in mind the difficult teen years may also have a knock-on effect on your relationship with your partner, because you are more likely to feel worn down or under siege with little time for yourself, let alone for your partner.

These hormonal shifts, as well as these converging environmental factors, may explain why women in this phase of life seem to be particularly prone to anhedonia. As feminist writer Susie Orbach points out: "The menopause arrives seeking out our vulnerabilities like a guided missile, just as we need all our strength to cope with daily life."

Dr Ferhat Uddin, a GP and menopause specialist at Liberty Health Clinics, says: "All the time, women tell me they've just lost their zest for life but can't quite put their finger on it because they know they should be happy because they've got everything set up in life. And yet, they just don't enjoy things anymore. Many end up blaming themselves, not realizing there's a biological reason. Lots of women present in perimenopause with flat mood and anxiety and GPs will prescribe antidepressants quite a lot. But all that usually does is numbs them more, without getting to the root of the problem or making them feel better. They are not feeling depressed or suicidal. It's more that they are feeling nothing really, no pleasure or joy, just 'blah'. They don't react in the same way and libido and orgasm can also be blunted. In midlife, there's often a few major life changes going on. Work may be stressful. Women may be dealing with older children moving out, as well as ageing parents. There's a lot to juggle on top of the hormonal changes, so that can lead to feelings of burnout. Everyone has different thresholds for burnout but if your hormones are going haywire, and you carry on doing the 101 things you were already doing, that point might come sooner rather than later."

For me, the most horrible thing was not being able to sympathize when my teenage kid shared their problems with me. I'd listen but I couldn't feel. I was like: "What kind of parent am I?"
Becki, 54

The good news is there are ways to make up for lost hormones with hormone replacement therapy, as well as lifestyle and diet changes. In time, the female brain will also recalibrate. According to Dr Uddin: "Studies show that women's brains at least partly compensate for these declines in oestrogen with increased blood flow and production of a molecule called ATP, the main energy source for cells. So, it seems the brain has the ability to find a new normal afterwards."

However, you navigate this period of your life, Dr Uddin says women should never believe that joy is an inevitable casualty of mid-life. She says: "The goal should always be to get a woman back to the way she felt when she felt her best. Life's too short to live it feeling like this."

In 2015, I was preparing to spend a girls' holiday in New York. There were five of us going and I should have been excited. I should have been beyond bursting with the plans that we had: a limo to and from the airport, a front row seat at Radio City Hall, a helicopter ride, a spending spree at the out-of-town retail outlet, an overnight trip to Washington. And yet, when we all got together one night a couple of weeks beforehand, I confided in my best friend that I was struggling to be excited or look forward. In fact, when I looked back on my life, I realized it had been that way for a while. I enjoyed myself in the moment but never felt gripped by anticipation. My mum had been diagnosed with cancer, so I put it down to that. Then when she died in 2016, I felt again like I was going through the motions. Everything was just OK but even planning for a trip was just a project. There were no real "too excited to sleep" moments.

Sarah, 49

Changing bodies

Another reason why women feel less able to enjoy this phase of life is self-consciousness about their changing bodies. Weight gain around menopause often feels out of control, making women feel self-critical and past their best. To make matters worse, research has found that hormonal changes may make women less motivated to exercise, thereby compounding the issue.

Yet at the same time, women are increasingly under societal pressure to fight the natural biological changes that come with age. Whereas in the past our mothers and grandmothers were relieved to get off the beauty treadmill well before they got to pensionable age, today's 50- and 60-somethings are more likely to suffer issues like body image anxiety and dysmorphia – an obsession with flaws in your appearance – as well as eating disorders.

In my 20s and 30s, I felt confident about how I looked. I still had a girlish figure. Then as I got into menopause my body felt as if it was slipping out of my control. I put on weight around my middle. I felt frumpy and matronly. I couldn't go to social events without worrying someone would take a picture of me and put it on social media. If they did, I'd go into a decline because I was trying so hard to fight it. I stopped wanting sex with my partner too because I was too self-conscious about my body to let go anymore.

Cara, 52

The Mental Health Foundation says many women feel more and more disconnected from their bodies as they age because how they look no longer matches how they feel. While they do not feel old, they have to face the fact they are seen like that by others. In short, they feel like they can never age in peace.

Psychologist Deanne Jade, founder of the UK's National Centre for Eating Disorders, believes part of the reason women no longer grow out of their insecurities about appearance is because the old certainties, such as life-long marriage, are less assured. Such worries are contagious and exploited by the plastic surgery industry, adds Deanne. "If you see someone else having an anti-ageing procedure that automatically provokes the anxiety that you should be having one too."

Of course, as the population lives longer and stays healthier, it's inevitable that older women want an appearance to match their active lives. But when appearance becomes the dominant concern rather than a transient worry, Deanne believes this can come at the cost to a woman's enjoyment of life. "Feeling grateful for all the good things in our lives – having purpose, hobbies, good relationships – all these things will offer some protection from poor body image," she says. "Instead of thinking of age as a downward spiral about the loss of looks, we need to think about what we are accumulating in terms of wisdom."

Psychologist Dr Cynthia Bulik, professor of eating disorders at the University of North Carolina and author of *The Woman in the Mirror: How to Stop Confusing What You Look Like with Who You Are*, also believes body image has become a cradle-to-grave issue. Instead of growing out of such worries, she has come across women in their 70s who have welcomed chemotherapy as a way to suppress their appetite and lose weight. These have included a 76-year-old woman with terminal cancer who weighed little more than 32kg (5 stone), but told her family to make sure she'd didn't look fat in her coffin. "In our research, the most common complaint we heard from older women is: 'Where did my waist go?'," says Dr Bulik. "But in menopause our bodies are changing the way they naturally should. Women are asking themselves: 'What is wrong with me?' – when changes to our shape over time are perfectly normal." It's a finding that has been echoed by the University of the West of England's Centre for Appearance Research in Bristol, which has found women in their 80s still suffering with low self-esteem because of their looks.

> *As I lost my younger figure, it made me feel older too.*
> *If I was in the mood to so something silly or fun, I'd get*
> *nagging voice in the back of my head saying: "You'll*
> *look ridiculous. You're too old for this."*
> Rebecca, 55

Societal changes

So, when did women start becoming so anxious about a process our mothers and grandmothers accepted as a natural part of getting older? And how can we stop this worry constantly nagging away at us, making us feel self-conscious, and getting in the way of feeling joy?

Professor Bulik believes women's expectations of how they should look in later life have altered profoundly over the last 20 years because of other societal shifts. She says: "Many of us will remember having a well-padded grandmother who was seemingly content with her body (at least on the outside). More important may have been her role in the family as cook, baker and babysitter. She had a sense of belonging and relevance to her family."

According to Dr Bulik, the loss of this traditional role means many older women are unconnected to their families and the marketing experts have identified them as prime targets for anti-ageing campaigns. She adds: "The modern grandma is supposed to be slim and fit – as long as she does not show too much cleavage, bare arms or, god forbid, her neck."

Painful though it might be, Dr Bulik says it's time to wake up from the myth that it's possible to stay youthful looking forever. "Once the ageing train starts, the truth is there's nothing you can do to get off it. Yes, we have celebrities who are in their 70s who look like they are in their 30s – until you get up close and the digitally manipulated photos, flattering lighting and heavy make-up is no longer there." Instead, she suggests older women ask themselves: "What percentage of your self-esteem does your body image take up? If it's taking up 80 or 90 per cent of who you are, then it's time to find some other ways of finding peace with your body and yourself so you can enjoy your later years."

The good news is that after this transition, Deanne believes many women can look forward starting to enjoy their lives more – and be liberated by their decision to change their priorities.

"How we feel about ourselves is always a trade-off between our expectations and our reality.

After menopause, I do think women take less notice of appearance and to take stock of other things that come of value: their relationships with loved ones, the excitement of seeing their children become parents. We know that our grandchildren care nothing for our looks. That helps takes the focus off appearance and move towards flourishing."

Andropause

While we are talking more than ever about the effect of menopause on women's ability to enjoy life, we often forget that men are going through hormonal shifts that can have similar effects. In mid-life, the demands on males can also be overwhelming – they too are facing economic uncertainty and surfing the same shockwaves of Covid, yet are often offered less empathy and support. And if they are fathers, they are also trying to juggle the same worries about their children's wellbeing and mental health. Furthermore, the research shows men have traditionally been much worse at asking for help.

In females, however, the hormonal changes of menopause get much more attention because 100 per cent of women will get to a point where their ovaries are no longer producing oestrogen. In men the drop is more gradual. Over time their pituitary gland sends fewer signals to the testes to produce testosterone and this can result in symptoms known as the andropause. This happens over the course of their lives, decreasing by around 3 per cent a year after the age of 30 (though health issues like weight gain, high blood pressure and heart problems can speed that loss up). What is often missed is that this decline can also cause feelings of "blah", brain fog and a loss of interests in activities men used to like too. They may also become more anxious and irritable. Just as oestrogen buffers stress in women, testosterone does the same in men. For example, in studies of rodents, middle-aged male rats were found to be more vulnerable to the effects of chronic stress than young ones – an effect researchers put down to the loss of testosterone and its antidepressant effect. These older rats were more likely to develop anhedonia, possibly because falling testosterone levels are also linked to a fall in activation in the striatum, part of the brain's reward system. In human studies, men aged over 45 with depression have been found to have lower levels of testosterone – though it's unclear which came first, the lower testosterone or the low mood, as it works both ways.

Checking testosterone levels

Checking testosterone is easily done with a blood test, but the challenge is interpreting the result. A man's testosterone level can change a lot over the course of a day, let alone a week or month. As men generally don't have their levels tested before they seek help, it's hard to work out what's normal for them, as baselines can vary. But if you have unexplained mood swings or memory lapses, investigate whether low testosterone may be a factor.

It was my wife who noticed it first. As I hit my early 50s, she pointed out I was turning into the proverbial miserable grumpy old git. I could see what she meant. I'd been getting anxious about everything and that was making me short-tempered and touchy. Plus, I was drinking more to self-medicate. My wife suggested a Wellman check and that I get my testosterone checked. I slightly resented it to be honest as I felt my masculinity was being questioned. I had to do a lot of blood tests at a private clinic to find out what my levels were and what I needed. But when I got the right dose, I started to get back a more positive outlook and sense of confidence

I didn't realize had quietly slipped away. It's not easy to get the balance right, but I'd say to other men suffering with unexplained low mood, it's worth looking into it further.
Daniel, 58

Thyroid Issues

So far you might get the impression that dopamine, oxytocin, oestrogen, testosterone and serotonin are all you need to make you happy, but the thyroid hormones can also have a key role in causing a feeling of "blah". We rarely think about the gland that produces them until it stops working.

Most of the time this small butterfly-shaped organ at the base of the neck gets on with its job in the background, pumping out the hormones the body needs for regulating its metabolism.

Over time, and for various reasons, it can stop working as efficiently. It seems constant stress doesn't help because cortisol also inhibits the release of thyroid hormones.

When the thyroid gland stops producing enough hormones, the effects on mental health are often mistaken for low mood. Indeed, it's estimated that 20 per cent of major depression is undiagnosed hypo-thyroidism. So why does this gland have such an influence on how we feel and how can it contribute to anhedonia?

Even when I was supposed to be having a good time, I couldn't. I'd go out with friends and feel stuck in a glass box. I'd wake up wondering how I was going to face the day. I started to resign myself to thinking I was just

*one of those people doomed to find life difficult. After
a lot of blood tests, I was diagnosed with low thyroid
function. I started waking up and looking forward to life
again. After I'd spent ages just feeling numb, it was like
I'd woken up again.*

Rona, 51

The thyroid and anhedonia

The hormones the thyroid gland sends out, triiodothyronine (T3) and thyroxine (T4), are in a feedback loop with the brain's hypothalamus and pituitary gland and help to control energy levels and metabolism. They are also critical for the development and maintenance of neurons, helping brain cells regenerate, and they affect the mitochondria, the powerhouses of the cells, slowing their energy output. One of the thyroid hormones, T3, also increases serotonin levels in the brain, which are important for a balanced mood.

If the thyroid stops making as much of this feel-good hormone, it can dampen its activity, as well as the action of GABA, which helps to calm anxiety in the brain. At first your body will try to make up for declining levels by telling the thyroid to make more, but your mood will gradually go downhill – and you are more likely to be vulnerable to stress too.

As thyroid issues often surface in the 40s and 50s, and occur much more often in women, they are often blamed on menopausal symptoms or stressful lifestyles. As many as half of thyroid patients don't know they have the problem because the signs are so common and slip beneath the radar. Indeed, it's so prevalent that it's estimated that as many one in five women over 60 (about ten times the number of men) have some form of thyroid dysfunction and will struggle to enjoy life as a result. Yet thyroid issues take an average of seven years to diagnose.

If you are suffering persistent unexplained low mood, together with other symptoms like rapid weight gain or loss, more sensitivity to hot or cold temperatures, or hair and skin changes, consider getting a blood test to see whether the output of your thyroid hormones has shifted over time. Otherwise enjoying your life more is going to be like pushing a boulder up a hill because your brain chemistry is working against you.

The good news is, once diagnosed, an underactive thyroid is relatively easy to treat because the failing levels can be topped up with medication, like levothyroxine tablets, a synthetic form of what's missing. According to GP Dr Ferhat Uddin: "Thyroid issues are in that grey space between psychiatry and endocrinology and so often gets lost between the two. But if you're constipated, if you're feeling cold, or sluggish, it's definitely one of things that need to be tested for because the thyroid's effects on mood can often be missed."

The food-mood connection: the gut-brain axis

Though it may seem counterintuitive, there's now a growing body of research showing that our moods are also created in a less obvious place – the gut. For a long time, the alimentary canal was a shadowy world which we didn't know that much about (mainly because gut bacteria could not be cultivated in lab conditions). But the 9m (30ft) tube which runs from our oesophagus to our bowels turns out to be an organ that has a key role in how we feel. This is because, as strange as it may sound, it contains our second brain.

Rather than being clumped together in one jelly-like mound in our skulls, this "brain" has 100 million neurons thinly spread over its surface. While this number of neurons is a lot fewer than in the brain in our skulls, and our gut brain won't be doing any philosophizing, it governs basic processes like feeling sick or nervous responses to stressful situations. This means all along, there was a biological basis for expressions such as "butterflies in your stomach" and "gut feelings".

From an evolutionary perspective the gut-brain axis makes perfect sense. We need some "intelligence" in our digestive tract picking up incoming information about what we are putting into our bodies. If our ancestors, foraging for food, ate a poisonous mushroom, the gut needed to send a message to the brain to tell us not to eat the same thing again. (This might explain why after falling seriously ill after eating mussels at the age of eight, even the smell of them made me gag for the next 20 years. The whiff of whiskey, which was the cause of my first major teen hangover, still does too.) After all, the gut is where we process the food we take from the outside world – and where we turn this fuel into "us".

I was feeling "meh" and lacking in energy and
wanted to see if my diet had a role to play. I can't
say I absolutely loved having to mix my faeces with
chemicals at home to send off to a lab for a microbiome

test, but the results gave me a whole new perspective
on what was going on inside me. I couldn't believe how
many different types of bacteria were in there, what they
were all up to and which ones I needed to encourage.
Now I don't just eat for me. I eat more fibre, less
sugar and less processed foods to help the little guys
who are busy making my feel-good chemicals too.
It's the least I can do.
Maya, 34

An essential eco-system

There's one more important way that what happens in the gut makes a critical difference to our moods. The dark world of your alimentary canal is also home to up to 1,000 species of densely packed micro-organisms – mainly bacteria, fungi and viruses – which have been colonizing your body since birth. At first this also sounds odd because we are brought up to believe that any bugs we ingest through our food are bad for us, and trigger stomach upsets. While a tiny number do, the truth is that the majority living inside us are largely beneficial and have a key role in mood.

You started building this essential eco-system the moment you came out of the birth canal; you breathed in and ingested bacteria teeming in your mother's vagina – or if you were born by C-section, as soon as you came into contact with the doctors and nurses who handled you.

Then, as you got older, you would have collected still more for your personal collection as you moved through the world around you, from playing in the garden, stroking pets and from the food you ate. By the time you got to school, you would have been host to a writhing forest of about 100 trillion visitors, which lumped together would have weighed 1–1.5kg (2–3lb) and outnumbered your own cells by about 10 to 1.

Knowing you have a tiny jungle of micro-organisms competing to eke out an existence inside you isn't just a weird fact. It's now been discovered that these gut bacteria perform the critical role of taking the food we eat and converting it into feel-good chemicals you need to enjoy your life. About 95 per cent of our serotonin is made in the gut. Some by our gut bacteria; some by species stimulating the cell lining of the intestines to produce it or sending certain messages to the brain. The gut is not just a factory for serotonin either. As much as 50 per cent of our old friend dopamine is also made here – and so too is GABA, another neurotransmitter which helps to calm anxiety.

A good selection of microbiota will protect the gut wall, stopping toxins passing through it and causing an immune system reaction. This can cause inflammation in the rest of the body, which can affect your brain and contribute to depression.

All this activity in the gut is communicated to your brain via the vagus, or "wandering", nerve, which stretches all the way down from the base of your brain to the spinal cord to your gut. Along the way, it reaches out to most of your organs and connects your stomach and intestines to your nervous system, so it can carry signals back up to you brain. This major highway for the nervous system allows your brain and the rest of your body to be in a constant two-way conversation. In short, what you eat isn't just filling your stomach and feeding your body. It's also making your mood.

How our diet is lacking

There is an onslaught of ways in which modern diet and lifestyle – as well as life – get in the way of your microbiome keeping you feeling good. For a start, to function at its best, your gut microbiota needs a wide range of foods – and in particular fibre – to feast off. It then breaks these down into the beneficial molecules needed to make neurotransmitters, like serotonin. However, over time our diets have become processed and lacking in this kind of plant material.

Not only does 75 per cent of our food come from just 12 plants and 5 animal species. In the UK, on average, we eat only 18g (0.6oz) a day of fibre, 60 per cent of the recommended 30g (1oz). Plus, heavily processed foods, containing refined flours, cheap oils and fats, sugars and starches, now make up 50 per cent of the foods we eat in the UK and 70 per cent in the US.

These tend to contain emulsifiers, chemicals that are added to extend shelf life by keeping in the moisture and preventing them from separating. Inside the gut, these chemicals disrupt the mucus layer of the intestines, killing off beneficial microbes and encouraging the growth of bad ones that produce inflammatory chemicals. Artificial sweeteners, found in diet drinks, and colourings added to make food look more marketable, also seem to have a disruptive effect on gut flora and can wipe out some probiotic bacteria.

High-fat and high-sugar foods also seem to create a more porous intestinal wall. This means that toxins and undigested food particles can pass through into the bloodstream, causing inflammation in the tissues. And then there's antibiotics which have a catastrophic effect on the microbiome, wiping out huge numbers of good bacteria. These are not just the antibiotics that doctors prescribe for chest infections or acne; they are the ones given to animals to help them fight disease in industrial farming and, in some parts of the world, to grow faster. Global meat consumption is now the highest it's ever been. As well as being in the animals' body, antibiotics enter the human food chain via their excrement which gets flushed into waterways and so also passes into fish. According to a 2018 study in the journal *Molecule*: "Antibiotic resistance is of great public health concern because the antibiotic-resistant bacteria associated with the animals may be pathogenic to humans, easily transmitted to humans via food chains, and widely disseminated in the environment via animal wastes." The likelihood is that this influx does even more damage to the delicate ecology of the human gut, compromising our ability to make happiness chemicals even further.

Stress gets felt down in this dark world too. A number of studies have found that anxiety damages the growth of good bacteria, such as Lactobacilli and Bifidobacteria, which have been found to be helpful for maintaining feel-good dopamine and serotonin. These good bacteria also keep inflammation in the gut at bay, a factor which, as you'll discover below, is increasingly making low mood more likely.

Inflammation

If you are in a state of ongoing "blah", it's worth considering whether your diet consists of a lot of foods that create inflammation, particularly sugars, saturated fats and preservatives. These can throw off the balance of your gut bacteria, make your gut lining more porous and even enter the bloodstream, where they trigger an immune response which may reach the brain.

Professor Carmine Pariante, a professor of biological psychiatry at King's College London, has been looking into the use of anti-inflammatories for depression for the past 20 years. He says the brain's reward system seems to be particularly sensitive to inflammation in the rest of the body: "A third of people with major depressive disorder, for example, will show they have high levels of inflammation markers in their blood. Depressed people who have higher levels of this inflammation are also more likely to have physical symptoms, like fatigue and disrupted sleep, as well as anhedonia. You can even see it on an MRI, that the chemical release of cytokines in the blood seem to change the function of the neurons there and decreases activity in the reward areas."

Indeed, a range of studies by researchers at Emory University, USA, led by Professor Jennifer Felger, has found that regions of the reward system – the ventral striatum and the ventromedial prefrontal cortex – don't communicate as well in the brains of depressed people who have raised inflammation. She says: "We hope that this work will lead to new treatments for patients with high inflammation who show symptoms."

Sleep

We evolved to live on a spinning planet that revolves around the sun and on which we are wired to wake up with the sunrise and to retire to our shelters to sleep at sundown.

Everything from our hormone release to our digestion has evolved with these daily rhythms.

Then, in 1879, Thomas Edison invented the light bulb.

Now that humans could engage in work around the clock, Edison himself encouraged the idea that people who didn't sleep were the ones who got ahead. (He proudly claimed he never slept more than four hours a day himself, and he expected the same from his employees.)

He was not the last. Lack of sleep became a byword for productivity. Over the next century, politicians and business leaders bragged about being "elite sleepers", even though only a very rare subset of humans has the genetic mutation which allows them to keep going on four or five hours a night.

But it's a natural law that whenever we try to fight biology, we lose. It's only been in recent years that we have understood the science which explains why being unconscious for up to a third of the day is not such a waste of time after all. Studies have found that seven hours of sleep a day is the optimum amount to allow your brain to perform at its best the next day, though sleep specialists recommend aiming for a broader window of seven to nine hours.

If you've ever had to get by on a few hours' sleep, then you already know how bad-tempered it can make you feel. How you have slept determines how you will feel in the day ahead.

Considering that the brain is always working and never switches off until death, why does it punish us so much when it doesn't get the downtime it demands? There are a few compelling reasons ...

When I don't get the sleep I need, I immediately
notice it in my mood. It's like the whole world
turns to grey, my focus narrows. My voice gets flatter,
and I don't laugh as much. I get irritable, I eat more
junk, so I get angry with myself – and it feels like
if the slightest thing went wrong, it would tip me
over the edge completely.

Amrita, 40

What happens when we sleep

During sleep, we restore the serotonin levels needed to maintain an even mood, and this has a downstream effect on the delicate balance of other hormones and neurotransmitters. Lack of sleep also seems to destabilize dopamine levels and with that the brain's reward system. After one sleepless night, psychiatrist Nora Volkow found there is actually more dopamine release in two brain structures: the striatum, which is involved in motivation and reward, and the thalamus, which is involved in alertness, probably to try to compensate for the brain's tiredness. But it's a poor temporary solution. She has found that the neurons of sleep-deprived people can release dopamine but not receive it. So, hardly surprisingly, this stops its free flow and impacts mood.

Furthermore, sleep is when the brain does its own deep clean. Every night, it washes out the daily build-up of waste left over by the activity of the brain cells, with waves of spinal fluid.

It's also when the immune system releases cytokines which fight infection. This may help to explain why too little sleep is linked to high inflammation, which in turn is linked to depression.

Sleep deprivation also knocks out the brain's emotional regulatory control mechanism, the prefrontal cortex, leaving an essential part of the threat detection system, the amygdala, in charge. When two groups of volunteers were shown 100 pictures, ranging from neutral to alarming, their amygdala was found to be 60 per cent more reactive when they were sleep-deprived.

Tired people have also been found to react more emotionally to negative stressors, putting them at greater risk of low mood. Sleep scientist Dr Kat Lederle says: "This means the pre-frontal cortex is less able to control and regulate the activity of the amygdala. It's a bit like a parent being absent leaving the child to do what it wants."

Lack of sleep can also start a downward spiral. Russell Foster, professor of circadian neuroscience at Oxford University says: "When we don't get enough, we don't process some of the information from the day before. So, our mental processing speed slows down the next day and our mood flattens. People who are sleep deprived also tend to remember negative experiences, but forget positive ones. So, your whole worldview becomes biased, and your decision-making can be influenced by that too."

Seasonal Affective Disorder

Do you feel more "blah" in the winter months? If so, it's worth asking yourself if you are getting enough sun. It wasn't many generations ago that most of our ancestors were outside for most of their daylight hours. As they spent most of their time searching for food, they would have been exposed to natural light all day, even in winter. This cycle of light and dark directs our internal body clocks. Light passing through our eyes is the main way it sets our tempo for the day. This body clock, or suprachiasmatic nucleus (SCN), is actually a cluster of about 50,000 special nerve cells in the hypothalamus, the small structure which regulates the timing of many processes, like temperature and hormone release.

When natural daylight hits the back of the eye in the morning, signals travel along the optic nerves and go into the SCN, which is close to where the optic nerves cross behind the eyes, before entering deep into the brain. The SCN then uses this information to time the release of hormones like cortisol and adrenaline, which speeds up the body and wakes us up in the morning – and the release of melatonin, which slows us down and makes us sleepy at night.

Over the course of a day, this master clock will try to keep the body ticking as close to the 24-hour cycle of the day – or the body's natural circadian rhythm – as possible.

Professor Russell Foster says: "Without this synchronization with the environment, our biology would be in chaos. The SCN is like a control tower at a busy airport that has to co-ordinate the arrival and take-off of many different planes throughout the day and night. It is continually sending messages to the different parts of the body to co-ordinate its rhythmic timetable."

Roll on a few millennia and the average modern human spends about 90 per cent of time inside – either in buildings or vehicles – so we can lose our bearings. Even in summer, we probably get less exposure to sunlight than our ancestors did during the winter months.

When days get shorter and nights gets longer, this can throw our body clocks off so that it lowers levels of feel-good hormones, like serotonin.

One sign of Seasonal Affective Disorder, or SAD, is "diurnal mood variation" or morning depression. This means you feel lowest in the morning and cheer up over the course of the day as you get more sunlight. To see if your moods are being affected by light, keep track of how your mood changes with the seasons and also over the course of a day.

The good news is that if lack of sunlight is contributing towards anhedonia, it can be addressed with a lamp that mimics full-spectrum natural sunlight. Chronobiologist Dr Kat Lederle says "Get a light box and stick to regular sleep times. Make sure you spend time outdoors every day, ideally in the morning when light levels are highest."

When winter sets in, I just want to stay under the duvet and not come out. Nothing holds any attraction for me – not parties, social events or even Christmas. My Seasonal Affective Disorder started at university when I found it hard to get up for lectures and stayed in my room. So now I recognize the pattern – and how my energy ebbs away as the days get shorter. The good thing is it that I can see it coming – otherwise I turn into Eeyore from Winnie the Pooh. Before I lose my motivation to do anything, I take steps to get more sunlight and to get outside whatever the weather. I also take all my holidays in the autumn and winter, so I go can get some sun while it's dark here.

Aisha, 33

Addiction

You may be someone who has overloaded your dopamine circuits in some way, so nothing brings you as much pleasure anymore. The mesolimbic pathway is where your brain processes pleasurable, intoxicating and rewarding experiences. Any type of overstimulation which keeps releasing dopamine and leaves that system depleted can lead to feelings of anhedonia – because it becomes harder to get pleasure from anything.

Addiction has long been a contentious word, usually reserved for chemical substances like drugs and alcohol. But now it seems that researchers are increasingly willing to use it when they see how other habits of modern life, like looking at porn and video gaming, use the same reward pathways and how they can also get in the way of real life. After a while the brain gets used to the stimulus, it starts to need larger doses more often to get the same feeling of enjoyment. "Essentially, it's free-falling dopamine which doesn't just return to basal levels but drops to below them," says psychiatrist Professor Anna Lembke, who specializes in addiction. When your "addiction" no longer gives you the "highs" it once did, the problem is it can make it harder to find pleasure in anything.

6

What's Happening in
Your Brain?

Happiness is a term we use for a constellation of feelings – from elation to relief to feeling free. It's usually a place where we want to stay. Feeling "blah", or being in a state of anhedonia, is more like an absence of emotion or of feeling things less intensely – and that is where we can get stuck. It's a state that's harder to explain and understand.

The answer to why we slip into anhedonia has long been elusive. The brain is the only organ that tries to work itself out, yet it gives very little away. From the outside, this lump of grey jelly is inscrutable. As it sits in the black box of your skull, it receives input from the five senses, but it rarely reveals the alchemy which turns those inputs into emotions. To work out where those sensations might have come from, it will help to look at where moods are created in the brain in the first place.

Working out what the brain was for

Democracy, good weather, plenty of food and some healthy intellectual rivalry were some of the conditions that enabled the Greeks to be one of the first civilizations to consider where emotions came from. At first, philosophers like Aristotle in the fourth-century BC were far more taken with the red, throbbing, beating heart, which they assumed was the seat of all feeling. This must have felt logical given that its beat sped up when the body felt fear and slowed down when it felt relaxed. By comparison the brain looked dull and lifeless.

Over the centuries, humankind continued to come up with various best guesses for the brain's role. It was viewed as stuffing to keep the skull from caving in by the Egyptians, a coolant system for the rest of the body by the Greeks, the seat of the soul by Renaissance thinkers, a collection of bumps that gave clues to your character traits by the Victorians. However, over the centuries, dissections of animals and humans pointed clearly to the fact that the brain was the ultimate destination for all the neural pathways of the body – converging in the spinal cord and up to the base of the skull. Credit must also go to Roman physician, Galen. At the start of the second century AD he had performed enough post-mortems on dead gladiators to conclude that the brain was where all five senses "terminated".

But even after the brain had been identified as the seat of thought and feeling, historically it's taken us a long time to use our own brain to work out what it does. After all, we can hear and feel the beating of our hearts, the rumbles of our intestines and the breathing of our lungs. But the firing of the neurons in our skulls, or the many conversations different brain regions are having with each other do not register.

Even when we are the owner of the brain, it keeps much of that chatter out of our hearing. Our highly developed prefrontal cortex also has trouble correctly interpreting what the emotional and basic brains – the regions just below it – are up to. It makes the best guesses it can, but often gets the wrong end of the stick, despite being part of the same organ. By the time we can "hear" a thought, positive or negative, in our conscious, higher brain, a great deal has already gone on. And though these feelings originate from our own brains, most of the time we really haven't got a clue how they got there.

It was naturalist Charles Darwin who first worked out there was an evolutionary point to happiness and sadness. He realized all mammals had to be able to experience positive and negative emotions to motivate them to mate and find food. Otherwise, they simply wouldn't bother to do the things they needed to do to keep themselves alive and continue their species.

But biologically, how are these good feelings actually achieved? It has been a question which has baffled scientists for centuries. Before he found fame as the father of psychoanalysis in the first therapy rooms of the early 20th century, Sigmund Freud dissected brains during a stint as a neurologist in a lab. But as researchers were still only on the cusp of understanding what neurons did, when he peered down a microscope at them, he wasn't entirely sure what he was looking at. By 1895, he had given up trying to find the connection between brain anatomy and the vagaries of the human mind, concluding they were not connected.

For the rest of the century, psychologists and psychiatrists made many more hit-and-miss attempts to try to work out how emotions were formed in order to tackle mental illness. But because the origins of pleasure were not understood, this usually took the form of numbing emotions of patients instead with either drugs or lobotomies.

The discovery of the reward system

Though its full meaning wasn't immediately understood, one of psychology's great eureka moments came in 1954 in a lab at Canada's McGill University. It was here that two psychologists, James Olds and Peter Milner, were trying to grasp the psychology of motivation.

In experiments with rodents, they realized that rats would press a lever as many as 7,500 times an hour to get stimulation from an electrode implanted in their brains, even passing up food and sex. By trial and error, they learned that it only had this effect if it was placed in a very specific area of the brain. Moved just a few millimetres away, the animals lost interest in getting the stimulation. That pleasure hotspot turned out to be the nucleus accumbens, an area which has turned out to be a key hub in the dopamine reward system.

Where does pleasure come from?

Suddenly, it seemed that stimulating a particular area of the brain could be the answer to human happiness. Newspaper headlines trumpeted that scientists had discovered the elusive "pleasure area", dangling the possibility of a world where endless joy might soon be on tap if you triggered the right part.

That utopia never came to pass. But humankind was still one step closer to identifying some of the structures in the mammal brain which produced good feelings. Those lever-pressing rats had heralded in what was to become the golden age of neuroscience. But there was still much to be done. While Olds and Milner discovered that stimulating a specific part of the brain could produce good feelings, they couldn't see why. A better understanding seemed so elusive that in 2002 Milner told an interviewer: "It's probably something that we will probably be spending the next two or three centuries trying to understand." Thankfully, several discoveries were on the horizon which meant we didn't have to wait that long.

The discovery of dopamine

As we've heard, discovering what hotspot needed to be triggered to cause pleasure was just the beginning. The nucleus accumbens is just one hub on the pleasure superhighway, also known as the mesolimbic pathway, running through the brain. How many other hubs were there on the way, and what was fuelling them?

Even though it had first been discovered in the 1950s, it took until the 1970s for researchers to fully understand that dopamine was the main driver of the brain's reward system. Without it, rats might still press the lever if you stimulated the pleasure centre, but if researchers blocked the flow of dopamine in their brains, they lost interest. This isolated it as possibly the main neurotransmitter needed to allow signals to pass rapidly between neurons on this track. As one scientific paper put it, dopamine was where "Sensory inputs are translated into the hedonic messages we experience as pleasure, euphoria or 'yumminess'." It still wasn't the whole picture, but it was a start.

Seeing under the bonnet

There was still one major obstacle to understanding how good feelings formed in the human mind in real time. Slicing through a deceased human brain didn't give up many secrets as the owner would have to be dead and so not thinking anymore. For most of human history, the workings of the brain have been as mysterious as the outer reaches of the universe. There had been electroencephalography (EEG), used since 1929, which could detect brain wave patterns with electrodes attached to the scalp, but these machines were mainly used to diagnose conditions such as epilepsy.

Then, in September 1980, *Newsweek* excitedly trumpeted the arrival of "a machine that reads the human mind". Called positron-emission tomography (PET), it spotted abnormal regions of brain activity in serious mental illnesses, which it described as a crude first step toward putting brain processes on film. It was a start, but a limited one. By injecting a radioactive tracer into the body, the scanner could track how dopamine was circulating in the brain. The images were slow and fuzzy, and the procedure was too invasive to be used for large-scale research. It was another decade before neuroscientists got the breakthrough they needed – the functional MRI scan (fMRI).

This went beyond static images of the brain captured by more basic MRI scanners. The updated version allowed magnets to track the movement of iron-rich haemoglobin in the blood in real time. It meant that people could be put into the circular machines, asked questions or be shown pictures, and the machine could track the flow of blood as different regions were activated. The dopamine reward path could now be seen and mapped.

It was cheaper and non-invasive and while the machines were expensive, almost anyone could be popped inside. Within 20 years of its discovery, the findings of fMRI scans had been cited in more than a quarter of million research papers worldwide.

Chocolate, tacos, sex or drugs

For researchers still trying to piece together the science of motivation and pleasure, an obvious first place to start was people who had the most intense kind of wanting of all – drug addicts. In one set of experiments in the late 1990s, crack addicts were shown images of butterflies, then pictures of people preparing the drug.

According to a report in Newsweek describing these early experiments: "For two minutes, images of monarch butterflies flitted by; the fMRI, which detects active regions in the brain, saw nothing untoward. Then the scene shifted. Men ritualistically cooked crack ... an addict handed cash to a pusher ... users smoked. It was as if a neurological switch had been thrown: seeing the drug scenes not only unleashed in the addicts a surge of craving for crack. But [it] also triggered visible changes in their brains as their anterior cingulate and part of the prefrontal cortex – regions involved in mood and learning – lit up like Times Square." Non-addicts, it was observed, showed no such response when shown the image of crack-taking.

Dr Scott Lukas of McLean Hospital in Belmont, Massachusetts, who led the study, explained that even just imagining or thinking about a reward, could trigger dopamine in the addicts. "These cues turn on crack-related memories, and addicts respond like Pavlov's dogs."

But as more experiments showed, it wasn't only drugs that got a strong reaction. Chocolate, tacos, sex, winning a competition, getting good marks in a test, getting praise, listening to music all triggered a rise in dopamine around the reward circuits, albeit in varying amounts.

Why pizza is so pleasurable

Although every brain is structured slightly differently, fMRI scanners showed that the brain's main mesolimbic reward pathway follows roughly the same route through the brain – and has the same stops along the way.

So, let's go on a simplified journey of the route that "pleasure" takes through your brain.

Take the example of pizza. Imagine it's a Friday night after a long week at work, you're sitting on your sofa and there's no food in the fridge. The process of enjoying that end-of-the-week treat is set in motion when levels of the hunger hormone, ghrelin, start to rise. This message is then picked up in the brain by the internal thermostat, the hypothalamus. This alerts your amygdala, which decides what to do with incoming sense messages, that a survival need has to be met. Now as the neurotransmitter of anticipation (not simply reward, as was once believed), dopamine is starting to flow. Also chipping in is another brain region on the route, the anterior cingulate cortex, which helps you decide how to meet that need.

So, why is it likely that pizza has popped into your head? There's a reason it's the world's most popular food. Early humans were hardwired to load up on carbs, fat and salts whenever they came across them, as the threat of hunger was always just around the corner. So even though, unlike our ancestors, we are never likely to starve, we are still wired to get the most pleasure from fatty, rich foods.

Add to that the reminders of the good times you've had with friends eating pizza, stored in your hippocampus, and that yearning for that thin crust with mushrooms and extra cheese gets more intense. Meanwhile your higher brain region, the prefrontal cortex, adds to your drive by helping you plan ahead and imagine that first bite. All this craving is releasing more dopamine from the ventral tegmental area – one of the main factories in the brain.

Dopamine: The molecule of anticipation

But that pizza isn't going to appear out of nowhere. You need to move, if only to pick up your phone and search for the best place to order from. Unbeknown to you, dopamine – which drives movement – is behind that too. Finally, with a bit more help from the cognitive skills built up in your cortex, you find a pizza parlour you want to order from, scroll through the menu and pay. Your order is on its way. With half an hour wait, your dopamine is continuing to "flow" in anticipation, stimulating your salivary glands, and narrowing your focus, making it hard to think of anything else but the arrival of that thin crust with extra cheese and mushrooms.

Finally, there's a ring on the doorbell. Your food has arrived. You open the box, unpeel a slice from the base of the cardboard box and move it toward your mouth, while trying to contain those trailing cheesy strings. You take your first mouthful. It tastes good. More than that, this pizza tastes amazing. The perfect marriage of tomato, gooiness, and crispy crust. That means you will get an extra surge of dopamine to help you remember the experience and learn what to do next time.

Although dopamine is "the pleasure chemical", which gave you a shot of intense pleasure, there's more to it. Dopamine is also a neuromodulator, which means it acts as a central domino that stimulates other chemicals in the reward system to make you feel good.

According to research by neuroscientist Professor Kent Berridge and his lab at the University of Michigan, the main pleasure of enjoying that pizza comes from the activation of "hedonic hotspots" – where both dopamine and the body's own naturally produced opioids work together. Each of these spots – so far found in the outer shell of the nucleus accumbens area of the brain – is around 1cm sq, making up no more about 10 per cent of that area of the brain. The nucleus accumbens is the location where Olds and Milner stuck electrodes to make rats pursue pleasure at any cost – and found the "hedonic hotspot" was no more than a cubic millimetre in a rat's brain. "Like the islands of an archipelago, the hedonic hotspots link to one another, and to other brain regions that process pleasure signals, to form a powerful, integrated pleasure circuit," Professor Berridge tells me. This is what creates "the Pleasure Gloss – a value-added sensation. The dopamine is the anticipation and looking forward to the pizza coming. When you bite into the pizza, it is still dopamine, but it's now also the opioids and cannabinoids. The experience of enjoying pizza is a combination of these things."

But as good as that first bite made you feel, you can't go on eating pizza forever. To ensure you are not lost in a never-ending cycle of pleasure that would make you eat more than would be good for you or your waistline, your conscious mind also puts the brakes on the process.

It might whisper to you: "Yes, this pizza's good. But if you eat more than I need, I'm going to feel sick or put on weight."

At the same time, your gut is also sending messages via the nervous system central highway, the vagus nerve, to report that your stomach is filling up. Plus, with each bite, the dopamine release is going down as the novelty is wearing thin. This is because dopamine-secreting neurons are always on the lookout for surprising new experiences that feel good.

And to save energy and time, the brain is constantly predicting what's coming next based on our previous experiences.

When we get what we expect, there's no particular change to dopamine levels. When we are pleasantly surprised, we get rewarded with an extra spurt. When experiences exceed expectations, it teaches the brain to do it again. Indeed, neuroscientist Wolfram Schultz, who has long studied this effect, says that "unpredictable rewards" may be as much as four times as exciting as ordinary ones.

Remembering what's good

Now you've decided you've had enough pizza and start putting the empty box in the recycling, there's one final stage in the reward process. If you've found a great new place to get take-out pizza, the hippocampus will help lock the experience in your memory. If it wasn't a great pizza, this will also remind you not to order from there again. And as you start to feel like you've had enough, your dopamine levels are not only dropping back to baseline, but they are also actually sinking a bit below so they can find that state of balance, ready to make you seek out the next meal.

What can go wrong

Looking forward, and then enjoying an experience, like eating a pizza, might seem like the most obvious and natural process in the world. But as we've seen even from this simplified summary, it's more complex than it looks. As with any journey, many things can go wrong en route, and stand in the way of pleasure.

Anhedonia, like any other mental state, comes in many forms – and there can be many ways the reward process in the brain can get thrown off course. To start with, dopamine is a very precious commodity. It's a Goldilocks molecule. Having too much or too little can derail the process. Some brains will make less dopamine. Some will make too much. Some brains will have fewer receptors for it, or have receptors that don't grab onto it as well. The dopamine could also be broken down too fast or reabsorbed by the synapses too rapidly. Or the flow of dopamine could be inhibited by other neurotransmitters. In some brains of

119

people with anhedonia, the amygdala seems to over-react from the start, disrupting the journey.

Research studies have found that there can be a breakdown in communication between the different hubs on the reward path. Inflammation, caused by factors like stress or poor diet, may also interrupt dopamine's release. As with any research into emotional states, there isn't one simple, easy answer. After all, your brain is a dense, complex mass of interconnecting neural circuits. Many regions and chemicals work in tandem to add up to good feelings.

Even the slightest tinge of pleasure could involve up to 20 to 30 small regions across the brain and body. Other neurotransmitters and hormones like oxytocin, norepinephrine and serotonin, will also play a role.

How pleasure varies

Some nights, that pizza may not taste as good. So why does enjoyment vary? Your mood is all the inputs of your senses, hormones and bodily functions. Your cortisol could be running high because you had a bad week with family stresses. Perhaps another brain chemical that modulates your mood, serotonin, was running low because your boss is sidelining you at work.

The ongoing challenge for researchers is finding out at the different points of the journey where the reward system can break down – and why. And that may be helped by the discovery that having pleasure is not one single process. As we will hear, it's *three*.

The joy of ... anticipation

Imagine going back to that first bite of pizza. What made it pleasurable? You might assume that the pleasure was all in that first moment, when your teeth sank into the crust and the flavours hit your tastebuds. But though this may seem like a simple moment in time, the pleasure you felt was half an hour in the making.

The first phase was anticipation. It started as soon as you started to get hungry and dream up the idea of pizza in your mind. One theory about anhedonia is that as well as the loss of pleasure in the moment, there's the loss of the ability to anticipate and look forward to experiences that will make you feel good.

In experiments, rodents whose brains are tweaked so they don't release dopamine stop seeking food to the point where they would die of starvation, if left to their own devices. The effect has been noticed in humans.

Studies of people with anhedonia find they lose the initial desire to chase rewards. But if the things that are pleasurable are given to them, like a favourite food or experience, they still enjoy it. However, if this does not happen, they stop enjoying their lives because they no longer do the activities that make them feel good in the first place.

Professor Berridge's research points to the fact that "wanting and liking" are distinct from each other in the reward system. He points out that this can be clearly seen in drug addicts who keep craving the substance that makes them feel bad – even though the high has worn off and they no longer get satisfaction from taking the actual drug. Professor Berridge says: "'Wanting' is the moment you become ensnared by the thought of food or its aroma. 'Liking' is the moment you put a bite of that food in your mouth and think, 'This is good'. 'Wanting' and 'liking' pizza may sound like the same thing. But these two processes can be separated out."

So, instead of looking at anhedonia as something that just happens when you don't enjoy life anymore, ask yourself a different question. Is it your motivation that's gone missing? Is it not so much the fact that you don't enjoy an experience, more that you no longer look forward to it and so don't take part in the activities that would make you feel good, trapping you in a downward spiral? According to Professor Berridge: "In cases of anhedonia, this can mean that feelings of pleasure may still be intact. If you give people with anhedonia an ice-cream and ask them to rate the pleasure of it, they give normal pleasure ratings. But that ice-cream isn't particularly valued by them. So, as well as anhedonia we now have a separate term – avolition – to describe the loss of wanting."

There's one more part to consider in the process after "wanting" and "liking". This third stage is learning or memorizing how you enjoyed the experience. When you finished that delicious pizza, your brain would have encoded the fact that you'd enjoyed that pizza so you'd know where to order it next time.

Wolfram Schultz, a professor of neuroscience at Cambridge University, says that as well as the anticipation beforehand, and the satisfaction when the need is met, there's a third stage in the reward system – the learning phase – so you can decide if you want to order the pizza again.

So, another question to ask yourself is whether you are looking back on an experience negatively, when, in the moment, you enjoyed it? This could also be explained by something called "mood congruency", which basically means if you are in a bad mood, you tend to recall more negative memories of an event, reinforcing the cycle.

In summary, the reward system is like a complicated system of pulleys, being used to raise a bucket of drinking water. When the system works well, it drives us to seek out what we want and then remember how to meet that need again. If the system stops working well, the bucket wobbles on its way up, the water spills and the reward isn't as great as anticipated.

Then, in some forms of anhedonia, if we get that refreshing drink, we may not remember how the system worked well in the first place. Indeed, it may be this which makes anhedonia so insidious. Anhedonia keeps you stuck so you stop trying. For example, when stuck at home with "blah", doing some exercise might seem like a good idea. But then if a breakdown in your reward system means you don't remember it making you feel better, you're less likely to do it. Or, say, you've been invited out with friends, but you discard the idea because the last time you socialized you got stuck at the end of the table with a person you got bored of talking to.

If you don't foresee the prospect of enjoying an experience – and you've also forgotten why you enjoyed it – you may not bother in the first place. Anhedonia can turn a party animal into someone who no longer enjoys socializing. It can turn a talented gourmet into someone who can't be bothered to cook. It can turn the sports fan who fanatically follows every loss and win of their sports teams into someone who no longer cares whether they've dropped a division.

Feeling numb

There is an important distinction to make about anhedonia when it is not part of depression. Anhedonia is often described as having a numbing effect, a dulling of emotion, a void where feelings used to be. By contrast, depression hurts. Usually when we are deeply depressed, we feel in pain too. For many people, feelings of low mood, hopelessness and despair also activate somatic sensations in the body, like feelings of pressure or tightness in the stomach, chest or head. Why could this be?

> I don't feel depressed or sad. I just feel numb, and on
> autopilot. Sometimes it even feels quite useful not to
> get upset like other people do about the state of the
> world and the bad things that can happen.
>
> Freddy, 34

Pain has its own pathways through the brain – and studies show there are lots of crossovers in the pain and pleasure systems. The anterior cingulate cortex, for example, is part of both. (It's also worth noting that people living with chronic pain can also develop anhedonia – possibly because the constant stress and cortisol interrupts the reward process.)

Researchers have yet to find all the biological mechanisms that underlie anhedonia. One explanation could be that it's caused by a partial breakdown of the reward circuits, but one which hasn't triggered the same physical pain circuits sparked by depression. People with depression don't always have anhedonia. So, could anhedonia be depression without the hurt?

My life has become dull, grey and drab. I used to be
laugh easily. Gradually it felt like there's a wall that has
come between me and the stuff I care about.
Hannah, 37

Whatever form anhedonia takes, neuroscientist Professor Carmine Pariante says it's important to take it seriously. "Anhedonia spreads across different disorders. There's a spectrum of severity. You may have it as a transient reaction to difficult circumstances, but, if it is prolonged in time, it can indicate a problem. It could be burnout, or it could be mild or severe depression, or another mental disorder that you don't realize you have. People tend to blame themselves or think they are weak or bad for feeling this. But it can always be part of something else. It's important to find out what it is, because it's a major shift in the way people experience the world and if it is part of a mental disorder it can be helped by treatment."

My emotional flatlining came on very suddenly
after a hospital stay. I lost interest in my friends or
family. They'd be talking and I'd think: "I wish I cared
but I don't. I just wanted to sit and stare at the wall."
But because you can still talk and function, people
think you're fine. You keep trying to explain it to
them and they don't get it.
Joely, 56

Fleeting pleasures

Another possible reason you might feel "blah" is that you don't hold onto pleasurable feelings long enough to appreciate them. When you enjoy an experience, signals travel down from the prefrontal cortex to the nucleus accumbens.

MRI scans by researchers at the University of Wisconsin have found that people with depression found it harder to sustain feelings in this pleasure hub and got less enjoyment when looking at pleasant pictures. In other words, the good feelings passed too quickly to really make a difference to their mood.

It's as if I can feel a little spike of satisfaction – like a "well done" from my boss – really briefly. But it lasts about five seconds before it disappears, and then I am back worrying about the next thing.

Katya, 33

In another experiment, the brains of people who had won online games were monitored. The people with more activity in the ventral striatum part of their reward circuits were able to feel better about their wins for longer. So, if your reward circuit is not working as well as it should, joy will be fleeting.

But even if we have trouble cherishing a beautiful sunset when we don't feel good, all is not lost. We can still learn to re-train our attention, says Aaron Heller, assistant professor of psychology at the University of Miami, who led the research. "The brain is plastic, and through choices and experiences we can become better at savouring or sustaining positive emotions or recovering from things like anxiety and depression." And as we shall hear, when we start paying attention to different things in our lives – and giving our brain better experiences – it's in our power to lift our mood too.

7

How Anhedonia Can Affect Different Pleasures

If your reward system is no longer working as well as it might, you may also notice some changes to the way you perceive the world. Our senses are how we interface with the environment. They are inputs we feed our brains, to help us decide what action we should take next. Every sensory input is run past the radar of the amygdala to decide whether it's a desirable feeling we want to repeat or a warning sign that should trigger our threat system.

If it's desirable, the reward system should kick in. If that's not responding as strongly as it should, due to anhedonia, those incoming senses may no longer give you the same pleasurable feelings they once did. If you are in a state of "blah", this can dull your sense of taste, touch and smell, and even dial down your appreciation of music and sex.

I have realized that at age 40 I just don't like going out drinking or even just a meal chatting with friends like I used to. Not because I am depressed, but just because I would much rather relax at home and call people for a chat without having to dress up, pay a fortune and plan it all. I see going out as another chore and don't get any excitement from it.

Annette, 40

Music

Music is the soundtrack to much of our lives. The advent of earbuds – which can wirelessly pump any song we like into our ears at any time – means we now listen to it more than ever.

So why does our brain crave something as intangible as music, which is nothing more than oscillations of compressed air, so much?

A dose of Mozart, or even Ed Sheeran, may be pleasurable enough. Our favourite tunes can give the most mundane of experiences, like our commute into work or a walk in the park, a cinematic grandeur. But considering music isn't necessary to our survival, our brains give it a lot of attention.

Music is so rewarding that it's also processed along the same main reward pathway as food, sex and even drugs, like cocaine and amphetamine. Professor Robert Zatorre, a cognitive neuroscientist at McGill University, USA, who has led the understanding of music's effect on our brain, points out that music "engages all our higher order cognitive mechanisms – from the neck up. Music is remarkable in that it links together the most highly evolved parts of our brains and links with our reward system to give us pure physical pleasure."

*I used to listen to music most of the time. Now it just
feels boring or annoying. It's so frustrating.*

Seb, 36

The power of music

Long before the first human decided to hit an improvised drum in a repetitive pattern, rhythm and melody existed in nature – whether in the sound of waves hitting the shore, birdsong or our own heartbeat. One theory is that, just like fire, humans learned how to harness a natural phenomenon and bend it to our own purposes. In our hunter-gatherer days, dancing to the beat of the same drum with other members of our tribe was the ultimate bonding activity. Over time, we learned it could be used to soothe a baby to sleep, to inspire romantic feelings or even to incite soldiers to fight.

Whatever its purpose, listening to music has become one of the easiest and cheapest ways to metaphorically "mainline" good feelings into our brains. Part of this enjoyment comes from anticipating and looking forward to what notes will come next. When we listen to a melody we've been looking forward to hearing, our brains release dopamine into our reward circuits when that expectation is met. If there's a big build-up and release of tension toward a climax of a song – or a catchy chorus – you may also get an extra dopamine dose when it hits.

*It felt like colours, noise, smells, tastes were so far away.
I felt like a player in a video game, walking through the
world but not connected to it. Then one morning. I put
in my earbuds and music didn't move me either.*

Harry, 25

Music and dopamine

The importance of dopamine in our appreciation of music was highlighted in a landmark 2019 study. In this experiment, researchers played music to volunteers who had been given either a drug which raised dopamine – or one that reduces it. Those who had their dopamine release blocked reporting enjoying music less.

Getting the chills in music seems to be the moment that people who love a song have the biggest release of dopamine. One 2011 study in the journal *Nature Reviews Neuroscience* found a nine per cent increase in levels when people heard songs that gave them chills. But there are physical changes too, like when your hair stands on end or you get goosebumps. Theories as to why this happens vary. It may be that the amygdala mistakes the emotional reaction you are having for fear and responds with some of the same physiological changes that would happen if you were scared. Professor Zatorre suggests it may be your reward system's way of labelling the experience as important to earmark it.

Such is music's power that we can even get more of a dopamine release when we are in a sad mood and listening to a sad song, probably because we feel comforted by being understood and empathized with.

Musical anhedonia

If listening to music has always been your go-to way to feel better, noticing that you don't get as much enjoyment – or the same chills that you once had – can, not surprisingly, make you feel like a part of your life is missing. In interviews, people with anhedonia report finding music no longer moves them emotionally or makes them want to dance in the way it once did. People who once felt "the chills" are surprised to feel nothing. Some report enjoyment of music disappearing for a year or more before it returned, along with their improved mood. When their enjoyment did come back, it was also one of the first signs their anhedonia was lifting.

I adore music. All my life, I have been listening to and music. But for a couple of years, it felt like something important in my life had got up and walked out of the door.

Sali, 24

What might be happening if you no longer enjoy listening to the songs you loved? About three to five per cent of people have simply *never* had any pleasure in music, but still enjoy other rewards, like art or food, according to research by a team at Spain's University of Barcelona. These people were found to have weaker connections between their auditory cortex – the part of the brain that first processes music – and their reward systems. (It therefore makes sense that big music lovers, who get a lot of chills when they listen to music, have been found to have stronger connections.)

If you once loved music and you no longer enjoy it as much, it's likely that this loss is part of a general decrease in the activity in your reward system. "It's not terribly surprising that people with generalized anhedonia don't enjoy music," says Professor Zatorre, who points out that enjoyment of music is processed in the same common mesolimbic pathway as other stimuli. "I would expect it's a disorder of the reward system itself."

You just might notice it more, says Carmine Pariante, a professor of Biological Psychiatry: "If you were once really passionate about music, you are more likely to notice that that particular passion has gone."

I used to love to dance. But then music became just noise, and I didn't feel like moving my body to it at all. My response was deadened. I could hear the sounds, but I couldn't connect to them. It felt so frustrating I wanted to cry.

Rosie, 37

Taste

As early Homo sapiens wandered the Earth, it was almost a full-time job to forage for all the fruit, seeds and nuts needed. Excavations of ancient encampments have found that hunter-gatherers grazed on anything from 50 to 90 different types of plants. This meant that a strong sense of taste was essential if humans were to tell the difference between foods that were safe to eat and those that were poisonous. To discriminate, our tongues have between 2,000–8,000 papillae, or bumps, on their surfaces, depending on our age and genetics, which get replaced about every two weeks.

On the sides of these papillae are around three to five tastebuds, each with up to 50 sensory cells. When these come into contact with food, they send signals up to the gustatory cortex of the brain. Here, different areas of the region distinguish between bitter, salty, sweet, sour and savoury, which in various concentrations and combinations can add up to 100,000 different flavours.

Taste is more than just our appreciation of food, though. Phrases like "sour grapes" and "bitter pill" are reminders that this is a sense intimately linked to emotion. One of the changes you may notice in anhedonia is that you no longer enjoy the flavour of food as much and this can be yet another casualty of your dampened reward circuits. When we taste food we love, as with the pizza example (see page 115), it should stimulate the release of dopamine and opioids to give pleasure.

> *I can still taste but I don't enjoy what I am eating. I eat much less because I don't care about it. Wine was once one of my favourite treats, but now I don't enjoy it.*
> *It tastes bitter.*
> Edward, 39

But taste sensitivity is also moderated by changing levels of hormones and neurotransmitters, and, ultimately, by mood. If less dopamine is being released, you won't crave or enjoy the foods you usually do.

Serotonin and noradrenaline also play an important role in taste, helping to send messages from the mouth to the brain. In one experiment, depressed volunteers were given medication that raised levels of one or the other. Researchers found that raising the serotonin improved the ability to recognize sweet tastes. Noradrenaline made volunteers more sensitive to bitter and sour tastes. This was echoed in another study in which sports fans were asked how sad or happy they were after their teams won or lost. They were then given lemon-lime sorbet. The happy fans whose teams were victorious rated the dessert as tasting sweeter. The fans of the losing team, who had produced more noradrenaline from seeing their side lose, rated it as more sour and not as pleasant.

Over time, our taste responsiveness can also dim. As we age, our tastebuds decline in size and number and don't regenerate as quickly. This means the older you get, the more flavouring you might need. One study found that elderly people needed two to three times more salt in tomato soup to taste it.

Falling oestrogen levels in midlife for women also means a woman makes less of the saliva needed to break down food into individual chemicals so they can be tasted. Research by Turkey's Ankara University found that 35 per cent of women said their palate was not as sensitive during menopause.

The easiest way to explain it is that it's like eating food when you have a cold, and you can't taste anything. You know you're eating. You know you must eat something. But you stop enjoying the texture or flavour.

Oona, 65

Smell

Smell is the sense we are most likely to say we would sacrifice, the one which we take most for granted, until it's gone. We are so casual about it, one survey found that students would rather give up their smell than their phones or laptops.

When one of the symptoms of Covid 19 was anosmia (loss of smell), it proved to be a bracing lesson in learning how flat the world can be without this sense. Smell is closely connected to taste, but only because we also smell the food that is going into our mouths and that's part of the experience.

When molecules in the air go up our nose, they trigger olfactory nerve cells in the nasal epithelium (the only part of the brain to be exposed to fresh air). Despite the crossover, smell is still a separate system – and also has the unique ability to form powerful memories. This is because, whether it's the aroma of freshly ground coffee or the cookies you once made with grandma, a whiff goes straight to the heart of our emotional brain. The signals then go to the olfactory bulb and trigger responses across the emotional and memory circuits.

This intimate relationship of smell and emotion means that smell is strongly bound to mood. For example, just a sniff of linalool – the compound found in clementine and lavender – has been found to interact with the neurotransmitter GABA to calm the brain and nervous system.

But it's a delicate relationship.

Studies have found that your sense of smell is also particularly vulnerable to changes in neurotransmitter levels. Over time, the size of the olfactory bulb in depressed people has also been found to shrink, which in turn reduces their enjoyment of life, creating a vicious circle.

One study in the journal *Chemosensory Perception* gave a group of women lots of smells to try – from vanilla to lemon pie and mint and fuel oil. The researchers found the flatter a woman's emotions were, the worse they were at smelling.

Smell is also linked to levels of feel-good chemicals in the brain. Rats who had their ability to smell removed were found to have lower concentrations of dopamine and serotonin, which also helps explain why blunting of this sense is linked to feelings of "blah".

There's a link between how I feel and how much I smell. At times, when I feel good, it's like I can smell things around me more deeply. Even the air smells better.

Alice, 39

Sight

When you are feeling "meh", you may see the world in more muted shades too. But then colour is not absolute. It's made in the mind. So, our emotional state will also determine how we see it.

In one experiment by researchers at the UK's University Hospital of South Manchester, it was found that people with anxiety and depression were more likely to use the colour grey to describe how they felt. The "greying" effect for the people with lower mood was so clear that researchers now suggest it could potentially be used as a test to work out whether someone is depressed, according to the study published in the journal *Biological Psychiatry*.

Intuitively, you could say we've always known this. It's why filmmakers, artists and writers have always veered toward using greyer tones to create sad scenes. The reasons are not yet completely understood, but one reason may be that the photoreceptors in the retina are the most energy-hungry cells in the body. If brains of people with depression and anhedonia are already running at a low ebb or getting a reduced blood supply, they may not have the processing power to interpret the full range of colour coming into the eye, making the world look more drab. Professor Russell Foster, head of Oxford University's Department of Ophthalmology, says: "We know that a tired brain can't process information as effectively, so the complicated task of colour processing might get marginalized."

All the colours I saw felt toned down, as I lived in a world which was always under grey skies.
Patrick, 36

I can see colours, but they are not vibrant. They don't stand out.
Finn, 24

Touch

When I was a foreign correspondent working In New York in 2004, I took part in a cuddle party. This involved 20 complete strangers meeting in an Upper East Side apartment in their pyjamas. According to the organizers, who charged a $20 entrance fee, it was a way to solve the problem of touch deprivation in inner city living. However, the fact that one of the house rules was "no dry humping" was a clue that previous guests had come for more than just their "recommended daily allowance of welcomed touch". Back then, it seemed like a crack-pot idea, but as time would tell, the organizers were onto something.

Touch has an evolutionary purpose because grooming is important between primates to show trust – and for reassurance that all is well. It also creates a sense of relaxation because if other members of our pack have time to groom us, it means there is no imminent danger. From birth onwards, kind touch activates reward circuits, releasing opiates in the brain.

Still, it took the Covid lockdowns to help us wake up to how important touch is for our mental health, says Professor Francis McGlone, head of the Somatosensory & Affective Neuroscience Group at the UK's John Moores University in Liverpool. "For the first time in human evolution, human primates were not allowed to touch each other. It's only that absence of touch that made them realize that something was missing in their lives. Now it's become widely acknowledged that humans need touch. The activation of these nerve fibres has a number of direct effects we can measure. It releases oxytocin, the bonding hormone. It releases endorphins. It lowers heart rate and cortisol, the measure of stress. So gentle touch is having a direct effect on processes that all factor into wellbeing."

Yet despite its detrimental role in feeling good, anhedonia can also rob you of your responsiveness. Disruption to the reward circuits can also mean that hug you once enjoyed may no longer feel as good, making you feel more isolated and down.

I used to love hugs. Now they feel weirdly uncomfortable any annoying. It's like: "Is this going to go on this much longer? I have things to do."
Maryon, 54

Sexual anhedonia

If anhedonia makes touch feels less rewarding, it's unsurprising that sex and, beyond that, orgasm, may not feel as intense. Scans of women and men having orgasms show how, at the moment of climax, as many as 80 different brain regions come "online". These include all the areas along the dopamine reward pathway, with activity in the nucleus accumbens – a key part of the reward system – reaching its peak at the moment of climax.

Meanwhile in the endocrine system, the hypothalamus, responsible for keeping your bodily internal functions in balance, also releases oxytocin. This triggers the muscular contractions in women. Men release oxytocin too but less of it and in shorter bursts.

As this is a cascade of hugely complicated, interlocking chemical processes, just a few of which I have mentioned here, lots can go off the rails. Sexual anhedonia can take several different forms. Some people may lose the motivation to have sex, for others sex may not feel as pleasurable or they may have orgasms which don't feel as good as they used to. One reason may be disruption to dopamine levels. Dopamine seems to have a key role not only in sexual craving – better known in this context as lust – and it also seems to be an orgasm accelerator, making climaxes faster and easier to achieve. So, if it's not flowing well, it could be another reason your orgasm is felt more like a faint tinkle than a tremor.

Less enjoyment of sex can also happen against a background of hormonal changes in both men and women. In women, oestrogen helps make orgasms stronger. It's the reason why women who have monthly periods have the biggest climaxes mid-cycle when oestrogen levels are at their highest. So, oestrogen's fluctuation over the menstrual cycle, or complete disappearance during menopause, will play a part. As oestrogen also helps to make oxytocin, another chemical crucial for sexual pleasure, enjoyment of sex also drops off in menopause. To add insult to injury, it's another reason climaxes may take longer to achieve, fade more quickly or may not feel as intense.

> *I used to love having sex with my boyfriend, but now the hugging and kissing feels like I am going through the motions. It's almost like: "Are we done yet?"*
>
> Flo, 27

> *I know I am having an orgasm, but it doesn't give me any pleasure. It's like a reflex, but it's toned down and disconnected, almost like it's not wired up to me.*
>
> Polina, 37

Childbirth and age can cause physical changes that make orgasm more challenging. The optimum distance between the clitoris and vagina for orgasm is 2.5cm (1in). Over time, a woman's anatomy can get slighter longer in this area, also making orgasm more difficult to achieve. Muscles in the pelvic floor, where the shock waves of orgasm are felt, can also weaken after pregnancy, surgery or weight gain.

For men, testosterone is also important for strong orgasms. As testosterone levels drop gradually with age, so does the amount of semen he makes. At around age 45, men start ejaculating 1.48 per cent less per year on average, according to research in the journal *Fertility and Sterility*. Other research has found that men over the age of 52 ejaculate half the volume of semen as those under that age (1.8 ml versus 3.2ml) which makes for weaker orgasms.

I watched so much porn, I lost my drive to do anything. Not just have sex but to go out and socialize. It was like my brain had frazzled all my dopamine receptors. Sex was boring and didn't feel as exciting as the stuff on screen. I decided to give it up the porn. After three months, I didn't just start enjoying sex again, I started laughing too. It was like the porn had sabotaged my whole pleasure circuitry.

Jeremy, 45

Social Anhedonia

A party invite comes through on email, but thinking you probably won't enjoy it, you stay in, bingeing on a Netflix series into the early hours. The next day you wake up past midday. You check your phone. No messages. After that, you're half deflated, but also feel half justified in telling yourself it would have been a waste of time. Next time you get asked, you feel no one will notice if you are there or not. The more you stay in – or even under the duvet or parked in front of your screen – the bigger effort it feels to get yourself out there, and the less you feel you have to say.

Earlier this year, I went to my best friend's 50th. It was a glamorous costume party and there were people there I hadn't seen for ages because of Covid. If I laughed, it felt shallow and forced and like it was for appearance's sake only. Probably from a distance, I looked like I was being the life and soul. Really, I was counting down the minutes before I could leave.

Kathy, 50

We all have moments when we don't really feel like socializing. A lot of the time we go anyway. Sometimes it's a fun experience, sometimes it's boring and awkward. Social events are hard to predict. If you develop social anhedonia – a sort of "I don't want to go", rather than FOMO – you might be less willing to take that chance.

Social anhedonia can take many forms. You may start to avoid social meet-ups with friends, feel more negative about other people, or feel like you have to fake having a good time with others. Even worse, you may start to pull away from your intimate relationships, including partners or children, because your feelings of love may feel blunted. Drops in the bonding hormone oxytocin may help to explain why you no longer feel like being with other people as much. We also get dopamine rewards from socializing, so if that's in short supply your urge to go out and mix may dry up too.

Brain scans have found that people with social anhedonia have difficulty even imagining they will have a nice time (though some may enjoy it once they get there). While they may still be motivated to keep trying for rewards that are certain – like earning money – they are less interested in bothering if they don't know what's going to happen; they seem to have less motivation to take a risk. "People with anhedonia cannot anticipate the pleasure they could get from certain activities or sensations, so they cannot motivate themselves to seek them out," says Carmine Pariante, a professor of biological psychiatry at King's College London. "Even if they do, they won't feel any pleasure."

These days, I prefer animals to people because you don't have to have a conversation with them.
Francesca, 36

A tough childhood made me defensive and on my guard. In my late teens and early twenties I had some good times with friends, even though I always felt a bit on the sidelines. But gradually life's inevitable knocks and my more cynical view of life meant that people found me a bit of a downer. It hurt when people made comments like saying I was only fun to be around if I'd had a few drinks. I was trying my best, but it just didn't come naturally. It was almost like there was a glass ceiling that stopped me enjoying myself.
Heidi, 63

Afterwards, research has found they also tend to remember their experiences of an occasion less fondly, making them less likely to want to go out and do it again. It doesn't help that if they do turn up, they don't mingle or interact as well. They may present with a blanker expression or a flatter voice. Some studies have shown that their reaction to others in social settings is also less enthusiastic. They are more likely to interpret social cues negatively, and even more likely to view others as less attractive. A loss of sense of humour is also a symptom. Research has found that people with anhedonia judge fewer things as funny and make fewer jokes themselves.

I recently finished my degree. I tried to be excited at my graduation ball. But even though I should have felt a huge sense of achievement and relief, all the celebrations felt fake.

Ted, 22

Part Two summary

As we've heard, anhedonia is a breakdown in the reward system, which is made up of three parts: wanting, liking and learning. To get your reward system fully back online, all three need to be working well together. To experience joyful moments, first you need to decide what you want to do and look forward to it. Secondly, you need to be fully present in the moment, and free from worry and self-consciousness, to make the most of the experience. Thirdly, you need to remember the event and be grateful for it, so you recall it positively, and want to do it again. In this final part of the book, we'll be looking at ways to get all three phases working in harmony together, so you can start experiencing life to the full again.

PART THREE

How to Feel Fully Alive Again: Solutions to Feeling "Blah"

8

Getting Back on the Same Side as our Brains

Imagine you have woken up in an alien country with no feeling in your arm. To everyone else, it looks fine. But you know these pins and needles just don't feel right and you're stressed by the fact that although your limb moves, it seems dead. The problem is that you lack the words to describe this numbness, so you feel unable to do anything to address it. Then imagine you found a name for it. You'd stop feeling you were the only person who had this experience, and you could find out what was wrong.

In the same way, if you've long been feeling emotionally numb and unable to enjoy life, you now have the term for it: anhedonia. By giving it a name, you're already taking charge of it. You now have a new word to add to your vocabulary, one that describes an emotional state which, until now, has been hardly talked about outside the therapy room.

A gradual change

You probably didn't develop anhedonia overnight. Gradually the enjoyment is likely to have drained out of your life, like water down a plughole. For many of us, the realization of how much we are missing out on came on slowly. It may have taken some time to wake up to the fact that you'd hadn't laughed, really laughed, in months, or even years.

Or perhaps you realized you couldn't really remember the last time you could relax and sink into the experience of a holiday. Maybe you started to notice the ratio of sad to happy feelings had become seriously out of balance. Or blah had become the "wallpaper" to your life.

Over the years, stress may have gradually eroded your capacity to have fun.

Just as anhedonia crept up on you, it won't vanish immediately. It may take some time to get your reward circuits running at full capacity again – or to get your feel-good chemicals back in balance. However, by making tweaks, changing your priorities and feeding your brain more positive inputs, those small changes will gradually add up.

Creating new thought patterns

Anhedonia may have become your default setting. You may have lived with it so long that it feels like part of your character. So, first of all, you need to believe in your capacity to change and get control over your mood.

As you are reading this book, there are around 86 billion neurons in your brain, linked together potentially by up to a quadrillion synapses. Individually each brain cell can't do much on its own, but if you have a lot of them communicating you end up with an activity pattern, which is also what we colloquially call "a thought", says neuroscientist Dr Henning Beck.

Thought formation is like the performance of an orchestra, says Dr Beck. "If you look at an orchestra from the outside, seeing all the musicians sitting next to each other, but not playing any music, you have no idea what melody the orchestra is able to play. Just like the brain, you have no clue what thought this system is able to think. In an orchestra, the melody begins to emerge when the musicians start to play together and synchronize with each other. So, the music, the melody, is among the players. Just like a thought in the brain is among the brain cells. A thought is not located anywhere. A thought is how the brain cells interact and how they process the information."

All these musicians (aka neurons) need to be ready to play their part at a moment's notice.

This means they are constantly on standby, which is why your brain consumes so much energy to run. (Even though it takes up just 3 per cent of your body mass, it uses up to 20 per cent of your energy. The firing of neurons alone is believed to use up to two-thirds of your brainpower.) The underlying melodies are formed in our emotional or limbic networks. This is more like a hum which is running all the time, but beneath our conscious awareness. When these emotions are processed in the cortex, the more complex, evolved part of your brain, we can put words to these feelings, like adding the lyrics to a song.

This view of how thoughts are made is a long way from the way the brain used to be seen, as a kind of grandfather clock with interlocking cogs, which operated in a fixed way. Now we know that thought patterns can be changed. Of course, like that orchestra we just talked about, the brain finds it easiest to replay the same thought patterns, which are like the melodies an orchestra has played again and again. But, if required to, with practice it can be trained to play other tunes.

Although it's easier for the orchestra, and your brain, to keep playing its core repertoire, over time our conscious mind – the conductor – can give their musicians new scores to learn, and your brain cells can join together to create different circuits.

Believing happiness is in our control

If you've ever tried to lose weight, you probably know there's a number on the scales your body always seems to return to. Even if you exercise and eat differently, it takes a lot of effort to move that dial away from the place it seems to "want" to rest. Research suggests there's a reversion to the mean, or "set point", in happiness too.

Estimates vary but some studies suggested that around 50 per cent of this state is decided by our genes and our childhood experiences, about 10 per cent is what happens to us. That leaves around 40 per cent in our control. Other researchers claim it's less. But there's one factor which makes us more likely to be able to decide how happy we are – and that is our belief that we do, in fact, have influence over it.

In a survey from Tracking Happiness Index, used to compile the World Happiness Report, over 1,000 people answered the question: "Is happiness something that you can control?" Next, they were asked: "If you look back at the last year of your life, how would you rate your happiness on a scale of 1 to 10?" It was found that an encouraging 89 per cent believed that happiness is something you have power over. Tellingly, the people who believed it was in their control, were a *third* happier than those who thought it wasn't. On the other hand, the people who thought happiness was *not* something they could change were *five* times more miserable.

So, let's say now, a growth mindset is essential if you are to move out of anhedonia. In other words, you have a better chance of beating "blah", if you believe you can. Psychologist Matt Killingsworth investigates how people's circumstances, behaviour and other factors contribute to and detract from their happiness. He believes that we are freer than we realize to influence how much we enjoy life – by changing the conditions around us.

He told me: "Some people are happier than others, but everyone is influenced by the conditions of their lives. By changing the conditions that affect happiness there is every reason to expect happiness itself to change." Indeed, it's never too late for your brain to grow new neurons in the area related to learning and memory, which may mean it's never too late for your perception of the world to change.

Neuroscientist Professor Hana Burianová of the UK's Bournemouth University tells me: "Once we thought that you were born with the same number of brain cells you were ever going to have. But the good news is that we now know we can grow new ones. The hippocampus, the area key to learning and memory, is able to make 700 neurons every single day, which is great, particularly if you expose yourself to new experiences." In short, it now seems that our future enjoyment of life lies more in our own hands that we ever realized.

We can't go back and ask the ancestors we met at the start of this book how much they enjoyed life. Even if we could find their fossilized remains, they wouldn't give much away after 100,000 years. What we can say for certain is that your relatives' brains were far more attuned to their environments than yours is now. As we've heard, their lives were certainly challenging. For a start, they were a lot shorter – average life expectancy was around 30 years of age.

But it's safe to say that, as your relatives negotiated their environment, they felt *alive*, rather than apathetic or zombified. They spent life outdoors, among a close-knit band of about 50 friends and relatives, bonded together to outsmart predators and by the common goal of making sure their tribe survived.

Getting our brains onside

In the 21st-century world our basic survival needs – and then some – are met with so little effort. Our reward circuits are triggered so relentlessly that they become overloaded, and nothing feels pleasurable. In other word, we feel "blah".

It's too late to turn back the clock. After living in the wilderness for a week or so, even the hardiest and most nature-loving amongst us, are keen to return to comfortable homes, with their mod cons and relative safety. But we do have one major advantage to help us find a middle way. For most of our existence, we humans didn't even know what our brains were for. Despite the fact that modern life can make enjoying our lives harder in many ways, we now have a big advantage. We now have more knowledge about how our brains work than any generation which has ever walked the planet.

Over the last decade, we have been able to see how our thoughts are formed in real time and view the circuits which underlie our feelings and moods. In short, we can finally peek "under the bonnet". When we see how good feelings in the moment can "light up" circuits in the brain, life no longer seems quite as conditional on having the holy grail of a happy childhood as it once did. No longer do we believe that we need to excavate every nook and cranny of our past before we can start to feel consistently good (although that's still a useful exercise).

It's this emerging understanding which means we are on the way to getting our brains back "onside" once again, instead of working against us.

Seeing how good feelings are physically created allows us to focus on the here and now. It's a shift toward viewing joy as something that's in our conscious control.

Broadening our view

At this point it helps to remember that happiness is a rather vague umbrella term. It stands ahead of us like some glowing unicorn state, a lofty goal which popular culture tells us we must be constantly striving toward. To feel like we are getting somewhere and hold more realistic expectations, the first step is to start seeing happiness in a more nuanced way. This means breaking this broad term into different types of feelings – and noticing any moments that help us feel "good" and valuing them.

That could be feeling relieved when you find something you'd lost. Or the security of lying in your partner's arms. It could be the appreciation of the smell of coffee in the morning. It could be putting your hand out of your car window to feel the wind as you listen to your favourite song at full volume. Or the sensation of slipping into freshly changed sheets. The snug feeling of putting on a favourite sweater. All are valid ways to feel great. There's no denying that happiness is a difficult overall state to achieve consistently, but in all these smaller moments, it's perfectly possible, as long as we recognize them. One of the reasons we fall into "blah" is because we stop noticing good moments when they happen.

We don't give ourselves time to feel their reward, or savour and remember them. This is either because we feel we don't have time or because our reward system has become blunted and it doesn't feel good. To notice and hold onto these good moments for longer, train your body in "interoception", which means noticing how your body reacts in response to the inputs it's getting from your five senses. So, in the case of "blah", start noticing when something makes you smile or laugh or feel good. Take that as a cue to pay it more attention, stay with it for longer and take note of it.

If we don't take deliberate steps to drink in the positive moments, the hard truth is the human brain is designed to be impacted much more by the uncomfortable, unpleasant moments of our lives much more.

The reason is that when something negative happens – say we get a parking ticket or have a row with a loved one – it feels like a crisis we have to respond to. Just as your ancestors took more notice of the snakes in the grass than the view of the sunset from that ridge, difficult moments grab more of our attention to help us head off danger the next time. In doing so, however, they narrow our focus, so overall we notice the good things even less. However just being aware of this bias too can remind yourself how outdated it is and why it's important not to give into it.

Psychologist Professor Barbara Fredrickson has combined neuroscience and anthropology to work out how and why people feel good. Her experiments show that when people are shown images which they like looking at, such as pictures of puppies, compared to neutral photos of chairs or tables, scans of the irises in their eyes show they are more likely to look around at their wider environment afterwards. "Positive emotions open our awareness," Fredrickson says of her broaden-and-build theory. "They increase the expanse of our peripheral vision. We see more. Because we see more, we see more possibilities. People come up with more ideas about what they might do next when they are experiencing a positive emotion, relative to when they are experiencing neutral states or negative emotions." Feeding the brain positive emotions has the same effect that sunlight has on a flower at dawn, says Professor Fredrickson. "They make petals open up and take in more light."

In anhedonia and depression, our focus is also narrowed, so we tend to look inwards and away from experiences that could make us feel better. In the next chapter of the book, we will look at science-based ways to feed your brain positive emotions so that you can also start to unfurl.

9

Does Happiness Happen to You – or Do You Make It?

It's ironic that in English, we talk about things that "make" us happy. Yet, we forget about the "making" bit, thinking that happiness is something that should somehow happen to us.

But as you will hear, you don't need to wait for your external circumstances to change to feel a bit better, day by day. Before we set about looking at how to shift anhedonia and feel better, first let's address some of the road blocks that might be standing in your way.

The number one enemy of joy

Let's put the cards on the table first and accept that any move out of "blah" is going to be difficult if you are constantly stressed. In healthy amounts, stress motivates us and gets us going. It's the spike in adrenaline that makes us run to safety if we are in danger. It's the rise in cortisol that gets us out of bed in the morning and spurs us on to deal with challenges. But high, continuous levels of adrenaline and cortisol help keep our bodies in a high state of alert, swamping our feel-good hormones and dampening our reward circuits. When this stress becomes chronic and non-stop it puts us in survival mode, preventing us seeing the good things all around us which could make life feel better.

If you feel you never have time to enjoy your life, first you may need to take a step back.

Quite simply, stress is the greatest enemy of joy – and one of the main contributing factors to anhedonia. In survival mode, you are trying to lob back each new demand that comes at you over the net to stay in the game. If the balls keep coming thick and fast, you never get the time to stand still. You are just trying to return the smashes, lobs and volleys. You may tell yourself that you just need to get through the next match, but somehow the serves keep coming.

Cutting all the stress from our lives, forever, is never going to be possible. But knowing what you know now, this is a good time to take some time to work out your real needs. As family educator Rob Parsons has pointed out: "A slower day is not coming." We all have the same number of hours in the day. And, with some tweaks, we all have some power to change how we spend those hours and what we prioritize. (Hint: On your death bed, I doubt you will describe the best days of your life as the ones you spent bingeing on Netflix.)

Step out of the game long enough to allow yourself to catch your breath, even if it's just an uninterrupted weekend. Put your out-of-office message on, mute your social media and reset your cortisol levels, then try exploring a new environment to get some perspective. It's only in a state of calm that you can decide whether you want to keep playing by the same rules.

MAKE SPACE FOR GOOD FEELINGS

Suzanne Alderson runs a charity and support group called Parenting Mental Health for some of the most stressed people on the planet – parents of children and young people with mental health problems who often feel in a state of constant vigilance over their children's suicide attempts and self-harm. It feels physically painful sometimes to step into the group's Facebook community and see so much of the stress, pain and guilt such parents go through. But after living through a period when her own 14-year-old daughter was attempting suicide, Suzanne reminds these parents that they must also find some time to enjoy their lives, even in the most difficult of circumstances.

Suzanne says: "My return to joy happened, ironically, when my daughter attempted suicide in 2015. It felt the ultimate disloyalty to her pain to be focussed on fun, friends or the life we'd had or expected to, and any moments of pleasure left our lives as we focussed only on the essential – her waking up every day. I soon discovered that focus can be a good thing until it becomes all-consuming and, as what we faced seeped into every conscious moment, every choice, and every thought, I had never felt further away from the state I was trying so desperately to hold onto – aliveness. And with that came a sense that I was less capable of giving my daughter the care and compassion she needed.

"So, blocking out my self-judgement and the fear and grief, I committed to what I now call essential maintenance; anchors in my day to mitigate the sadness and fear and remind me that space for joy was how I would be resourced enough to be the present, patient partner she needed in her illness. These rituals didn't mean that I didn't care or that I was self-absorbed. They fuelled me to care more. There was equivalence between her needs and mine, even if I often needed to meet hers first. Meeting one didn't mean I couldn't meet the other.

"Gratitude became a daily practice after I started sharing it with the Parenting Mental Health community, I founded in 2016. For many parents, it was, and remains, hard to be grateful when there's so much pain and uncertainty to process. But the act of finding things we are grateful for can carve out much needed space for positive reflection, give us a glimpse of the sense of joy that is still possible even when we can't imagine seeing light again, and bring us back to ourselves.

"One of the greatest joys for me comes from community. Holding space for 30,000 parents might be some people's idea of hell, but connection fuels me and it has changed my life and how I view what is important. We don't always meet each other at our best but we always meet with compassion, and the truth of our everyday is where we create our deepest understanding. But we have to give ourselves permission to do this. Overload and overwhelm can mean even the mere thought of feeling joy feels indulgent and disloyal to the pain those we love are carrying, and we don't have the energy to go out and seek it. Being joyful and connected to ourselves is often low on our list; it's what we'll do when everything else is complete. But if we continue to live with a deep-rooted need to progress in all areas of our lives, there is never time. Until we're reminded that we've used it up worrying about the things that don't matter and doing things for people who aren't really bothered.

"Being burnt out, emotionally and physically, led me to rituals. These ways I can shoehorn in a moment of connection with myself and with nature as I stand on the grass barefoot before I go back into the heavy work of supporting parents in distress.

"These rituals are big enough to matter to me and small enough to go unnoticed to others.

"Not that I care now what anyone thinks about the time I spend finding pockets of joy in my life. They give me the fuel to continue to care. And whether it's a belly laugh with a friend about something really silly and inconsequential to most, the sense of accomplishment that comes when you eat something you've grown, or the quiet delight of a tidy knicker drawer, joy is available to us all right now, if we can only allow ourselves to have it."

How guilt stands in our way

Life is hard for many of us. The problem is that we tend to feel we have to be engaged in a non-stop battle to try to make things better. As Suzanne points out (see box), by turning down opportunities to enjoy ourselves, we sink into overwhelm and instead of fighting back against challenges, we make ourselves less equipped to face them. Furthermore, if we lose the joy of being with the people we love, we can also feel shame. We assume we must be horrible, heartless psychopaths if we are not moved by the pleasure of spending time with friends, parents, partners, children or grandchildren.

Psychologist Dr Rami Nader reminds people who are dealing with anhedonia that it's not a character flaw. He says: "Often when I am working with clients, they get down and upset with themselves. They tend to beat themselves up over the fact that if they were good parents, they wouldn't have to try and force themselves to enjoy playing with their kids. It can feel confusing, scary, or distressing. Or perhaps they haven't returned text messages to friends because they just don't feel like it. But there's not something wrong with them that they don't want to do these things. It's a symptom. The first step is for them to give themselves a break and accept it's anhedonia. It's not them being bad parents or bad friends."

What is your soundtrack saying?

As we learnt in Part One, your brain evolved to anticipate threats. This was great when it helped your relatives survive hostile, predator-filled environments. Although there are no longer any lurking, supersized carnivores behind the next tree, our brains tend to behave like there still are. We may be safe on our sofas, but we still spend a lot of time thinking about what might, or might not, happen.

Brain scans have even found the place where this inner fearmonger lives in the brain – a circuit of regions known as the "default mode network" that runs from the back to the front of the brain through the anterior medial prefrontal cortex, posterior cingulate cortex and angular gyrus.

This is the place you go to when your brain is not actively engaged in something it needs to concentrate on. So, if you had a difficult childhood, it may revert to a more cynical, apprehensive view of the world. Unless you become aware of it, it could be the source of the whispers that tell you that you don't deserve to be happy or that nothing in your life will ever be fun again. If you are experiencing anhedonia, it could be the inner critic telling you that it's selfish to enjoy yourself. Allowed to become too loud and go unchallenged, it can talk you out of feeling good.

So, why do we put up with it? For one thing, we mostly don't realize we don't have listen to everything it says. We think it's just "us" when in fact it tends to be the same patterns of thinking which we have tended to default to over the years. Another reason is that our carping inner voice can help us feel more in control. Our inner commentator fools us into thinking that by worrying about something, we are doing something to fix the problem, when most of the time we're just ruminating – or letting the same thoughts go around and around in our heads.

Start paying attention to what it's saying. If it keeps putting obstacles in the way of feeling good, move them aside. Decide it's time to live in the moment, rather than view life through the misted-up lens it presents us with.

We spend up to half our waking hours engaging in mind wandering, according to happiness researcher Matt Killingsworth. And while it's needed to plan ahead to a certain extent, too much activity in the default mode network is associated with lower happiness. According to Killingsworth: "[The] opposite of mind-wandering is being fully present – bringing all of one's attention and energy to the current moment. My research suggests that people are happier, more productive, and more socially connected when they are fully present."

You may want to try these ways to stop the rumination:

Find a circuit breaker: An Israeli study using MRI scanners found that people who silently repeated the word "Echad", meaning "One" in Hebrew, could deactivate their default mode network circuit and stop ruminating. "When people said 'one, one, one,' everything that had been active during the resting state in the default mode network was shut down," says psychology professor Aviva Berkovich-Ohana of the University of Haifa in Israel.

Change your environment: When you notice yourself spiralling downwards into negative thinking, change where you are. Places like bedrooms, where people tend to ruminate, can become associated with unhelpful thought patterns. The same environmental cues can lead you to having the same thoughts. According to Professor Ethan Kross, author of *Chatter:*

The Voice in Our Head (and How to Harness It), "If we make smart choices about how we relate to our surroundings, they can help us control our inner voice."

Try the 90-second rule: One tool to get more control over rumination when it's standing in the way of joy is the 90-second rule. This means becoming more aware when neurochemicals are released in your brain, observing how they make you feel and then waiting for them to pass. According to neuroscientist Jill Bolte Taylor: "When a person has a reaction to something in their environment, there's a 90 second chemical process that happens in the body. After that, any remaining emotional response is just the person choosing to stay in that emotional loop. Something happens in the external world and chemicals are flushed through your body which puts it on full alert.

"For those chemicals to totally flush out of the body it takes less than 90 seconds. This means that for 90 seconds you can watch the process happening, you can feel it happening, and then you can watch it go away.

"After that, if you continue to feel fear, anger, and so on, you need to look at the thoughts that you're thinking that are re-stimulating the circuitry that is resulting in you having this physiological response over and over again."

Pivot: Redirect your focus by going out into nature. Whatever is happening in our world, nature is a constant. When you pay decide to pay attention to it, you can always find something beautiful. It puts your life in perspective. One 2015 study found that when people walk through green space, they ruminate less. Even a quick stroll of 15 minutes or less can do the trick, probably because it's long enough to remind us that nature stays luminous and transcendent, whatever challenges we face.

And overall, distinguish between worry, anxiety and stress: Life will feel more manageable if you start tapping into and recognising what emotions you are feeling, rather than letting them swirl around in your head like a whirlwind you can't see through.

Let's look at how to differentiate between the three main enemies of joy: worry, stress and anxiety.

Worry is thinking about what might happen if we don't do something. In the right amounts it can stimulate you to act. Stress is a longer-term physiological response to something in your environment, like work, an on-going burden or a health issue which can make you feel, at times, like you can't cope. Anxiety is worrying about things you have mostly imagined or amplified in your mind, but which still trigger your nervous system as if they were real.

Simplistically, we can see a worry as an invitation to problem-solve. We can see stress as a suggestion that we take steps to reduce the load. We can see anxiety as a sign we need to work out what's really a problem that can be dealt with and what's imagined. With all three, noticing, naming and talking back to these feelings and experiences, can help dissipate their power.

10

How to Get Going Again

The key to beating anhedonia is finding the motivation to go out and do things that will make you feel better and more alive again. After all, anhedonia is not depression. It's more of a gradual drifting away from the activities that make life enjoyable. It is that state you find yourself in when, on balance, you feel more negative feelings in your day, than good. Those who live with it also describe it as feeling "dead inside". This means identifying what's important to you in your life – what makes you feel alive – and understanding what's standing in your way.

When you enjoy yourself, you are not just "having fun". As we've heard, feeling good is the result of the co-ordinated movement of several types of feel-good neurotransmitters and hormones around your brain and body, some of the best-known being dopamine, serotonin and oxytocin.

Feeding your brain

The good news is that unless your brain's reward system has been so disrupted by addiction, brain injury or long-term major depression (in which case you should be seeking specialist help), there are plenty of steps you can take to help recalibrate those levels. By consciously setting out to feed your brain a range of more positive experiences, via those five senses that make your emotions, you can change your overall mood state.

Think of it as setting out to spoon-feed your brain a new kind of diet, or self-administering experiences, that will boost your happiness hormones. Remember, you have biology on your side now that you understand it. Our brains are always striving for neurochemical balance, because no neurotransmitter works in isolation – they all have a knock-on effect on each other.

By creating joy from within, we can allow our own brain to find the balance it naturally craves. As neuroscientist Candace Pert said: "Each one of us has his or her own finest drugstore available at the cheapest cost; to produce all the drugs we ever need to run our body and mind."

It's hard to motivate yourself when you can't see the point. It was hard at first, but I kept going by seeking out new experiences to get out of my environment. Once a week I made a date for myself to go to places around me I hadn't found time to visit before, like museums and parks. I enjoyed going on my own so I could appreciate everything without having to worry about anyone else. I made a point of focussing on small details and even took a sketch pad so I could really savour the things I enjoyed seeing instead of taking a quick snap for Instagram and forgetting about it.

Jana, 55

Feel-good factors

When people are asked to list the things that make them happy, the answers in the modern industrialized world tend to be remarkably consistent. Here's a compilation of some of the most common responses when people were surveyed to find out what made them feel good:

- Getting into a freshly made bed
- Feeling the sun on your face
- Having a cup of freshly brewed tea or coffee
- Curling up with a good book
- Having time to yourself
- Smelling fresh bread
- Getting a massage
- Looking at the sky
- The clean feeling after having a shower
- Putting on your favourite song
- Finding a bargain
- Listening to rainfall when you're inside
- Having a long hot bath
- Smelling freshly cut grass
- Browsing in a book shop
- Tasting chocolate
- Going outside to do something active
- Doing some exercise
- Seeing dogs stick their heads out of car windows
- Using a new cleaning sponge
- Waking up and realizing you have a day off

- Enjoying the sight of a room you've just tidied
- Baking a cake
- Popping bubble wrap
- Swimming in the sea
- Dancing like no one's watching
- Opening a new book
- Smelling fine wine
- Putting your out-of-office message on when you've finished work
- Putting on a new pair of socks or underwear
- Singing in the shower
- Getting a seat on a crowded bus or train
- The "pop" when you open a new jar
- Complimenting other people
- Looking at beautiful photographs
- Ticking off items on your to-do list
- Feeling safe and warm at home
- Making something with your hands
- Using new stationery
- Watching comedy clips
- Having dinner around a table
- Tidying out a drawer
- Late night conversations with friends
- Getting home after a long day
- Planning a holiday or treat
- Watching a musical performance or music video
- Going to a farmers' market
- Revisiting a favourite film

- Stroking a pet
- Looking after plants
- Drawing/doodling/colouring in

Look through the list and see if you agree with any of them. Tick the ones that make you feel good, then double tick the ones that you could do today if you wanted to or, failing that, the next day.

What do they have in common? Many employ the senses. Others involved some seeking out, enable a small sense of achievement or contain a small element of surprise. Many take no more activation energy – or the basic motivation to get something done – than you need to get out of bed in the morning.

This list also shows how quickly we can pivot to activities that make us feel good. Too often we convince ourselves we need to take life-changing actions, such as rebooting our careers or relationships, to get happy chemicals flowing again. We also tend to believe good feelings must arise spontaneously. This is a misconception. According to a 2010 study in the journal *Clinical Psychology Review* by researcher Eric Garland and colleagues, most people simply don't realize that "Positive emotion can be intentionally self-generated. If 'savoured', even the most fleeting everyday moments can add up to upward spirals in positivity." Put another way, you can give your brain a better chance of finding happiness if you feed it more uplifting experiences.

Indeed, it's easy to underestimate the value of making small improvements daily. As your brain circuits and chemistry start to change, so will your mood. You probably won't notice when you feel one per cent better every week, or even every month, but over time, these improvements add up. Furthermore, now you can visualize how feel-good chemicals move around your brain, you are likely to feel more in control of them. Indeed, research has found that it can take as little as seven weeks of self-generating positive emotions to reduce symptoms of low mood.

> *I worked out that even if I didn't feel joy at new things,*
> *I could be curious about them. That was an attitude*
> *that helped me while I waited for good feelings to*
> *come back into my life.*
>
> Nathan, 43

> *I have stopped doing the things I don't enjoy and*
> *do more of the things I do. I have taken up activities,*
> *small steps at a time, like joining a local running club*
> *and going out to the theatre, until they have become*
> *habits I enjoy.*
>
> Jon, 43

This is also known as Behavioural Activation Therapy – and there are two simple principles. The first is that doing something – anything, no matter how small – is always better than doing nothing. The second is don't wait until you feel better to do something. In other words, do the opposite of what anhedonia is telling you to do. "We know that people with anhedonia don't look forward to things other people might find enjoyable, and unless they put themselves in the position to try something they won't have the opportunity to enjoy it," says Erika Forbes, a professor of psychiatry at the University of Pittsburgh. "If it sounds like fake it, till you make it, you're right," says Dr Ellen Hendriksen, a clinical psychologist at Boston University's Center for Anxiety and Related Disorders. She says: "The reason it works is because it sets up a positive feedback loop. The brain affects your behaviour, but behaviour also affects your brain. So do the thing you love, even if you don't feel the effects right away. Whatever it is, it doesn't have to be big. It may feel like a drop. But drop by drop, you can fill an ocean."

Tracking your progress

Before you start behavioural activation, take note of where you are, because it's hard to notice you are feeling better when the improvements come in small doses. If you don't chart your progress, you may genuinely not notice how much your mood is subtly shifting. After all, if you had broken your arm and needed physio, each session your therapist would compare your strength and flexibility to the last time – and let you know how you were improving. That would feel tangible and help you celebrate your progress and encourage you to keep doing the exercises.

But it's just as important to track our mental health to keep doing the things that make us feel better. By taking the average of your mood every day, with the tools we talked about in earlier chapters, you will notice any gradual changes. If you haven't started monitoring your mood, now is the time to start.

Enjoying life again tends to sneak up on you. The shifts will be subtle. For the first time in ages, you may feel like you want to dance or sing when you hear a song you like. Your skin may get goosebumps again when you hear an old piece of music you love. You may even cry more easily; a sign that your emotions are unblocking. Fleeting moments of happiness may not fade away as fast as they used to.

Overcoming other barriers

If I asked you one simple question: "What do you enjoy doing?" you could probably dig deep and find the answer. The question is why aren't you doing more of it? This is why anhedonia is so crafty. It creates a sense of helplessness and hopelessness that robs you of your motivation. After all, if it were that easy to do things that make you feel good, you'd already be doing them, right? And if you've been feeling "blah" for a while, now you probably have a ticker tape running through your head saying, "Why bother?" and "What's the point?"

As well as sapping your motivation, anhedonia tells you to stay put. "We often feel that we need to feel motivated to do something in order to do it," says Navit Schechter, CBT therapist. "Whilst this can be helpful, if you're experiencing anhedonia and a lack of motivation, doing things even when you don't feel motivated can break the cycle. Working toward a goal or doing something potentially rewarding or fulfilling can impact on the body and hormone activity and change the way you feel as a result."

How long will it take before I enjoy life?

Psychologist Dr Rami Nader compares behavioural activation to using an old-fashioned water pump to get water from a well. "There's water way down at the bottom of a well and you want to bring it up. At first you pump the handle, and nothing comes up. But keep pumping because even though you can't see it yet, the water is still coming. Eventually the reward will come. So, if you used to enjoy painting, the way to resume it again is in small steps. Say you start just spending five minutes painting. You may not enjoy it one bit. The key is to focus on the doing, not the feeling. Then you bump the painting up to ten minutes and then 15 minutes. A lot of my clients will say: 'I can't mindlessly sit down and paint for five minutes. If I am not enjoying it or having any fun, why should I continue?' But the point isn't to enjoy it. It's to persevere. This is how you bring the enjoyment back." In short, if your reward circuits are interrupted, it will take time for them to reconnect.

Overcoming the nay-saying telling you to do nothing

As we've heard, when our inner voice speaks, we tend to listen. After all, this is the narrator which gives a blow-by-blow commentary on everything you do. We tend to think it's being helpful and it's helping us work out what's happening and what steps we should take next. But, over time, it may have developed its own tone and character. And if its timbre has become negative in tone, it can be hard to escape from its constant downbeat subtitling of your life. Often, we have fallen into such a habit of automatic negative thinking, we don't even notice when we are doing it anymore.

One method to stop the spiral of negative thoughts which stand in the way of you enjoying your life is a process which can be summarized as "Catch it, check it, change it." For example, you may have fallen into the routine of thinking: "Nothing makes me happy" or "I never really enjoy myself at social occasions" for so long that it has become a self-fulfilling prophecy.

Say you have a big social event coming up, but you are already worrying it won't live up to your expectations. You might believe anticipating any problems that could happen means you won't get any nasty surprises. Perhaps you want to save yourself from the pain of disappointment.

Maybe in childhood you never saw a lot of fun around you – or you felt left out and unconsciously cast yourself as an outsider – so you don't expect anything to be different in adulthood. This can become a vicious circle – because you never think you will enjoy social occasions, you don't. Who would have fun with this kind of gloomy dialogue running through the back of their minds? Whatever the reason, it will help if you can start to notice and challenge these thoughts, pass them through a fact-checking process and grant yourself more freedom to open yourself up to new experiences.

If you are opting out of experiences that could make you feel better because you are feeling so "blah", CBT therapist Navit Schechter says it helps to train yourself to reframe those thoughts. She says: "Understanding the relationship between thoughts, feelings, behaviours and physical symptoms can be really helpful if you need to respond differently. We often feel that we need to feel motivated to do something in order to do it. Whilst this can be helpful, if you're experiencing anhedonia and a lack of motivation, doing things even when you don't feel motivated can break that cycle. The act of working toward a goal or doing something potentially rewarding or fulfilling can impact on the body and hormone activity and change the way you feel as a result."

Going back to that social occasion we were just talking about, imagine a few days before, you feel a lurch in your stomach every time you think about it. But because you are feeling "meh", you are so convinced you won't enjoy it, you are now thinking about not going. Notice that physical feeling first. See it as a clue that this is a thought you need to address. Instead of allowing it to circulate, the first step is to register it, capture it and write it down.

For example, you could sum up this thought by writing: "I really don't want to go to this event because I never enjoy parties, I always feel left out, I feel judged, and I bet no one will want to talk to me. When I see everyone laughing and having fun, I feel left on the sidelines." By getting your thoughts down on paper or onto a computer screen, you are now ready to examine how helpful and accurate these thoughts are. Next, ask yourself what feelings underlie this thought. To help this process you can run your summary against the main types of unfair and negative biases that often crop up, listed below.

Never and always thinking

This is a tendency to overgeneralize and see one single negative experience as a general rule.

Applied to this thought: "I've been to loads of rubbish parties. So, I think all parties are over-rated."

How to reframe: "All parties are different. Some are better than others and they've not all been completely rubbish."

Catastrophizing

In this distortion, you immediately jump to the worst conclusions, causing anxiety to quickly escalate.

Applied to this thought: "If I don't have someone to talk to at any point, it will be absolutely awful and embarrassing."

How to reframe: "There are always moments at parties when you have no one to talk to. It's not just me and it usually doesn't last long if you are friendly and open with other people."

Discounting the positives

Your negative bias means you ignore anything positive that happens and tell yourself it doesn't count.

Applied to this thought: "It was fun dancing at the last party I went to, but I had a really bad hangover and felt terrible the next day. That means overall it wasn't a good experience."

How to reframe: "It was fun dancing at the last party I went to, I had a really bad hangover and felt terrible the next day. That was horrible but the party itself was really good fun."

Fortune-telling and mind-reading

You believe you can predict how things will turn out and people will react and jump to the worst conclusions.

Applied to this thought: "Not everyone at the party will be happy to see me or be friendly, so I'd rather not go."

How to reframe: "I don't know how people are going to react to me. There's no reason to think they won't be happy to see me. Chances are there will be some nice people who will be friendly."

Personalization

In this distortion, you tend to believe that anything you feel is real and is about you when really other factors are involved.

Applied to this thought: "One person I spoke to at the last event ignored me later in the evening, so that means people don't like me. They must think I'm boring."

How to reframe: "I had conversations with people during the evening who were interested in what I had to say and seemed to like me. I don't know why that person ignored me or what they were feeling."

Emotional reasoning

This is best summarized as "Because I feel it, it must be true."

Applied to this thought: "I was uncomfortable at the party so that means everyone is judging me."

How to reframe: "Just because I am meeting new people, it doesn't mean they are judging me negatively. Most people are more worried about themselves than others. I am a unique person. Some people will gel with me. Others won't."

Should statements

You have a script running in your brain with a lot of expectations about how people *should* act and how situations *should* turn out. You then feel annoyed and disrespected when they don't live up to them.

Applied to this thought: "Parties should be loads of fun, but I avoid them because sometimes they don't live up to the hype."

How to reframe: "It would be great if all parties were nothing but fun, but that's not always possible. Most parties have at least some fun parts."

Now having given yourself some distance from your thoughts, and after running them past some of these biases, you could ask yourself: "Was I judging this situation fairly?" It takes practice and at first it can help to get into the habit of reframing with a therapist. To make it easier, keep a screenshot of the most common thinking errors above on your phone or your desktop, so you can run any worries you feel in your body past this fact-checking process.

Only work on one thought at a time. Over time and with perseverance you can learn to change the way you think – and start to believe you are as entitled to enjoy your life as anyone else.

Now supercharge it

People with anhedonia have been found to benefit from a more targeted version of behavioural activation, called Positive Affect Treatment. This means working out what you like to do the most in life, thinking about the positives so you look forward to doing them, and then really sinking into the experience.

As you read this chapter, collect a toolset of at least four pastimes that you can call on, such as playing an instrument or going to a museum. Choose activities which usually make you feel good, happy and satisfied when you've done them.

If you still find it hard to get going and get out of the house, for example, visualize yourself doing it. The human brain often can't tell the difference between reality and imagination, so you'll be halfway there. The power that imagined experiences have over the rewards system is why anhedonia researchers at UCLA have given people virtual reality headsets. As they look through the goggles they can see themselves "swimming" with dolphins, "riding" trains through forests or "celebrating" a victory by their favourite sports team. By training volunteers to really take in the positive things happening around them, the scientists believe they are more motivated to plan fun activities in real life and notice what's good about them.

Back in real life, say your planned activity involved going out to a local comedy club.

Beforehand get your clothes ready, plan what you are going to wear and arrange your travel, so you are more likely to do it. Once you've made it to the comedy night, look around, take stock. Notice all the people laughing around you having a good time. When you remember the event, focus on the parts of the evening that you enjoyed. Was it easier and more enjoyable than you thought? By getting into the habit of anticipating fun activities, savouring them when you are out and then appreciating them afterwards, you will be waking up all three phases of your reward system.

Holding onto good feelings

It's been said that "change the moment and the rest will follow". You may not be able to alleviate all the stress in your life, but you can put it to one side for moments, minutes, or even an hour or two at a time. It will take intention, practice and patience to shift your focus.

Once we start to experience any pleasure, the next challenge in anhedonia is learning how to hold onto those feelings. This means taking active steps to train your brain to notice and prolong them. Linger more over low-key moments. Place them under the microscope. Put them in perspective by remembering they are the ones you would miss if they were gone. This is more than just advice to "smell the roses". One study found that prolonged activation of a brain region called the ventral striatum is directly linked to sustaining positive emotions and reward. And people who managed to sustain these levels by concentrating and savouring uplifting moments reported high levels of psychological wellbeing and were found to have lower levels of the stress hormone cortisol.

The brain can only process one thought at a time. So, stay in the moment for five seconds or more, noticing everything about the experience. Try to come back if your mind starts to wander. In a 2012 study, college students were asked to take part in a savouring activity called "mindful photography". The students were asked to take at least five photos of their day – of their friends, their favourite views of the campus, books they were enjoying – twice a week for a fortnight. The result? They enjoyed their college life more and had more gratitude for their university.

When I was in a state of anhedonia, I often preferred to stay in bed than go anywhere. While that felt better for a few seconds, it didn't last long before I felt icky and stuck. Even if it killed me to pull myself out of bed, I

*knew if I could just make that push, I'd usually feel a bit
better. The same with leaving the house. Even if I didn't
initially want to go for a walk, once I summoned some
energy to get up from my desk or sofa, I recognized that
after ten minutes, almost everything felt better. I soon
realized there were very few times when a walk didn't
help me feel better afterwards.*

Tori, 52

Find your flow

If you are in anhedonia, it's important to start enjoying activities
as you do them. While this can feel elusive at first and take some
practice, one way is to aim for 'flow'.

Over recent years, flow has been seen as the holy grail of
brain experience because so many feel-good chemicals are
involved in getting into that state. According to Steve Kotler, in
his book *The Art of the Impossible: A Peak Performance Primer*,
"Flow may be the biggest neurochemical cocktail of all: the state
appears to blend all six of the brain's major pleasure chemicals
(dopamine, norepinephrine, oxytocin, serotonin, endorphins
and anandamides) and may be one of the few times you get all
six at once. This potent mix explains why people describe flow
as their 'favourite experience' while psychologists refer to it as
'the source code of intrinsic motivation'."

Because the brain is such an energy hog, this state of
concentration means there is no energy left for self-critical
voices. It feels good because you get a sense of freedom. If
you think about it, you are probably happiest when your mind
is completely absorbed, like during sex (which has in fact been

found to be the activity in which your mind wanders the least), during a good conversation, or during exercise when you need to stay focused.

To find flow look for activities that require you to be 100 per cent present. Turn off email and social media and settle down to a task which stretches you but that is not so challenging that it's stressful.

Like orgasms, flow can be hard to achieve because a few different conditions have to be in place. But if you get the conditions right by finding an activity you enjoy, often a hobby, which involves a small challenge, and then close down all distractions, you'll get there.

Locking in good moments

As we've heard, anhedonia is what happens when you no longer look forward to things, you don't enjoy them and, even if you did, you don't remember your experiences positively – so you are less likely to do them again. One way to lock in experiences is gratitude. If you are doing a small inward groan, I hear you. I did too until I saw the impressive amount of science showing the outsized effects.

I understand the reason why talking about gratitude puts people's teeth on edge. The society we live in socializes us to keep striving and not just to accept what we have. It feels more protective to think about the future and anticipate the next threat. From a distance, gratitude can sound like "good vibes only" toxic positivity. After all, if someone tells you to be grateful, it's easy to hear it as a hint that you are not and that you should be counting your blessings.

Even if that's a little bit true, your first impulse might be to want to tell them to go away.

Being told you must be grateful can also sound like a trite dismissal of anything difficult that you have been through in your life. But while it may need an image makeover, this cynicism stands in our way of reaping gratitude's very real benefits. Time and time again, it's been found to be the single most effective way to feel better and appreciate experiences. The beauty of it is that it can take just a few minutes. At its simplest, gratitude involves writing about an experience you appreciated at the end of the day.

Done every day, gratitude works to beat "blah" in several key ways. Studies show it can increase your brain's production of dopamine in your reward pathways, boost serotonin and tone done your memory of negative events, bringing the positive ones into sharper relief. Gratitude is also associated with an impressive 23 per cent drop in the stress hormone and happiness disruptor, cortisol. Being grateful also helps you to record the good times so you are more likely to do the same things again; you learn that feeling good is in your control. Over time, this retraining of the brain to see the positive can rewire your thought patterns. Studies show gratitude can help turn "blah" days into better ones and, over time, counteract innate negative bias.

When did counting your blessings go so badly out of fashion? Every day I now wake up grateful to have a safe home, and a balcony where I can see the sun or the moon. If I catch myself grumbling, I change tack and think about what makes me fortunate instead.

Leah, 58

How gratitude helps in other ways

Gratitude is a practice which is nothing less than the best buffer we have for dealing with the cortisol-raising nature of modern life. It can also be an antidote to the type of entitlement we have developed in the modern world, in which we have grown spoiled into believing that all our needs should be met immediately.

Lack of appreciation is what happens when our default thinking always homes in on what's wrong with our lives, not what's right. Gratitude brings back our focus to the appreciation that there are already things around us that can make us feel better if we start to take more notice. The convenience of modern life has also resulted in making most of us feel entitled to everything on our terms. We can easily slip into habits of moaning, so it becomes second nature. Gratitude tones down your worry circuits and powers up your feel-good ones. If you are still sceptical, there are even impacts on you physical health that can be tangibly measured. Research has found that gratitude reduces blood pressure and inflammation in the body, which is believed to have a role in depression.

A 2021 study found that women who had a regular gratitude practice showed a fall in amygdala activity and the production of inflammatory cytokines. Grateful people have also been found to experience fewer aches and pains, according to research published in the journal, *Personality and Individual Differences*.

Not surprisingly, grateful people are also more likely to take care of their health. They exercise more and go to the doctors for regular check-ups, so they are also likely to live longer.

SIMPLE PLEASURES

Anhedonia researcher Jackie Kelm, who coaches people who are dealing with anhedonia and flatlining, advises them to do a 15-minute daily exercise. This involves doing whatever they enjoy and writing down what they appreciated about it. "Even if you address the root cause, it can take some weeks for the feeling circuits to come online again," says Jackie. Each day, think about "simple pleasures" in your life and write them down. "A simple pleasure is anything that you would appreciate, find comforting, or enjoy if you could feel any of these positive emotions. Examples could be drinking a cup of coffee in the morning, a cat sitting at your feet, laughing at something. It's important that you write it down because it reinforces it in your brain. Ideally set it as a routine. As far as possible, try to come up with new things but you can repeat the same things. It's the searching for the good things which seems to reactivate the brain circuits."

The two biggest mistakes Jackie sees are people becoming frustrated and giving up because they think it's not working when it can take weeks to feel the difference. It may help, instead of expecting to enjoy it right away, to focus on the fact you're doing the activity in the first place. "If you find it difficult at first to do the exercise, or it seems pointless, just keep trying," says Jackie. "You won't see any difference at first, and this is the hard part. This doesn't mean it is not working. In fact, any time you look for good things you are building positive pathways. It's just that most of us stop and go back to the bad feelings of flatlining and un-do the good feeling pathways."

Jackie, who overcame depression followed by emotional flatlining a few years after she was given huge doses of antibiotics to save her leg after a serious post-surgery infection, says most of all it's essential to develop a "growth mindset" – or the belief that you have the power to take steps to change how you feel for the better.

"Joy is available to everyone. I spent many years in therapy being told that I could only be so happy. That I could only *manage* my issues. That things could only get so good. But I don't believe there is a limit. Keep trying."

After I was diagnosed with breast cancer, I started paying attention to things that made me happy and prioritizing them. You'd think that by the age of 58, I'd already know what food, art, films and pastimes I liked? Wrong. Like many of us, I relied on habit and outdated ideas. If you'd asked me before all this started, I'd have said I liked impressionist paintings best, because I visited the Louvre as a teenager, and they blew me away. But I've been visiting galleries with my daughter during my illness, and we've found the most joy and fun in the medieval art galleries, which are full of vividly painted humans, annoyed-looking saints and pleased-with-themselves dragons. What's not to like? Try new things – or return to old pleasures – and truly pay attention to how you feel and how much enjoyment you really get from them. Make a list if you need to. Then include as many of them as you can in your day-to-day life.

Leah, 58

Other ways to show gratitude

Write a letter: As well as writing down what we are grateful for, gratitude also works well if you give it to others. In one experiment, 100 or so participants were asked to write a short "gratitude letter" to a person who had affected them in some way. Sample letters included appreciative messages to fellow students and friends who offered guidance through the college admissions process, job searches and tough times. "Saying thanks can improve somebody's own happiness, and it can improve the wellbeing of another person as well – even more than we anticipate, in fact," said study co-author Amit Kumar, an assistant professor at the University of Texas. "If both parties are benefitting from this, I think that's the type of action we should be pursuing more often in our everyday lives." On a smaller scale, give someone you meet during the day positive feedback about how well they are doing their job – or take the time to rate something you enjoyed. The benefits are two-way.

Remind yourself of the long odds of your existence: The odds of you being born at this moment in time is 1 in 400 trillion according to one calculation. Reminding yourself that our time on Earth is not unlimited – and the average life is only around 4,100 weeks long – is a reminder that the moment to start enjoying your life is now. As Dr Gabor Maté has pointed out: "We are all in the process of dying."

Falling back in love with music again

Ration yourself: Not long ago finding and playing music took a great deal of deliberate effort. It sounds quaint now, but if there was a song you liked, you had to find a record shop, flick though boxes of vinyl, pay for the record, take it home, remove it from the inner and outer sleeves, put it onto your turntable and then, with some precision, and after de-fluffing it, lift the needle onto the revolving piece of plastic. On top of that, every 15 or 20 minutes, you had to get up and turn the record over. We now know there is one very important precursor to reward in the brain – and that is the first phase of anticipation. This will inevitably dim now you can get any track you want in seconds streamed via your phone. As anticipation – and dopamine release – are such a major part of musical enjoyment, ration yourself. Reset your musical dopamine levels by putting off listening to a favourite song until next week and then listen with intention. Notice the pace of the music, the sounds of the different instruments. If external thoughts start creeping in, tell yourself you are entitled to take a holiday from them in your head.

> For over a year, I was indifferent when I heard music.
> Even my favourite artists would get on my nerves.
> When I realized what the issue was, I tried listening
> to new music and get out to gigs, even when I didn't
> feel like it. When I noticed the hair standing on the back
> of my neck a couple of months ago when I heard a track
> I hadn't listened to for ages, I felt like someone had
> plugged me back in.
> Felix, 36

Prep for concerts: One of the best ways to have a positive emotional response to music is to surround yourself with others feeling the same appreciation. Try to see your favourite artists live. You will get a bigger surge of dopamine when you hear the songs you are looking forward to hearing – and research shows you will release more oxytocin if you are in a crowd who are singing along and enjoying the same music.

Listen to nature: Tune up your hearing skills. We are wired to take notice of the sounds of nature for our survival. Tune in to listen to the sounds of birds, breezes or water flowing. A recent meta-analysis study from the University of Michigan also found that sounds of nature lower stress, promote calmness and improve mood. According to a 2022 study by researchers at King's College, London, hearing regular birdsong will improve mental wellbeing scores in as little as two weeks.

Seeing the world in full colour again

Walk in sunlight: Bright, natural light triggers the release of dopamine from the retina and has been found to improve colour vision. Plus, sunlight appears to increase the number of dopamine receptors in the brain. One study of 68 healthy adults found that those who received the most sunlight exposure in the previous 30 days had a higher density of dopamine receptors in the reward and movement regions of their brains.

Try red light: One way to power up the retinal cells is to look at deep red light for three minutes a day, according to researchers at the UCL Institute of Ophthalmology. Red light has the longest wavelength of all the primary colours – 650 nanometres – and is thought to be better able to penetrate body tissue. The research found that red light seems to improve eyesight by stimulating the retina to release more dopamine. For the study, volunteers were asked to look at a deep red-light beam from an LED torch for three minutes a day for two weeks. They were then retested for their rod and cone sensitivity. The red light didn't affect people aged under 40, but there were clear improvements in those aged over 40. Their ability to detect colours had improved by up to a fifth.

Get more sleep: More sleep will help because it will give the brain more energy to do the very intensive work of processing the colours it sees.

I can always tell my mood by how colourful the world looks. If I am tired and depressed it's like I am looking at the world through a grey gauze. When I feel well rested and upbeat, I really notice colours like yellow, green and red.

Niamh, 37

Sharpening your sense of smell

When people who were depressed completed a course of smell training, in which they mindfully smelled strong odours for up to three months – their depression "decreased significantly". Smell training involves deliberately and regularly smelling distinctive scents, such as coffee, garlic, lemon or a favourite perfume. Or choose strong smells that bring back powerful memories. Concentrate as you make short "bunny sniffs'" and spend about 20 seconds on each scent. Researchers think that concentrating every day on the same range of odours increases the number of the receptors on the olfactory neurons, allowing you to experience sensual experiences – like eating the food you love, or having sex – more fully.

Chrissi Kelly, of Abscent, a charity for people with smell disorders, says: "Smell training is something that happens in the brain. It takes time and needs thoughtful attention every day. How well it works depends on your use of the technique. Like any kind of rehab, it needs to be done over a prolonged period." Chrissi also suggests giving yourself other opportunities to smell train throughout the day. She says: "This can include using scented plants around the house or savouring your scented hand cream or sampling the smell of foods in your kitchen, for instance."

I knew I was getting back on track when I could smell the lavender in my garden. I didn't realize how much I had missed it.

Tavi, 47

Reviving your taste

Eat mindfully: Pay attention to each bite of your food, on purpose, just for the experience. Eat without distraction. Take a small piece of food, like a raisin, look at it, pick it up, feel how heavy it is, feel the texture, put it between your lips, then into your mouth and concentrate on what you feel and taste. Bite it once and then notice each and every chew. Don't judge it or think about calories. Make sure it's fully dissolved in your mouth before you swallow. Think about how it made you feel. Try this exercise at least once a day with different food tastes and textures.

Add more flavour: Herbs and spices – and sharp-tasting foods like vinegar and lemon – are flavours which can cut through and be strongly registered by our brains, even when our sense of taste is blunted. Other options are pepper, chilli, cinnamon, garlic powder (as long as it doesn't contain too much salt) and ginger.

Ginger, miso, chilli. I covered my food with all of these just so I could taste something.
Chris, 61

Turning on your touch

Get a massage: Professor Tiffany Field, founder of the Touch Research Institute at Miami Medical School, says: "We know that depression can be reduced by massage therapy, and we think that's because of the reduction in cortisol and the increase in serotonin that accompanies the reduction in depression following massage therapy. Moving the skin (as, for example, in hugging, massaging and exercising), stimulates pressure receptors which are transmitted to the vagus nerve, the largest cranial nerve that has many branches in the body. Increased vagal activity calms the nervous system. It also reduces levels of the stress hormone cortisol."

For a while, it felt like I had lost all sensitivity in my skin. Only the firm pressure of massage seemed to register.
Mika, 63

Take the sexual pressure off: How much we want and enjoy sex is closely linked to our mental state. If your anhedonia is linked to anxiety, self-judgement and rumination, it will interfere. But it's also hard to enjoy yourself – if you're stressed about

NOT enjoying yourself. Start by taking the pressure off. Start a conversation with your partner so they understand you are not rejecting them and so you can work on building back sensuous experiences together. Once you do feel the first inklings returning, think about ways you could enhance the anticipation, like making a date early in the day to spend time in bed together to feel close and connected. Check your hormone levels and that any medications you are taking do not affect sexual response.

Hold off: If touch during sex doesn't feel as good, try sensate focus – or being mindful about what you are experiencing when you are caressed by your partner. The idea is that by letting go of the expectations of sex, at least for the initial sessions, you will have more freedom to relax, appreciate it and enjoy the sensation. Each partner takes up to 15 minutes to touch the other, at first avoiding the breasts and genitals, but varying the speed and pressure of the stroking so the other can say what feels good. Even if you don't have sex, keeping up regular non-sexual touch which will reduce the cortisol build-up that could be compromising your dopamine levels.

Play music: Touch and sex can be enhanced by music. In experiments, robots were used to stroke the skin on the forearm of volunteers with a brush. When music was played that the participants found sexy, they rated the touch as feeling more sensual.

Check your speed: Being touched at the rate of 3cm (1.2in) per second has been rated as the most pleasurable because it triggers a special nerve fibre called the C-tactile afferent. Neuroscientist Professor Francis McGlone, of Liverpool John Moores University, says: "The nerve fibre fires up areas of the brain that connect to reward. There's a release of oxytocin, a hormone that plays a fundamental role in our social behaviour. It has an effect on our dopamine levels, which is the brain's reward system; it impacts on the release of serotonin, which is connected to our happiness and wellbeing; it has an impact on our stress system; and it helps lower our heart rate."

11

How to Harness Your Happiness Chemicals

When some of our key neurotransmitters and hormones are out of balance, enjoying life will be more challenging. While we can't micromanage them, it still helps to understand more about their ebb and flow – and what we can do to help them stimulate good feelings and overcome "blah".

Dopamine

"Step into a world of totally irresistible happiness," announced the Facebook ad for Dopamine Land. For a 30- to 50-minute trip to this interactive museum just off London's Kings Road, visitors were promised the opportunity to be immersed in a space which would delight their senses (and which would conveniently also look good on Instagram). Cynical though it may have been, when this exhibition launched at the start of 2022, Dopamine Land tapped into the concept that dopamine levels could be easily tweaked. Whether you should pay £17.50 to look at walls projected with images of popping popcorn and landscapes that look like computer screensavers is subjective.

But there's a reason dopamine has become regarded as the new currency – and "dope" has become teen slang for "anything good in life". While there may be more than 100 different kinds of neurotransmitters circulating in your brain, dopamine is seen as the most pivotal because it drives the most important brain pathway for reward. (For this reason, if needed, antidepressants targeting dopamine levels are more likely to be prescribed for anhedonia. SSRIs, targeting serotonin, are more widely given for depression.)

When brain scans are done, they tend to show that in cases of anhedonia, dopamine response is blunted in the ventral striatum, a hub for dopamine neurons and the anticipation and processing of rewards. However, because such tests can't be widely given, dysregulated dopamine is more often diagnosed by symptoms. So apart from feeling "meh", signs your dopamine system is out of balance may include:

- Finding it harder than usual to get up in the morning
- Having difficulty concentrating
- Procrastinating and finding it hard to start and complete projects
- Having a declining sex drive

Despite the hyperbolic way it's often talked about, dopamine isn't like a drug, such as cocaine.

It's circulating all the time in the brain because more is released when we anticipate getting something we will enjoy. For example, if you decided you were hungry and ate some food, some research has suggested that would raise your dopamine levels by 150 per cent above your baseline. Video games would spike it by 175 per cent, sex by 200 per cent, cocaine by 450 per cent and amphetamine by a staggering 1,000 per cent.

But dopamine is not designed to stay raised above its baseline for very long. It takes just two minutes to break down again. With so many activities and products which stimulate it in the modern world, the best way to maintain an optimum level is to moderate your dopamine-triggering activities. This is because over time too much stimulation wears out dopamine receptors, making the brain less sensitive to reward, so nothing feels quite as good anymore.

HOLIDAYS

Take holidays seriously: As we've heard, anticipation builds dopamine. So much so that researchers have found that planning a break can give you more happiness than taking it. Boost this anticipation and start your holiday in your head by researching where you are going and immersing yourself in books and films about your destination. "As humans, we spend a lot of our mental lives living in the future," says happiness researcher Matt Killingsworth. "Travel is an especially good thing to have to look forward to. In a sense, we start to 'consume' a trip as soon as we start thinking about it. When we imagine eating gelato in a piazza in Rome or going water-skiing with friends we don't see often, we get to experience a version of those events in our minds." The holidays we look forward to also have an advantage over other experiences in that we are more likely to value them, adds Killingsworth. "Since we know a trip has a defined start and end, our minds are prone to savour it, even before it's started."

There's no need for an expensive holiday to the other side of the world either. The human brain is wired for novelty. So anywhere that's new will trigger dopamine. To get the most rewards, plan for short breaks. You might think that a fortnight's holiday should feel twice as good than a week, but research has found that wellbeing peaks after two days – and lots of mini-getaways provide a greater number of happy memories. The variety of going to more places has also been found to activate the brain's reward circuits more powerfully.

If you don't have the time or money to get away, treating weekends as "mini-holidays", rather than catch-up time has also been found to increase happiness levels. To savour and remember your best holiday experience, sensory expert Professor Charles Spence, of Oxford University, suggests that rather than taking a picture for social media, try sketching what you see. His study of 2,000 adults found that more than half of the population suffer from "digital amnesia" – relying on smartphones or other devices to "store memories" for them.

Professor Spence said: "Much of the pleasure from holidays comes from remembering. But our love affair with the digital image and our growing affiliation to the 'if it's not on social it didn't happen' mantra, could be inadvertently fuelling a memory bank deficit."

According to Professor Spence, this means that on average holiday memories fade after less than two weeks. "Scientific evidence even suggests the more senses we stimulate, the more robust the multisensory memory that is formed," he adds. "Technology keeps our eyes occupied. But while it plays to our dominant visual sense, it fails to connect with our emotional senses. Typically, only one sense – sight – is stimulated when taking a photo and at most two – sight and hearing – are triggered when filming something. However, drawing something you want to remember on holiday activates up to three, including sight, touch, sound and 'proprioception' (or position sense), enabling the brain to solidify the memory, and embed it in your memory for longer."

Here are some ways to get your dopamine circuit back on track:

Give your dopamine reward circuits a break: Many clinicians recommend mindfully disconnecting from activities that artificially raise dopamine too easily, like social media overuse, online porn, marijuana or video gaming. This break is designed to give the brain time to get used to finding pleasure in more "natural" real-world activities. Based on her work as an addiction specialist, psychiatrist Anna Lembke recommends taking a 30-day holiday from the habit you are indulging in the most to reset the dopamine release into your reward pathways. For more serious drug addictions, many specialists believe it will take more like 90 days.

Set yourself micro goals: If you feel "blah", you may feel less excited about future events, but scheduling small, regular treats, once a week will help to build anticipation and dopamine in a more measured way. Researchers have found that people who look forward to good things get a significant bump in their mood. Make a list of things you want to do, put them in your diary and make a date with that plan every week. It's always better than sitting home and doing nothing. Rotate the enjoyable experiences you do. Just as the first bite of food is always the most rewarding, look out for novel experiences when you feel yourself getting bored with the regular ones.

Keep goals specific: Vague abstract goals like "I want to be happy" won't help you get there, according to researchers at the University of Liverpool. Dopamine works best if you're seeking something specific and just within reach – for example, "I'd like to go for a 5km bike ride this weekend." Raise levels of anticipation by scheduling it beforehand.

Create a manageable to-do list: Even crossing off a single task take can boost good feelings. Create small projects you'd enjoy, and which feel rewarding, whether it's a DIY task you can complete in a couple of hours or tidying out a cupboard. Loretta Breuning, founder of the Inner Mammal Institute, which helps people manage the ups and downs of their brains, recommends the following: "Embrace a new goal and take small steps toward it every day. Your brain will reward you with dopamine each time you take a step. The repetition will build a new dopamine pathway until it's big enough to compete with the dopamine habit that you're better off without."

EXPOSE YOURSELF TO COLD WATER

Are you one of those people who can get into a swimming pool whatever the temperature? That was never me. Even though I had seen the considerable body of science on how cold water resets the dopamine system, I politely avoided friends' invites to go cold swimming in the sea and opted for cryotherapy instead. This was roughly akin to the experience of walking into a vertical freezer for three minutes for £15 a minute. Thanks to clouds of nitrogen which could take the temperature down to minus 160°C (320°F), I got to guess what it must be like to start to freeze to death in an avalanche. It was certainly cold enough to be uncomfortable, so I can see how it probably released some pain-relieving endorphins.

Another theory for why cold therapies work is that as your core temperature drops, and your body goes into physiological stress, the body compensates by releasing more dopamine and noradrenaline. One study found that immersion in cold water raised people's blood levels of dopamine by 250 per cent and noradrenaline by 530 per cent.

If you want to try cold swimming in the sea or local lake, how cold does it need to be? According to neuroscientist Dr Andrew Huberman: "The key is to aim for a temperature that evokes the thought, "'This is really cold (!), and I want to get out, BUT I can safely stay in.' For some people, that temperature might be 15°C (60°F), whereas for others it might be 7°C (45°F)." For an easier everyday option, having a cold shower can also do the job, say dopamine experts. Thirty seconds is fine at first, but over time your body will adapt and get used to the shock and you'll need three minutes to get the same impact.

Serotonin

Serotonin is a particularly busy molecule with roles all over the body, helping with everything from digestion to sleep. In the brain it works as a neurotransmitter, where it seems to tone down the threat-detecting amygdala and make sure dopamine's relentless drive for reward doesn't get out of hand. Serotonin is also important to our mood, and how we think about ourselves. It increases when we feel seen and respected and rise up the pecking order. It takes a hit when we feel inferior.

Once serotonin is raised in the brain it gives us only a flicker of satisfaction, dispersing in a matter of minutes. Apart from feeling "blah", signs your serotonin levels are out of balance may include:

- Your mood changes quickly
- You wake up during the night
- You are less interested in sex
- You compare yourself negatively to others
- You often feel beaten, defeated and like a failure
- You feel more anxious
- You have digestive issues

Serotonin is the neurotransmitter most often targeted by antidepressants which aim to boost the amount circulating in the brain. However, if prescribed in cases of milder depression, it also tends to blunt feeling of joy.

The good news is there are other natural ways to raise serotonin:

Get more sunlight: Studies have found that people have higher levels of serotonin on bright sunny days than cloudy ones, whatever the temperature. Autopsies have also found that people who die in the summer (of non-psychiatric causes) have higher levels than those who die in the winter, when there is not as much sunlight.

Curate your social media: Choose fair comparisons. It's normal to look to others to try to work out where we stand, but due to social media the number of people we compare ourselves to has become too vast. Yet despite how it makes us feel, studies show we don't look to others at around the same level. We tend to torture ourselves by measuring ourselves against the most successful person in that field who we know. The bad news is that spending time trying to work out why we don't stack up has been found to be linked to lower self-esteem, body image and poorer mood. In short, comparison really is the thief of joy and the direct opposite to gratitude, which allows you to feel good about your life.

Remember that your diet isn't only what you eat. It's what you watch, read, listen to and surround yourself with. If you want to feel better with immediate effect, put this book down for an hour and curate your social media feed.

Apply the principle of "spark joy" to the people you follow: Unfollow, block or mute any people or accounts that make you feel stressed, insecure or "less than". Then create a new online experience for yourself. Social media is not all bad by any means. Many activities that make us feel good, such as looking at accounts for animals, photography, comedy, awe-inspiring places, or nature, can be done online. As long as you are looking at those images of puppies and kittens as a break and not as a distraction, or as a way to hide from life or procrastinate, go ahead and enjoy the boost of serotonin or oxytocin. One study even found that people felt more energetic and happier after watching cat videos.

Collect good memories: People who look at sad memories have been found to have lower levels of serotonin in their cingulate cortex, the area of the brain linked to attention. When they looked at happy images, their serotonin went up by 11 per cent and even lifted their spirits more than chocolate. So, keep a stack of feel-good resources on hand, like a photo album full of your favourite moments, for when you become aware that you need a mood boost.

Dial down competitive friendships: Although we don't like to talk about it, humans live in constantly changing hierarchies. One minute you might feel superior to a friend for sticking to a New Year's resolution when they haven't. The next you may feel snubbed when you hear about a party they are invited to, and you aren't. Be aware of competitive dynamics in friendships and opt out or don't engage. After all, the foundation of a true friendship is that you can relax and be yourselves with each other. When you are constantly worried about where the next subtle put-down is coming from, your guard is up all the time – and so are your cortisol levels.

It's likely that you already know who the competitive people are in your life, so mute them on social media and distance yourself in real life. Let your mantra be: "You do you."

See the bigger picture: It's been suggested that depression is a disease which affects people who feel defeated. Could it be that in today's highly competitive environment many of us are folding our cards and refusing to play? If you keep buying into a comparison culture that is created to make you feel insecure so that you keep coming back for more, it's no wonder many of us feel like we can't keep up. Ask who is really profiting from the messages in our culture telling us we can never earn enough, own enough or be enough.

Oxytocin

Humans are a social species and oxytocin is the hormone which helps us bond to one another.

It also helps to reinforce any good feelings we have toward people we like and love. (But it also turns up dislike on those we don't like. Less cuddly-sounding studies believe it also helps people view others outside their tribe, as the "out" group.)

Among our hunter-gatherer ancestors, having the time to stroke and groom each other was a sign that the coast was clear and there were no imminent threats. This may help explain why oxytocin works so well to dampen down the activity of the brain's alert system, the amygdala, as well as the stress hormone cortisol.

Signs you could be running low on oxytocin include:

- You don't enjoy hugs as much
- You don't feel close to your partner during sex
- You don't enjoy going out and meeting people as much
- You find it hard to empathize when you hear other people's problems
- You find it harder to orgasm

So how do you improve your levels of the so-called "bonding" hormone?

Get or give a 10 to 20 second hug: Just beneath the skin are tiny egg-shaped pressure receptors called Pacinian corpuscles. When these feel pressure, they send a signal to the brain which releases oxytocin. A range of studies have found that hugs of between 10 and 20 seconds raise oxytocin levels in the body and reduce cortisol, though the effect seems to be more marked in women. A compassionate touch from a well-meaning stranger, compliments and gifts will all move the oxytocin dial in a positive direction.

Call your mother: Even a few words from the right person can help spike oxytocin. Researchers at the University of Wisconsin-Madison found a few words from loving mums over the phone eased a daughter's worries. (Of course, it's likely that words from a loving dad would have a similar effect, but this particular study focussed on mothers!)

Have meaningful conversations: Listening empathetically to what someone else has to say will raise oxytocin levels in both you and the person you are talking to. One way to supercharge this effect is "reciprocal self-disclosure". This means revealing personal information about yourself while the other person does the same. In studies where two people who had just met were given a list of revealing questions to ask each other, they liked each other much more than those who had not shared personal information. Seek out a friend you can trust with whom you can talk openly without feeling judged or censored.

Talk to strangers: Having small talk with people you don't know may sound awkward, but it can also boost your mood, says psychologist Dr Sarah Jelbert, a lecturer at the school of psychological science at the University of Bristol. For a series of pre-pandemic studies, published in the *Journal of Experimental Psychology* in 2014, researchers from the University of Chicago surveyed commuters about to board trains and buses – places where we are typically surrounded by others, but rarely interact. "One group of commuters were asked to predict how happy they would feel at the end of their journey if they either 'kept to themselves' or had to talk to the person who sat down next to them," says Dr Jelbert. "Another group put this into practice – either enjoying their solitude or trying to get to know the person next to them. People who hadn't tried it out predicted that they would feel happier if they kept to themselves and would be much less happy if they had to talk to someone. In reality, it was the group that tried to connect with a stranger who reported being happier once they got off their train. In later studies, the researchers asked the people who had been spoken to report how they felt, and it turned out these 'talked-to' individuals had also enjoyed their journey more than usual."

So why does talking to strangers boost our mood? Dr Jelbert says: "We are an extremely social, group-living species. We expect this effect with friends and family, but this shows it's often a positive experience to interact with new people too. Essentially, that means that we all hold the mistaken belief that other people don't talk because they don't want to. In fact, many people would be quite happy to talk. It's just not the norm." So, it seems that when we have these friendly interactions, it allows us to let our guard down in public and trust others, feelings that will also spike oxytocin.

Endorphins

Even though humans no longer need to run to catch prey, we continue to do so anyway – for pleasure. One of the reasons many of us run recreationally is to chase "the runner's high" – a flutter of home-grown euphoria. Bear in mind, however, that the main job of endorphins seems to be not to create pleasure, but to mask pain. They are intended to give you a fighting chance of getting away if you are wounded by a predator or an enemy.

Other kinds of physical stress can also trigger endorphins – and when this happens, they bind to the body's opioid receptors, along with other endocannabinoids. Endorphins also help release nitric oxide, a chemical that helps relax tense muscles and dilates blood vessels, helping to reduce levels of the stress hormone cortisol too.

Signs you may not be producing enough endorphins may include:

- Aches and pains
- Feeling stressed
- Hunger pangs you can't ignore

So how can you raise you endorphin levels?

Find things to laugh about: The physical act of laughter seems to trigger endorphins because of the way it pumps the diaphragm up and down and makes us take deep breaths, like when we exercise. Even the anticipation of laughter, like looking forward to watching your favourite comedy movie later in the day, can boost endorphins and reduce stress hormones, compared to people who don't have a funny film to look forward to. So, make a regular date with funny activities, whether it's visits to your local stand-up club or making comedy part of your TV diet. Researchers have found young children laugh about 300 times a day. By adulthood that has fallen off a cliff to about 17 times a day. The more you boost that number, research shows that the less likely you are to be affected by stressful events.

Let yourself cry: Crying raises endorphin levels possibly because it's a release of pent-up stress in the body and because sobbing also makes the ribcage rise and fall like intense exercise. If you feel the need for an emotional release, seek out a song or film that will give you a chance to let go. The release of endorphins also helps to relieve both physical and emotional pain.

Stretch: When you stretch, it triggers endorphins possibly because you are putting your body through minor stress. Look for ways to incorporate stretches while you are watching TV, waiting for the kettle to boil or whenever you have a spare minute. These don't have to be full body stretches – you can stretch your fingers or toes or any part of your body. Consider doing activities like Tai Chi and yoga which allow you to stretch in a more systematic, guided way and release endorphins on a regular basis.

Oestrogen

How oestrogen affects a woman's mood is complex and not yet completely understood, but in recent years, we've come to realize how closely they are linked. This fluctuation of oestrogen, along with progesterone over the course of the female menstrual cycle, may help explain why until puberty boys and girls have similar rates of depression, according to a 2017 study in the journal *Psychological Bulletin*. After that, girls' depression rates double.

What is also being recognized is that, as oestrogen falls away in menopause, there is often a significant impact on women, making them feel flat, hopeless or unable to cope. This is likely to be because oestrogen is key to helping make feel-good chemicals in the female brain and balancing levels of serotonin.

Signs that your falling oestrogen levels may be affecting your mood include:

- Having trouble concentrating
- Moodiness
- Anxiety about things you didn't used to worry about
- Brain fog
- Loss of confidence

As women's health physio Christien Bird told me, oestrogen is the "water in the garden" for many of the processes in women's bodies including mental tasks.

Considering it's so essential, how can we address its disappearance in menopause?

Track how you feel over your menstrual cycle: If you have periods do you sometimes feel more "blah" at some times of the month than others? If so, start tracking how you feel over the course of your menstrual cycle, suggests hormone expert Gabrielle Lichterman, author of *28 Days: What Your Cycle Reveals About Your Moods, Health and Potential*, which has a mine of information on how to do this. Gabrielle says: "Our moods can be impacted based on which day of our menstrual cycle we're on. That's because levels of our reproductive hormones rise and fall throughout the 28 days or so between the first day of our period and the day before our next period. These hormonal rises and falls spur changes in levels of brain chemicals, such as serotonin, that can spur either positive or negative moods. Knowing about these cycle-related mood changes is incredibly useful. That's because in healthy menstrual cycles, these hormonal rises and falls follow the same up-and-down pattern cycle after cycle. This means that you can predict when your hormones will be likely to prompt certain moods, such as cheerfulness, irritability, excitement or sadness. All you need to know is what day you're on in your menstrual cycle and you'll know what kind of mood to expect from your hormones.

"As a result, you'll know when to take advantage of hormone-fuelled improvements in good feelings (for instance, by planning to hang out with friends on 'happy' days in your cycle) or when you'll need to prepare for hormone-triggered declines in mood (for instance, by planning to treat yourself to self-care on 'sad' days in your cycle)."

Tracking these mood changes will help you anticipate any feelings of blah, says Gabrielle: "Writing down how you feel as your cycle progresses means you can predict when your hormones will be likely to prompt certain moods, including sadness and irritability. It will help to know these feelings could just be due to hormones, they will pass and in just a few days you'll be feeling optimistic again."

Consider HRT: While it's not for every woman as they enter menopause, studies have found Hormone Replacement Therapy – which can top up your oestrogen and progesterone levels – can help beat feelings of "blah". In one study, post-menopausal women were given HRT containing transdermal oestrogen and micronized progesterone. Only 17 per cent of those on HRT developed any depressive symptoms compared with 32 per cent on the placebo. If HRT is not for you, look into supplements which have human clinical trials showing they can also support mood in menopause, like Vitamin B complex, which helps make the feel-good chemical serotonin.

Reframing menopause: This generation of woman is fortunate in that we are finally living in an age when menopause is being talked about and understood like never before. Indeed, a more positive attitude toward this phase of life seems to have a protective effect. One review found women with higher self-esteem and positive attitudes toward menopause experienced fewer negative symptoms, whereas women with negative attitudes experienced higher levels of shame about their bodies. Dr Jen Gunter, author of *The Menopause Manifesto: Own your Health with Facts and Feminism*, believes there's no reason why menopause should be any more than a break in your stride. "Perhaps a good analogy

215

for the hormonal chaos of the menopause is like a computer loading a new program," says Dr Gunter. "During the upload (the menopause transition) things run a little slow. Once loaded there may be a glitch or two before the new program is running smoothly and then things settle as the new program takes over." Indeed, reframing menopause so it does not seem as negative can have a powerful effect on relieving menopausal symptoms, with a range of studies now finding that Cognitive Behavioural Therapy can relieve anxiety, hot flushes and night sweats.

Testosterone

Most of a man's testosterone – 95 per cent – is made in his testicles. Production in males is triggered by the brain's pituitary, the gland which controls the release of hormones and stimulates cells in the testicles to make it. From the age of about 30, a man's testosterone levels drop by about 1 per cent a year. By age 50, the effects can start to become apparent because by then the accumulating effects may start showing up in a falling sex drive, lower mood and forgetfulness.

But falling levels are not just an issue for men. Women also make small amounts of testosterone in their ovaries. As this drops off in menopause, they can also feel the effects as its loss can undermine their confidence and dampen their "get-up-and-go".

So, what are some of the signs of lower testosterone?

- Lower libido
- More difficulty getting erections for men (and possibly orgasms in women)

- Loss of muscle mass
- Weight gain
- Tiredness
- Low mood
- Brain fog and irritability

More doctors are prescribing testosterone for both men and women. However, it can take some time to get the dosage right – and the side-effects may outweigh the benefits.

There are also some natural ways to keep testosterone levels higher:

Lead a more active lifestyle: Researchers at the University of California found when men did traditional (dare I saw macho?) activities, like chopping wood with an axe, it significantly increased their testosterone levels, even more than competitive sport. Cutting up trees for an hour raised the testosterone levels in their saliva by no less than 47 per cent, compared to just 30 per cent playing football, according to the study published the journal *Evolution and Human Behaviour*. Of course, you don't need to behave like a lumberjack to get benefits. A range of studies has found that moderate, consistent exercise – and particularly strength-training – will boost levels, in both men and women. Reducing body fat, as well as drinking and smoking, also helps keep up testosterone levels.

Get more sunlight: One study found that men who spent half an hour in front of light boxes, usually used to treat Seasonal Affective Disorder, managed to increase their testosterone levels by half. For a study by Italy's University of Siena, male volunteers were split into two groups. One group stood in front of a box that gave out 10,000 lux units of light, the same given off on a sunny summer's day. The other group received just 100 lux, the equivalent of the light on a dark, overcast day. Researchers found that the men exposed to half an hour of the 10,000 lux light daily for two weeks saw their testosterone levels increase more than 50 per cent, and their sexual satisfaction levels more than triple.

If by now you have started tracking your daily mood score (see page 10) – a simple number at the end of the day will do the trick – how are you getting on? Even if you are simply scheduling things you want to do, taking more notice of small moments that made you feel good, allowing yourself time to appreciate them, and then writing them down so you remember them, after a month or so, you should see a subtle upward trend in your mood, whatever life is throwing at you.

Remember that enjoying life can sneak up on you, and we can quickly forget how we felt before. If you take note of any improvements that you have helped to create, you will feel more in charge of your moods and more confident that you can create your own joyful moments. Like little drops of mercury, these will attract each other and eventually join together. In the final chapter, we will look at more ways to make these moments part of your life.

12

How to Create a Lifestyle That Beats "Blah"

Beating "blah" doesn't mean you have to turn your present life upside down. In my own journey out of anhedonia, I found that making different choices gradually added up to a big difference. Gradually seeking out experiences that made me feel better for a few seconds or minutes a few times a day accumulated and helped me retrain my brain and redirect my attention.

While all the targeted strategies in the previous chapters will also help light your way out of anhedonia, they will work better as part of a bigger picture. Of course, you're bored of hearing that exercise and a healthier diet could work wonders for you, but I am going to frame this slightly differently and give the compelling evidence that these things aren't just a nice idea. They will have more powerful and long-term effects than any mood-boosting drug ever invented. Beyond this, I will bring together the research which shows how to supercharge their effects to create a lifestyle that offers a better chance of contentment.

This is not a one-size-fits-all prescription for feeling good. Your psychology and physiology are unique to you, but what is on your side is that your body is always seeking balance – or homeostasis. It just needs *you* to be on its side.

Get more sleep

We've already talked about how it's pretty much impossible to be sleep-deprived and feel good. At one end of the spectrum, it can make us feel like zombies and at the other like grinches. The impact on your mood is real. There are biological reasons for feeling "blah" if you are not getting enough sleep. The less you get, the less likely you are to enjoy the good things in your life. Studies have found that sleep-deprived people feel negative emotions more intensely and enjoy positive moments less.

Decide a set bedtime: Part of the much longed-for freedom of being an adult is that we get to set our own bedtimes. But once you've experienced the freedom of staying up as long as you like in your teens and 20s, a return to a childhood routine is no bad idea. Until the 1980s there was no TV past midnight. Yes, it was boring, but the present-day habit of binge-watching into the early hours is taking its toll – and it's showing up in our mood. Set a bedtime that will give you the optimum 7 to 9 hours sleep you need a night. Set a nightly alarm to go off half an hour before bedtime to tell you it's time to wind down. Try it for a week and see if you notice a difference to how you feel.

Treat every day the same: Your hunter-gatherer ancestors did not wake up on Saturday or Sunday morning and think "Time for a lie-in." The obvious reason is that they didn't know it was the weekend (it wasn't until the 1930s that the two-day weekend became commonplace in Western societies) and neither do your brain's circadian rhythms. So, as far as possible, try to stick to your daily sleep schedule, even on your days off.

Challenge your brain: Giving your brain new experiences that tax it in lots of different ways will help to make it more "tired" at night, says Dr Kat Lederle, a chronobiologist who studies the rhythms of sleep. This is because difficult mental tasks really do demand more energy from the brain. Dr Lederle says: "Think about how to provide your brain with more variety and stimulation, even when doing normal tasks during the day. For example, try working out a new route to get to the supermarket to engage your problem-solving skills. I do this myself when I am cycling around London. I stop using the sat nav on my phone to make my brain work harder – or in the evenings try a new recipe even if I don't have all the ingredients. It means my brain is ready for sleep in the evenings because it needs that time to recover."

Have a warm bath: After light, temperature has the biggest effect on the body's wake and sleep cycles so manipulating it can help you sleep better. A 2019 study from the University of Texas, in the journal *Sleep Medicine Reviews*, found the best time to have a sleep-inducing bath is about 90 minutes before bedtime. They also discovered it speeded up the rate of falling asleep by an average of ten minutes as well as deepening sleep. According to the researchers, this is because warm baths and showers stimulate the blood to go from the body's core to the hands and feet, reducing the temperature to get it ready for sleep.

Sit by a window: In the back of our eyes, we have receptor cells that tell the difference between light and dark to help the brain know when it's time to go to sleep. Getting as much natural sunlight, particularly in the morning all year round, will help keep your body clock synchronized and increase the mood-boosting chemical serotonin. If you work indoors, top up these levels by sitting near a window, and go outside to get some sunlight during any breaks.

Work out if you're an early bird or a late owl: Though we live in a society geared up to early starts, it helps to recognize for some of us our biology makes it harder to get up early so we don't put unnecessary stress on the body. Professor Russell Foster, professor of circadian neuroscience at the University of Oxford, says: "Early birds prefer to wake early. They make up only 10 to 15 per cent of the population. Night owls prefer to go to bed later and make up about 15 to 25 per cent of the population. The rest of us fall somewhere in the middle. This means night owls often struggle to get off to sleep at a conventional time at night because their body clock is delayed. They can also feel groggier if they have to wake up at a conventional time in the morning, because their body clocks will want them to be asleep." Professor Foster suggests arranging more of your work life around your sleep chronotype, which is something he does himself: "As a late owl, for example, as far as possible I schedule meetings later in the day, rather than first thing in the morning, which are torture for me. So, if you are your own boss or do shift work, it makes sense to arrange your work life around your genetic chronotype to be happier, healthier and more productive."

Don't shun separate beds: If your partner snores, you're likely to lose an hour of sleep a night, according to a study in the *Mayo*

Clinic Proceedings by scientists at the University of Utah. And once your partner moves in their sleep, there's a 50 per cent chance that you will shift position too, and your sleep will be disturbed without even realizing it. Professor Russell Foster says: "The partner lying next to you in bed may be messing up your sleep without you even realizing it. If they are big snorers, get them tested for obstructive sleep apnoea (when the muscles in the back of the throat relax, obstructing the airways and causing gasping, snorting or choking noises). But also think about separate bedrooms. Sleeping together is not an indicator of the strength of your relationship and it may be bad for your sleep."

Deal with your night-time worries during the day: It's often our worries that keep us awake at night because there are fewer distractions when we are lying alone in the dark in bed and we feel less able to do anything about them. Don't leave it until bedtime to deal with them. Set aside time earlier every day to check in with any uncomfortable feelings that might be building up, so you are not dealing with them during the night. Trying to push worries away only makes them worse and fuels their strength, frequency and number. One way to do this is to look at your feelings as they arise in your body and imagine their shape, weight, colour and feeling. See them as sensations which will pass through your body, rather than feelings which can overwhelm you.

Use your spark

Recently, I saw a meme that said: "Don't ask me about my hobbies. I look at screens all day and then I go to sleep." In a nutshell, isn't that where many of us are – and why many of us are in anhedonia? To feel your potential, you also need to spend time doing activities that you love, which absorb you and make you feel good.

Giving up hobbies is seen as an early warning sign you are heading into "blah". Resuming them again is increasingly seen as an important way to overcome anhedonia because of the way they reawaken positive feelings and kickstart the reward circuit. Once we feel the pleasure of taking part, we release dopamine as we look forward to doing it again, according to research at the University of Reading.

Studies have found that people who take part in leisure activities they value have fewer negative feelings, lower blood pressure and are overall less stressed. Brain scans have also shown that the brain's reward circuits also become more active when people take part in activities, like art, just for fun. Indeed, hobbies are now viewed as a form of medication. Doctors now prescribe taking up pastimes, like gardening or art, as a way for patients to overcome mild depression, thanks to research which shows they have a tangible impact on life satisfaction.

How to find the best blah-beating activity for you

To find an activity that will help lift you out of blah, it helps to identify your "spark".

Everyone has sparks. They are activities that give energy and joy, and which when we do them make us feel alive and as if we are drawing on our potential. A spark originates inside you. It hasn't been forced or imposed. It can be any skill, talent or interest. According to the late Peter Benson, a pioneering youth worker who formulated the concept: "When we express our spark, we're not worried about how good we are or how it looks to others. Just doing it, or being it, is enough." Benson described spark as a "passion", which makes you feel like a lightbulb is switching on in your mind. It could be anything from "making things with your hands; to being in nature, to growing things, to volunteering, to helping people, to photography."

Sparks are most likely to fit into these broad categories: sport, creative arts, nature and the environment, volunteering, leading, spirituality, animal welfare, living life with purpose, reading. Benson, who originally developed the concept of spark to develop the talents of disaffected American teens, found that two-thirds of us can immediately name our spark, but most of us just haven't been asked, or thought about it enough.

The easiest way to identify your spark is to go back to the activities you were naturally drawn to as a child or teenager, and which you would have done anyway without adults getting involved. If it's not immediately obvious where your spark lies, have a think about the following questions:

- What was your favourite activity as child, which you did without being asked?
- What were your favourite subjects at school and when you left which ones did you want to know more about?
- What clubs did you join in your teen or college years when you had free time?
- What were your favourite holidays as a child?
- Is there a theme among creators you follow on social media?

Have a look through all your answers. Do they have anything in common? Once you've narrowed it down to an activity, think about how you could pursue it again.

One of the other obstacles to finding a new pastime outside of work may be the word "hobby", which sounds pointless and a bit nerdy. Instead, think of going back to your spark as nourishment or even an antidepressant. To others, frame it as your speciality or favourite occupation.

If you are afraid you have lost the knack of doing an activity you used to enjoy, consider taking an online course, or joining a club or evening class. Give it a few weeks to give yourself the chance to feel like you are mastering it again. If you still feel you haven't got the time, put a tracker on your phone to see how much you are spending pointless scrolling instead of creating or doing. Then decide to allocate that time to your new pursuit instead. This means intentionally setting aside a dedicated period each week. Commit to it by blocking out time in your phone calendar, with reminders.

Persevere even if, at first, it feels like you are not enjoying it. Eventually, as you learn to master a skill you are naturally drawn to once more, you will start to crave the uninterrupted moments of flow this activity will create for you – and the pleasure you once got from them will return. It will also be one of the clearest signs you are heading out of anhedonia.

I made a bucket list of simple, achievable things I wanted to do. I signed up for a pottery painting session to make a mug with a get-up-and-go message for the mornings and two online courses I'd always told myself

*I didn't have time for, on subjects that really interested
me. I also went to a Zumba class every week, where I
could really let go. I made dates with myself, so I had
always had something to look forward to.*

Darcey, 30

Diet

Feeling "blah" can often feel beyond our conscious control, so
it's comforting to know that what we feed our body can feed
our minds too. As we've heard, this is because many of our
feel-good hormones are made by the microbes that colonize
the gut. Your diet plays a huge part in their production, so it's
important to eat a range of foods which will sow your "lawn"
in the first place.

Here are some ways to do that:

Eat more fibre: All fibre is helpful to encourage a wider
range of gut bacteria. The greater variety of fibre-rich foods you
eat, the more varied your microbiome will be. Up your intake
to more than 30g (1oz) a day, particularly plants in the brassica
family, such as cauliflower, broccoli, kale and Brussels sprouts.
Artichokes, bananas, nuts, seeds, avocado, onions, lentils and
asparagus are also brilliant at helping your microbiome make
feel-good chemicals.

Try velvet beans: Velvet beans are natural sources of L-dopa,
a molecule that the body uses to make dopamine. Studies show
that they may be as effective as Parkinson's disease medications
at boosting dopamine levels.

Avoid refined carbohydrates: Sugar, artificial sweeteners
and highly processed grains, such as white flour, throw the

microbiome out of balance, and high-sugar intake is linked to depression, according to a range of research. One study of 8,000 men found that those who ate 67g (2.3oz) or more of sugar a day – about the same as three bags of sweets – were 23 per cent more likely to be diagnosed with depression, compared to men who ate 40g (1.5oz) or less. Apart from contributing towards an imbalance in your microbiome, overloading the brain with too much glucose causes inflammation which interrupts the reward system. Eating a lot of sugar can also trigger glucose spikes, which means sharp emotional highs followed by lows.

Eat less saturated fat: Research has found that eating too much animal fat, like the type found in fried foods, meat and dairy products may disrupt dopamine signalling. One experiment found rats who ate half their calories from saturated fat had a blunted response in the reward pathways, compared with animals who consumed the same number of calories from other types, possibly because it increases inflammation in the brain.

Eat enough protein: Dopamine is made from the amino acids tyrosine and phenylalanine, both of which can be found in protein-rich foods. Studies show that increasing the amount of these amino acids from foods like soy, nuts and legumes can boost dopamine levels. When both are missing, dopamine levels have also been found to drop off.

Reseed your (gut) lawn: You can also "reseed" and fertilize the "lawn" in your gut with foods that already have healthy, live microbes in them. These include fermented foods which have been left to break down in their own juices and include yoghurt, kefir, sauerkraut, kimchi and kombucha. These help because the fermentation process involved creates a slightly more acidic environment in the intestines. Certain bacteria thrive better in this environment, and these include lactobacilli bacteria, viewed as helpful in breaking down proteins to make short-chain fatty acids needed to make feel-good chemicals.

Consider taking omega-3 fatty acid supplements: As well as being essential for making cell membranes, these have been found to improve brain health by reducing inflammation.

MENOPAUSE AND DIET

Due to falling oestrogen levels in menopause, middle-aged women may have to pay particular attention to their gut microbiome to keep their mood up. Menopause specialist Dr Ferhat Udin says, "We know from studies that the microbiome plays a huge part in serotonin production. But during menopause it seems that falling oestrogen throws the microbiome out of balance. One of the things I talk to women in menopause about is the importance of having a diverse diet, and eating the rainbow of fruit and veg, because you are going to get more diversity and be producing more of the hormones and neurotransmitters which are helpful for mood."

While studies show that HRT to replace oestrogen levels can help improve mood in women in mid-life, it's also worth considering eating a diet rich in phytoestrogens – a substance found in certain plants which produce similar effects. Found in foods like nuts, seeds and soya, phytoestrogens appear to bind to oestrogen receptor sites. Women who eat them have been found to have fewer hot flushes, than those who don't.

One study in the journal *Menopause* found a plant-based diet rich in soy cut moderate-to-severe hot flushes by 84 per cent, reducing them from nearly five a day to fewer than one a day. Another study by Italian researchers in the journal *Fertility and Sterility* found that giving women more soy improved mood, as well as cognitive sharpness. Dr Udin says she often sees a real change in women's feelings when they reboot their eating habits: "Time and time again, I have seen women who change their diets start to feel better. It's not instant, but when they chart their moods, and start eating differently, they start to see changes over three to six months."

Exercise

We evolved to wander the landscape as nomads looking for food and, although life was stressful, our ancestors could dissipate the build-up of stress hormones with plenty of exercise. Until the industrial revolution, nearly every human engaged in some form of physical labour, which also kept us fit and healthy. Then, thanks in part to the invention of screens, humans gradually became glued to the flashing rectangles placed in front of them: TVs, computers and smartphones.

Instead of seeking out experiences, we sat waiting for them to come to us. The result is that the human body is no longer being used in the way it was designed to be. Yes, it's tedious to be reminded that you should move more, but looking at the positive effects on brain chemicals presents a compelling case for why exercise is one of the most essential components for mental wellbeing.

Exercise is as good as depression medication for improving mood because it triggers multiple positive changes in your body in many more ways than any drug can. Scientists at Duke University Medical Centre tested exercise – brisk walking, stationary bike riding or jogging for 30 minutes, plus a 10-minute warm-up and 5-minute cool down, three times a week – against the antidepressant drug Zoloft for four months. They found the ability of both to reduce or eliminate symptoms of depression were about the same. But when they checked back later ten months later, they found exercise seemed to do a better job of keeping depressive symptoms at bay. The group that had exercised as well had significantly lower rates of low mood than those who had only taken the medication.

Another 2018 review found that exercise, especially weight training, can reduce symptoms of depression at least as well as Cognitive Behavioural Therapy and medication for some people. Even if it can't beat low mood entirely, any type of workout, whether it's yoga or running, can tone down the symptoms.

The reality is that if you rolled all the benefits of exercise into a single medication, people would pay a fortune for it. Even small sprinklings of exercise can rapidly boost mood.

Any activity that gets you puffing and raises your heart rate, kickstarts the process. Adrenaline quickly starts to flow, setting off a cascade of downstream benefits.

For decades, the good feelings from exercise were put down to a rush of endorphins: hormones that act on opiate receptors in the brain. But moving your body energetically also increases dopamine release and encourages the growth of new brain connections, as well as decreasing the action of enzymes that break down your feel-good neurotransmitters. Into the bargain, it also reduces the build-up of that infamous enemy of carefree joy, cortisol. During exercise, your body makes nitric oxide, a molecule that circulates in the body and helps the blood vessels to dilate, increasing circulation. This allows blood, nutrients and oxygen to travel to every part of your body. It also encourages your brain's neurons to fire and grow. What's more it reduces inflammation, which is now seen as a major cause of depression.

So, it's time to stop thinking of exercise as a way to lose weight. That's when people give up and get discouraged because let's face it, dropping pounds is hard. Reframe it instead as a pastime that makes you feel good. To prove it to yourself, rate your mood before and after you exercise every day for seven days. If you're anything like me, my mood can quickly go from 4 to an 8. Also notice at what point you are starting to feel better during an exercise session. When I do a spin class or go for a run, I notice a clear improvement in my mood 10 to 15 minutes in. On mornings when I don't feel like it, it's a reminder that good things are coming. If you want an exact time when your mood will start to lift, a 2022 Iowa State University study found that half an hour of exercise will disperse feelings of anhedonia for 75 minutes afterwards. Don't feel you have to commit to hours of continuous exercise every week – it doesn't have to last that long to have benefits. A range of studies has also found that "exercise snacking" – or breaking up exercise into three 10- or 15-minute bursts throughout the day, anything from a brisk walk to quick strength workout – can be as good for your health and wellbeing than doing it in one fixed block. And of course, you're more likely to get it done.

THE POWER OF SINGING TO RAISE MOOD

Singing has been found to be the easiest way to boost your mood, whether you do it in the shower alone or in a choir. Simply listening to a song will kickstart the release of dopamine into your reward circuits. Putting your voice to it takes it one step further, boosting the levels of feel-good endocannabinoids in the brain – cannabis-like chemicals that your body naturally makes. Of course, if you are feeling very "blah" you may not feel like singing in the first place, but it's worth trying anyway. It's simply one of the easiest ways you can activate your pleasure circuits – and it helps to lift you out of any rumination.

Singing also relieves stress. One experiment measured the cortisol levels in people's saliva and found that when they were happy to join in a song, levels of their stress hormones dropped, whether they were alone or singing with other people. If you *do* get the chance to join a choir, consider it as a supercharged way to raise your mood. In a study of 375 adults, researchers found that people reported more wellbeing when singing in a group because of the connection they felt with others, triggering oxytocin release too.

Move your feet

Because it can also be strenuous exercise, ten minutes of dancing releases additional endorphins. When you listen to a song, your brain is constantly looking forward to the next note – and especially to the chorus – because you have a spike of dopamine and opioids at the moment of the melody's climax. When you dance, your body does the same and has to decide how to move to respond in time to the next beat, activating your sensory and motor circuits into the bargain. And once you've shed any initial self-consciousness, dancing also seems to be the easiest way to enter into a state of flow, because the repetitive movements absorb your mind.

When dancing with other people, the effect ramps up still more as we synchronize our bodies to the beat, improving the connection we feel with others, a state which has been called "collective effervescence". There are some other benefits. When we move our bodies, we feel more in control not only of our limbs, but also our lives, according to research.

Dancing is so absorbing it makes us live in the present. And dance has a longer-lasting effect on mood than many other pleasurable activities. According to studies of the reward circuit, we stay in the "liking" phase of the reward for longer. "Research studies have shown that four things happen when people dance together," explains Dr Peter Lovatt, author of *The Dance Cure: The Surprising Secret to Being Smarter, Stronger, Happier*. They report liking each other more, trusting each other more, they feel they are more psychologically similar in terms of their values, and they're more likely to help one another outside the context of dancing.

"When we dance, it creates an electrochemical firework display in our head and every move we make creates a new 'flash', 'bang' or an 'ooh' and 'aah'. As dopamine levels go up, we can shake off some of those negative feelings and float into a euphoric state."

So, considering the joyful benefits, it might be worth tackling any self-consciousness which might have been holding us back from the dance floor, especially as it's such a great way out of "blah".

How your phone is draining your joy

You probably view your phone as an essential. After all, they've deliberately been designed to serve our every need. But viewed another way, phones are also stress-activation systems that never switch off. (Many of us don't even know how to find the "off" button. Our biggest concession is to put it on airplane mode.)

Naturally, we kid ourselves that having our smartphone with us all the time gives us control. In reality, any feelings that we are on top of the situation are cancelled out many times over by the deluge of notifications, stressful emails, and the latest headlines from a news cycle, naturally biased toward the negative. This constantly raises our levels of cortisol and tells us we need to get ready for threats, even when we are in no immediate danger.

If we could take more breaks from our phones, they wouldn't affect our mood as much. But because most of us keep them within arm's reach nearly all the time, even at night – and we spend an average of four hours of our waking day on them – the interruption is relentless. Because it never stops, this leads to chronically elevated cortisol levels, which interfere with the production of feel-good hormones.

Ask yourself if time you spend on your phone is standing in the way of meaningful experiences you will remember? Instead of snapping more pictures for your camera roll, could you concentrate on experiencing what you are seeing instead? Our lives are our memory banks, but we have little chance of remembering those important moments if we are taking pictures for the entertainment of others or scrolling through other people's lives rather than living our own. If it seems your life is passing in a blur, could it be because you are distracted with so much mental clutter that you are never truly paying attention?

So, what can you do to put boundaries in place around your phone use and make time to experience life?

See the bigger picture: Phones were designed to be convenient, but they were also designed to target your vulnerabilities, so you stay on them for longer. We've now lived so long with the smartphone that we're starting to forget what living "in real life" is like. Take a step back and see how your time is being drained away by social media companies for their profit, not for your benefit. It's another adaptation of that old cliché, but it's fair to say that none of us will get to our deathbeds and announce: "I wish I'd spent more time on my phone."

Think about what you are missing out on: We spend hours a day scrolling, hoping to get dopamine hits, but often getting cortisol spikes instead. Track your weekly screen time to get an idea of how much time your phone is swallowing up. Set yourself a goal to reduce your screen time each week. Think about what you could have done and achieved instead.

Turn off all but essential notifications: Are you constantly being interrupted by messages you need to get or notifications that social networks and other companies want you to know about? Your attention is their currency. Turn off all but the most essential notifications from people you really need to hear from. The only messages that interrupt you should be important ones. Unsubscribe from non-essential mailing lists. If the answer to any email is likely to be more than 30 words, wait until you get to your computer. If it's important, you will write it faster and more coherently when it has your full attention.

Create friction: Most of us are in the habit of mindlessly looking at our phones when we get bored or distracted or don't want to deal with something uncomfortable. In her essential guidebook, *How to Break up with Your Phone*, Catherine Price recommends putting an obstacle in place to slow you down. Her suggestion is putting a rubber band around it. As you will have to remove it to use the phone screen, it becomes a brake that forces you to pause and ask if you really need to check it. Or set a lock screen that reminds you that the most important moment in your life is now, and not to waste it unnecessarily.

Go back to a basic phone: Often the advice for dealing with psychological addiction is to go cold turkey on the thing you crave but having no phone at all is challenging in our day and age when it is designed to be the ultimate multi-tool. Take charge of your phone, instead of letting it take charge of you. As far as possible, use your phone only as your phone. Change your screen to black and white so it's not as visually appealing. If you are still finding it hard, there's a growing trend in so-called "dumb" phones, which just do the basics like taking calls, texting and playing music.

Try a trial separation: Think you can't live without your phone? Reset your cortisol and dopamine levels by putting away your phone for an hour, then a day, and then a week if you can manage it and see how you feel. Don't make it feel like deprivation. Frame it as a treat and use that time to do something else you'd enjoy.

See how others see you: Ask for some radical honesty. Ask your friends and family if you seem distracted or they sometimes feel ignored. If you have young children do they seem to get upset when you are using it? Are the people who matter competing for your attention?

HOW TO CREATE A NO-DO LIST

Two hours is the amount of free time per day that makes people their happiest, according to research by the University of Pennsylvania. At the other end of the balance, people with no free time at all have been found to be the most miserable. So how do we find those elusive two hours of free time?

Your brain has finite resources. It can't multitask. It can only rapidly switch attention, which is exhausting. When it feels like you have too many tabs open, your cortisol level can stay permanently raised, interrupting the workings of your reward system. We are all familiar with the concept of to-do lists. But sometimes we need to write a *no-do* list to intentionally reduce our mental load and free up more time for joy.

The number of chores on your list may have built up because it feels easier to do them yourself, and you haven't had the time to train the people around you to share them.

When drawing up a no-do list, write a list of the things you do each week. With each, ask yourself: Do I actually want this or is it just expected of me? Then decide which ones you can cross off and which ones you can delegate. As you decide what tasks to drop, check first that there won't be any negative consequences for you, or anyone else around you, as a result.

How to talk to others about anhedonia

If anhedonia is difficult to explain when you are experiencing it, partners, children, friends and family may find it even harder to understand. If it's not depression, and you're still smiling and getting on with life, they might think you're complaining needlessly, and you should "just" cheer up.

Within relationships, anhedonia can feel like a guilty secret. One of the unspoken laws is that your partner is supposed "to make you happy". This means that many people who are in a state of "blah" often don't share how they feel with loved ones. You may be nervous of bringing it up because you're worried it will be heard as criticism or your partner will be concerned you no longer enjoy being with them.

If it's not part of debilitating depression, you may also assume anhedonia is not serious enough to talk about, even though emotional flatlining can seriously damage relationships. You may worry you're just "making a fuss". Even so, it's worth bringing into the open. You wouldn't feel embarrassed to admit a physical impediment, so why not a psychological one? If you don't raise it, it's going to be a lot more corrosive to your relationship. That's because if your partner doesn't understand how you feel, and you don't explain it to them, they may already be processing your lack of joy as a rejection. Your sex life may already be suffering and they won't understand why. Plus, if you are not enjoying your life, your feelings will be contagious, so your partner may be matching your tone. The result is the fun may have drained from your home, compounding the issue. If you are going to start enjoying your life, it will also help to tell your partner so you can tell them what you'd like to change and how you'd like to bring them with you – and create a happier, more fun-filled relationship.

> *I'm married with three lovely kids, and we are*
> *financially well-off. But I still feel worn down by life.*
> *There's very little fun or playfulness, just the day-to-day*
> *grind. When I hear myself laughing with my husband,*
> *it almost takes me by surprise!*
> Nita, 46

Psychotherapist Lohani Noor says: "Just as one person can lift another, so can they bring them down. It is very difficult to keep a positive motion going in a relationship if your partner can't meet you energetically." See telling your partner you are ready to have more fun as the ultimate investment in your relationship. Research from the University of Denver has found that finding moments to be together free of financial, family or other stresses – just to have fun together – is not a luxury. "The more you invest in fun and friendship and being there for your partner, the happier the relationship will get over time," according to psychologist Professor Howard Markman, co-Director of the Centre for Marital and Family Studies. "The correlation between fun and marital happiness is high, and significant."

Sharing new and exciting activities is also consistently linked to stronger relationships, according to findings in the *Journal of Personality and Social Psychology* by psychologist Dr Arthur Aron. "When you're first in a romantic relationship, there's an intense excitement. But then you grow used to each other," according to Dr Aron. "If you do something new and challenging, that reminds you of how exciting it can be with your partner. It makes your relationship better."

> *I realized my partner and I had to get some fun back in our relationship. We'd both fallen into the trap of moaning all the time and just getting stuff done. I realized I missed the way we used to laugh together.*
> Livi, 45

Here are some ways to talk to your partner about anhedonia:

- **Think about what you want to get out of the conversation:** Include how you'd like your partner to support you. You could start the conversation by saying, "I'm not looking for advice and I'm not looking for you to come up with a solution. But I would like to communicate how I am feeling so I can connect with you."

- **Talk about how anhedonia affects you:** Explain whether anhedonia is with you all, or just some, of the time. If you can, make a timeline of when you first noticed it and work out if it was related to any external stressors or circumstances. Was it extra pressure at work, having to care for a relative, difficulties with childcare or the onset of menopause or andropause?
- **State your intent:** Tell your partner that you want to do things that allow you to enjoy life together more – the type of activities you might have done as a couple at the start of your relationship, but you now no longer do together. Few partners won't want to join you there.
- **Share your load:** Research from Stanford University has found that the reason women *still* tend to take on the lion's share of childcare and household management and duties in heterosexual relationships is that they don't feel entitled to put their own needs and time first, a type of thinking known as "un-entitlement". In short, women tend to default to believing that housework or childcare should fall to them. Whatever your gender, if you feel your relationship has become one-sided, in an amicable, constructive way, draw up list together of all the little things you and your partner *both* do to keep your home going – something writer and time-management expert Eve Rodsky has called "the Sh*t I Do list". This may include micro-tasks, like being the one who always applies sunscreen to the kids, who arranges birthday parties, and organizes the childcare. Then compare your lists and look at ways to share the jobs more evenly. Point out

that having to remind your partner to do tasks puts more pressure on you and that if they take responsibility for a job, like the laundry, they should see it all the way through from start to finish. If the balance has become unequal, your partner may not have noticed the toll the build-up is taking on you.

- **Set aside regular time:** If you've fallen out of the habit of having fun, and life has got in the way, it is unlikely to happen unless you schedule it. Make a date in each other's calendars for a date night to discuss what you'd like to do together. Psychotherapist Lohani Noor says: "Pick a few things you'd both like to do. Put time aside in your diary just to do the fun things you have identified. Take turns at organizing the events, no matter how big or small."

- **Find some novelty in one another:** When you and your partner first dated, your relationship was unpredictable and that made it exciting. Would they text you back? Were your feelings reciprocated? But as you settled down, it was inevitable that, over time, you settled into more habitual ways of being together and the novelty wore off. No matter how long you've been together, it's still possible to bring it back. To do this, discover some new things to ask each other. Try some reciprocal self-disclosure, a form of mutual questioning that has been shown to make people feel closer. To help you find questions you probably hadn't thought off and help you feel a sense of connection, try 36 Questions for Increasing Closeness, devised by psychologist Arthur Aron. These have been carefully designed to be asked in order to help both of you share personal information and gradually appreciate each other more, without causing conflict. Try them at https://ggia.berkeley.edu/ practice/36_questions_for_increasing_closeness

- **Go small:** We tend to think we have to make grand sky-writing gestures to show love, like booking an expensive meal or holiday, but it's the small daily things you can do together which add up. When you see your partner after time apart, put your phone away and treat them as someone you haven't seen for a while.

- **Do something which requires you to rely on one another**: Studies have found that the joy and excitement people have from having new experiences rubs off on their feelings about their partner. If you are adventurous, choose an activity, like canoeing or rock-climbing, where you have to trust each other, to increase your closeness.

- **Increase eye contact:** You might find that when you are feeling stressed and "blah", you can go a whole day without actually looking at your partner, even if you're in the same room. Engaging in deliberate mutual eye contact boosts oxytocin and makes a clear statement you want to be emotionally intimate. Try facing each other for a minute and locking eyes to see how long you can hold eachother's gaze.

- **Do something with your shared interests:** As much as you might like to plan to take a campervan around Europe, the activities you plan together don't have to be vast or grand. I heard about a couple who, during lockdown, realized they were no longer having any fun together because any spare time was swallowed up by time on their phones or listening separately to music and podcasts. So, as they both loved the same band, and he played the guitar and she sang, every day they performed one of the band's songs together. Not to record or put on social media, just to enjoy feeling more connected.

- **Make fun a regular thing:** The joy starts with the planning and anticipation. Ensure there's always some time together scheduled in your diary, preferably once a week, to look forward to, whether it's a date night or a trip to get out of the house.

Above all, make it clear you want these discussions to improve your relationship. Explain quite simply that you'd like to enjoy life more – and you'd like to bring your partner with you.

Be prepared to listen without judgement if your partner shares they have had similar thoughts. Psychotherapist Lohani Noor told me: "Honesty is the best policy. If you are not quite feeling yourself, let your partner know. Talk about yourself and your own experience, don't make it about anyone else. Have some information ready at hand so that your partner can learn about anhedonia at their own pace."

But ... don't rely on your partner completely, advises anhedonia counsellor and researcher Jackie Kelm. "You won't ever get all your emotional needs met by just one person. If you put too much pressure on your partner to be everything you need to have fun, you are likely to be disappointed. All of us have personal differences in what we view as pleasurable.

So, cultivate friendships and spend time with other people who enjoy the same things you do."

It was hard telling my partner I'd been feeling flat for so long. I don't think she'd noticed. But she really appreciated it when I told I wanted to make some time for us to have fun together the way we used to at the start of our relationship.

Jon, 59

Making life more fun for kids too

Lack of joy in the world – and anxiety – can be contagious to children. Young animals look to cues from adults to show them how to be in the world and what to be worried about. For example, baby monkeys have been found not to be afraid of snakes until they are shown videos of adults being frightened of them. Having fun with your kids also makes them feel like the world is a safe place.

Research has shown that when rat mothers lick their pups, the pups show lower stress levels. Counsellor David Code argues that this is not just because they feel cared for, but because the mother is sending the message that the environment is safe enough to give her time to groom her offspring. "A mother rat is saying to them 'times are so good and predator- and stress-free that I have lots of time to lick you guys'."

Try to find more moments of genuine fun, not only to share in the unfettered joy that kids naturally have, but also to send the message that enjoying life is important, no matter how old you are. It doesn't stop when you reach adulthood.

Here are some things you can try …

For younger kids: When you are with your kids, really engage with them. Get down on the floor, make eye contact and let them direct the play. Don't try to teach them anything, so they can relax into it and be as silly as they like. Put your phone in the next room and join them where they are. Make playtime session daily and predictable, even if it's only for 15 minutes, so your children know they will have this time with you each day.

For older kids: Teens are particularly sensitive to facial expressions and tone of voice and can interpret even neutral expressions as negative or critical. If you have been feeling "blah" for some time, they may also interpret this as a rejection or a sign you don't like them very much. Tell your child you've realized you want to enjoy your life more and a key part of that is to have more fun with them. Teens do generally want to spend time with parents, whatever they say, as long as criticism is put on hold. Make it a deal that you will both take a break from judgement when you're together, so you can relax and have fun.

To reclaim your closeness with your tween or teen, psychologist Oliver James recommends a technique called "love bombing". (James began using this term over a decade ago to describe a technique to foster positive bonds with kids. Its use to describe unhealthy behaviour in adult relationships came later.) James' version of love bombing involves spending a period of time alone with your child, offering them unlimited love and control over what you do, in order to re-establish the trust between you. James believes that by taking your relationship back to its roots, you can stabilize the levels of the fight-or-flight hormone that may have built up over time – and reset your relationship. The idea is that by freeing your child, it will take you back to the closeness and intimacy you once shared when they were younger, and before other issues gradually came between you. It may sound mad to give a child total freedom to set the rules, but it's only for a short space of time – usually a weekend – and children usually make perfectly reasonable requests. Ask them to suggest fun activities – and say you'd like to join in.

Creating a joyful home

We once lived mainly outside in an ever-changing landscape, unencumbered, except for the most basic possessions. When your ancestor sought shelter, most of all he wanted a place that made him feel safe from the dangers outside. Even in the 21st century, that should still hold true. In an era, dubbed "The Age of Anxiety", the home should be a haven which reduces stress levels. That means that no matter where you live, how big or small it is, you should be surrounded by things that make you feel safe and good. It should be a feeling, as much as physical space. This entails tuning in more to the ways your body and nervous system is interacting with your surroundings.

Too often we accumulate "stuff" because we are told we need it. We may acquire possessions because we believe it will make us happy. And then we often fail to throw stuff out when we find it hasn't. The result is that according to one estimate, the average Western home contains 300,000 possessions.

As interior design expert Michelle Ogundehin points out in her book, *Happy Inside: How to Harness the Power of Home for Health and Happiness*, "Clutter is the arch-enemy of the restful home. It is the interiors equivalent of a to-do list that never gets completed, undermining any attempt at relaxation.

Physical clutter equates to emotional debris, stifling energy and dampening enthusiasm." It's not that we don't have enough space in our homes, Michelle points out. The real problem is that we have too much stuff.

One possible reason is mess is so stressful is that in our hunter-gathering days, our brains were designed to scan our horizons for immediate threat.

Too much stuff obscures that view, even if all we are looking for is our phones, rather than a predator. The build-up actively raises cortisol, which over time, reduces levels of feel-good chemicals like dopamine and makes us more anxious. Inside our homes, we can also end up arguing over space, and wasting precious time looking for things.

People in chaotic environments have been found to feel more out of control of their lives and less likely to make better choices for their health and wellbeing. In one experiment, volunteers were put either in a messy room strewn with old correspondence and papers, or in a clutter-free room. It was found that those in the tidy environment were more likely to choose healthier snacks and donate more money to charity. People have also been found to make more mistakes in an untidy environment than a tidy one. Furthermore, if your life hasn't felt joyful for some time, we can also associate our surroundings with these feelings. Changing the space around you and drawing a line under that period in your life can be a declaration that you now intend to prioritize different things.

Here are some ways to make your environment more joyful:

Remove what doesn't make you feel good: Imagine clutter as weeds. Removing it will allow space for more positive feelings. Start by scanning the room you are in for things that make you stressed. As well as bills and receipts, remove objects with difficult memories attached, photos or pictures that don't make you feel positive, and medicines or tangles of wires. Take decluttering slowly by addressing one shelf, drawer or cupboard at a time. Your dopamine circuit will be activated as you tidy up each area. By the end of the process, each room should feel lighter and your mood more buoyant. Curate every section until every object either serves a purpose or makes you feel good.

Cut down on your mirrors: Even too many mirrors can subtly raise your anxiety levels, according to research. If you are constantly catching sight of yourself and criticizing your appearance, you might want to go mirror-free in places like your bedroom, especially as few of us look our best when we get up. Replace mirrors with photographs of happy moments, or images of nature which have been found in research to have a calming effect on the nervous system.

Let in the light: After heathier food, and enough sleep, light is the next most important thing we can give our bodies to feel well because of the way it affects our circadian rhythms, and the chemical balance of our bodies. People who say there isn't enough natural light where they live are 1.4 times more likely to report being depressed than those who feel their homes are sunny enough. Other studies have found that people who work in a space with more daylight sleep better than those in darker spaces. Wherever you live, do what you can to bring the light in, whether it's raising your blinds first thing in the morning, or cutting back foliage that's obstructing your view.

Bring nature inside: One of the reasons people feel so disconnected is they live in cities that retain so few elements of the natural world. Unconsciously we try to make up for this by bringing plants inside. According to a study in the *Journal of Physiological Anthropology*, touching and smelling indoor plants can reduce physiological and psychological stress. People who have houseplants also tend to feel fewer negative feelings than those who have no greenery at home. Don't wait for others to give you flowers. If you can afford them, buy them for yourself.

No matter, how much money I have, every week I buy myself a bunch of flowers for the kitchen table. Every time I walk in, it's my reminder to myself that I am committing to making myself feel good.

Catriona, 37

I am so happy that my feelings have come back. I recently went to see a musical and instead of being critical and cynical, it genuinely brought a smile to my face. I have got my motivation back to do other things, like taking up swimming and eating better for my mood.

Ash, 60

I decided to break out of going around and around in circles and began taking up my old hobbies again even though I didn't feel like it at first. I was kinder to myself and less critical. It didn't always work but I persevered. It came back slowly until I started to feel fully functional again. There is light at the end of the tunnel.

Jules, 46

Spending time in nature

Think back to your favourite childhood memories – and the moments when you felt the most carefree and alive. It could have been looking down on the world from the branches of a tree, running through the snow or making a den in a hedgerow. It is a good guess that many of your most treasured recollections were when you were outside and playing with no adult supervision. It was in the moments like these when we played outdoors, away from adults, that we learnt to think of ourselves as independent beings who could make decisions, take risks and look after ourselves.

The phrase "nature deficit disorder" was coined by author Richard Louv, who first argued almost 20 years ago that the human cost of "alienation from nature" is the "diminished use of the senses, attention difficulties and higher rates of physical and emotional illnesses."

We pay a high price with our wellbeing when we cut ourselves off from the outside.

In her book, *Joyful: The Surprising Power of Ordinary Things to Create Extraordinary Happiness*, designer Ingrid Fetell Lee, points out that nature is the place where we are most liberated: "Some of the most joyful moments in life are when we gain a kind of freedom. Think of the ecstatic opening of the school doors on the last day before summer break or the buzz in the office when the clock strikes five on Friday. Joy thrives on the alleviation of constraints. The delicious stretch in your legs on stepping out of the car at the rest stop after many hours of driving is a joyful freedom. So is sleeping under the stars, riding in a convertible and skinny-dipping, feeling cool water against bare skin. Joy has a dynamism that doesn't like to be squashed in or pent up. We fight so hard for freedom because it enables us to pursue joy – as well as everything else that matters in life. For our ancestors, having room to roam meant a greater likelihood of discovering sources of sustenance, favourable habits and potential mates. This is why incarceration is a punishment second only in severity to death and in more prosaic terms, why the middle seat on an airplane inspires such universal dread."

A few generations of industrialized living cannot breed a species who spent many millennia as nomads out of our need to go foraging, climb trees and build dens. These benefits are still hardwired into our physiology and nervous system at the deepest levels. For instance, a 2019 study in the journal *Frontiers in Public* Health, by Japanese researchers, found that walking in a forest lowered concentration of the stress hormone cortisol, as well as lowering blood pressure, compared to walking in a city environment.

To magnify these effects, just add water. According to Professor Charles Spence, who studies the senses at Oxford University's Cross Modal Research Laboratory, swapping green space for blue space means people can supercharge their senses and get the ultimate wellbeing workout – something he calls the "blue gym effect". Following his research paper, 'Multisensory Well-being and Boating', Professor Spence, points out the Victorians were right to send patients to the coast to recuperate, because there are benefits for the immune system too. Visiting the sea or ocean also helps to combat burnout and Seasonal Affective Disorder.

Professor Spence, who is also author of the book *Sensehacking: How to Use the Power of Your Senses for Happier, Healthier Living*, says: "So-called blue space has even greater health and wellbeing benefits than green space. While the effect is often considered in terms of vision – perhaps unsurprising given that we are so visually dominant – there is a growing awareness of just how important the sounds of water and wildlife are to the beneficial effects of nature. The results of research conducted in national parks across North America revealed that the sounds of water had the biggest positive effect on health and positive affect outcomes. Water sounds have also been shown to provide an effective foil to the stress-inducing noise of urban, typically transport, activities." One possible reason, Spence suggests, is that the rhythmical sounds of waves crashing on the beach remind us of the sounds we heard when we were in the womb. "Layered with the sight and sounds, the impact of the smells of nature and being close to water on our mental and physical well-being is tangible. The added benefit for health are the negative ions given off by large bodies of open water. Ocean air and its ions are probably what is more beneficial for us physiologically than the tangy smell of the sea. The latter is caused by the release of dimethyl-sulphide from the breakdown of bacteria, and as we have just seen may be linked to psychological benefits due to its association with happy, healthy memories of the beach."

One thing I learned when I was coming out of anhedonia is that it's always better to do something than nothing. If I was ever in two minds about a walk, for example, I made it to rule to make myself go. I never regretted it because whatever mood I was in, I always felt better afterwards. I made a point of noticing the clouds, trees, ducks and squirrels. There was always something. I think after years of working too hard until I burnt out, looking out for the subtle changes in the landscape every day brought me down to earth again.

Lou, 55

Feeling good came back in tiny steps. I started to feel lighter. I made more plans. I got to know the things I could do to make myself feel better and take me out of myself, even if it was only for five or ten minutes. It feels like a guilty secret, but for me, it was knitting! It worked on so many levels. I could pick it up and put it down. I could see the progress I was making. I had done it as a child and had loved it then. It gives me satisfaction and that gives me joy.

Elise, 46

Awe Moments

Another reason why seas and oceans inspire us is that these vast unknowable expanses also give us a sense of awe. If there's one type of experience that will help shake you out of "blah", it is this, according to a growing number of compelling research studies. These are moments in life when you come across something which blows your mind. They don't have to be in nature, though they often are.

Mine were moments like seeing how the marble twinkled on the Taj Mahal at dusk, the sparkling lights which light up to the steps to Sacre Coeur in Paris at night, the desert dunes in Tunisia and the first glimpse of my newborn babies. Think back and you are likely to have had several of your own – and they will be clear, sharp memories which punctuate the story of your life.

Awe moments were first defined by psychologist Professor Dacher Keltner as "the feeling of being in the presence of something vast and greater than the self." You don't have to be in an exotic country or having a life-altering moment to experience them once you start scanning for them. Awe experiences can be found in the everyday. They can be discovered looking up at clouds or observing the intricate skill of a bee collecting pollen in a flower. They seem to have such a powerful effect because, in those moments, you realize there is something bigger than you and it throws the transient issues we all face into perspective.

Research shows that moments of awe can have profound effects on how you feel about the world, by reducing brain activity in the areas involved with self-focus and mind-wandering. In one experiment, scientists divided mentally healthy volunteers in later life into two groups to take 15-minute walks once a week. One group was asked to walk as normal. The other group was told to look out for moments of awe while they strolled. This meant going somewhere new, and paying attention to details along their walks, and "looking at everything with fresh, childlike eyes". "Basically, we told them to try to go and walk somewhere new, to the extent possible, since novelty helps to cultivate awe," says Virginia Sturm, associate professor of neurology at the University of California San Francisco (UCSF), who led the study. As an add-on, both groups were asked to take a few selfies during their walks, in order to commit them to memory. Otherwise, they were asked not to use their phones. At the end of their trips, the walkers in both groups uploaded their selfies to a website and were asked to write daily online diaries about how they had felt. After two months, the researchers compared the groups' experiences and selfies. It was found that the walkers who had looked for awe moments had become skilled at noticing magical moments in the details of nature. They felt happier and more socially connected than walkers in the other group. The others, in contrast, reported they had spent much of their time fretting about their to-do lists. The selfies the two groups took also showed key differences. The people who had not looked for awe mainly took close-ups of their faces. The group told to look for more transcendence took pictures of themselves in which they were smaller and less important compared to the context around them.

Altruism, humility and generosity are other qualities that come more readily when people become more respectful of the world around them, according to Associate Professor of Psychological Science, Paul Piff. In his research, he found that people who looked up at tall trees for a minute were more generous afterwards.

The climate catastrophe and mass wildlife extinctions are burdens weighing on my mind, especially with the scorching heat, fire and floods the world has experienced in recent years.

It's very easy to fall into an endless cycle of hopelessness, but it's important to use the strong feelings we have around injustices to spur us into action. I take joy in the little things. Being connected to nature is incredibly important to me, so I ensure that every day I take a walk with my dogs. I spend time with animals whenever I can. I have helped rescue pigs, cows, turkeys, chickens and ducks, and then had the privilege of getting to know them in beautiful sanctuaries or my home. There is so much joy that can be found in tackling issues that mean something to us, taking steps to challenge what we know to be wrong. Often it is only by experiencing despair that we feel motivated enough to take actions: it's important to harness these negative feelings to fuel positive changes.

Juliet Gellately, Director of Viva

Part Three summary

This may be the first book on anhedonia for the general reader, but I am aware it's not yet the whole story. Now that anhedonia is being treated as more of a stand-alone area for research, its many causes, and new ways of addressing it, are being discovered. As I write, more studies are being done on the possibility that hallucinogens, like psilocybin, made from fungi, may have chemical properties which free us from the negative rumination that can drive the false belief that joy is beyond reach. Ketamine, when used in safe environments and in clinically prescribed doses, is also being investigated further. Some trials have found that ketamine seems to directly address some forms of anhedonia, possibly because it blocks neuron receptors for glutamine, a neurotransmitter which is key in learning and memory.

In Spain, researchers are also looking at the role of galanin, another brain chemical that can act as a neurotransmitter, that seems to block pleasure and motivation in rodent brains.

All this shows how much serious thought and research is now being applied to an emotional state that is robbing too many people of their potential to live fuller lives. The prospect of beating anhedonia is exciting. It could allow millions to step out of the grey middle ground and into the light.

Conclusion

"Don't ask yourself what the world needs, ask yourself what makes you come alive. Because what the world needs is people who have come alive."

Howard Thurman, civil rights leader

Throughout this book, I have written about the latest research which shows that anticipation has a hugely important role in joyful experiences. So, I can't finish without addressing the elephant in the room, which is that it's hard to look forward when we are not sure what kind of future awaits us. It feels like we are at a precarious crossroads, but when we enter a new period of history, for a moment we are always lost. Often it can take some time, and some discomfort, before we reorientate ourselves.

What if the liminal spaces we are passing through (the type coincidentally being captured in countless spooky images of empty corridors on TikTok) can take us in a new direction? What if, having faced up to the toll human industrialization has had on our brains, we can use our new understanding of how it works to get ourselves back in synch? Have we finally got enough understanding of the human brain to work out how it flourishes best and how best to use it for the good of the planet?

In a guest essay for *The New York Times* based on his latest book, Oxford University philosopher William MacAskill recently offered a new perspective on how we can anticipate the future in a more positive way. If human history were a novel, he suggests, then we are barely at the end of the introduction. He asks us to consider looking ahead more optimistically, not just for the sake of our own wellbeing and that of our children, but also for the sake of future generations. If we can stick to some of the positive paths we are on – the growing equality movements, improved healthcare and the democratization of knowledge on the internet – MacAskill believes we have a lot to look forward to and that humanity could theoretically last for many more millennia.

He argues: "To be alive at such a time is both an exceptional opportunity and a profound responsibility: we can be pivotal in steering the future onto a better trajectory. There's no better time for a movement to stand up, not just for our generation or even our children's generation, but for all the generations yet to come." This could be just the beginning.

But if we *don't* start to take more note of the science of how our minds work, it will feel like we are just rearranging the deckchairs on the *Titanic*. How much more will we have to look forward to if we can start to really apply the new scientific understanding of how our minds and emotions work to the challenges we now face.

The Greeks were among the earliest to consider the nature of happiness – and they got it right the first time. As well as coming up with the word hedonism, on which the word anhedonia is based, they also coined "eudaemonia", or "a life with meaning". Modern research has repeatedly shown they were correct. Happiness depends on a balance between everyday joy on one hand and a sense of purpose on the other. Research has found that people who do something to support the causes they believe in are healthier both physically and emotionally. Often the good we do today, is the happiness we feel tomorrow.

To finish off this book on how to enjoy life, I'd like to pan out for a moment. Let's go back to your ancestors waking up hungry that morning, wondering how they were going to find something to eat. Then think about all the hundreds of generations that came after them and who led to you. Consider all their struggles and how far they travelled. How many love stories and how many heartbreaks did they experience so you could be sitting, right here, right now, reading this book? What if you set your mind to living a life of optimism for the generations who will follow you too? Imagine leading a life so fulfilled that you have more energy to make the world a better place for your future descendants.

The most important thing about you isn't your race, class, gender or education. It's whether you live by what thinker Leon Kass calls "The ruling passion of your soul." It was in 1890 in the first introduction to the field, *The Principles of Psychology, Vol.1*, that William James wrote a simple statement that's still packed with meaning: "My experience is what I agree to attend to. Only those items which I notice shape my mind." In other words, we are what we pay attention to.

My point is that for most of human history we have instinctively known what it takes to be happy. It's only in the last half century that consumerism – and the orthodoxy that every country's economy must keep growing at the cost of everything else – which has diverted us.

Already change is happening. We are realizing there are other measures of growth and achievement.

There's the growing FIRE Moment – "Financial Independence, Retire Early" – in which the goal for a growing number of young people is to save up to three-quarters of their income by the ages of 30 or 40 so they have the freedom to live their lives on their own terms.

Then there's the "quiet quitting" movement in which workers, tired of being exhausted by the daily grind, stop subscribing to the "work is life" culture and start considering what's good for them, not for the shareholders and profits of the companies they work for.

We want a different life for the next generation too. More parents than ever are deciding not to put their children through one-size-fits all school systems that dehumanize them, and turn them into league table statistics, and are instead creating alternative education systems.

Are we in the middle of "The Great Resignation?" or "The Great Re-prioritization"? What all these movements have in common is a decision to put freedom first, instead of the material success which we have been conditioned to believe we must all strive for. When we prioritize our mental wellbeing, it links to improvements in the environment too. The more we realize that stuff doesn't make us happy, the less we consume.

As psychologist Barbara Fredrickson has pointed out: "People who have positive emotions rather than negative or neutral ones, can see the bigger picture. They turn their gaze outwards." At a fundamental level, when we feel good, we can step back and see the world's needs. We have more bandwidth to do something about it.

In the short term, on your way out of anhedonia, I hope you have more days when you can't stop dancing to your playlist or singing in the shower, and you can't take your eyes off a full moon.

From my own experience, I know these may seem like small moments, but, over time, they add up to big changes in the way you will feel about the world. Life will never be perfect, and you don't have to enjoy yourself every second of the day to find contentment. The point of being alive is not just to feel happy, but to feel the whole spectrum of human emotion. At the same time, you shouldn't feel so bowed down by modern life that joy feels like a luxury you don't have time for.

While I was researching this book, I came across a quote from the 14th-century Persian poet Hafez: "I wish I could show you when you are lonely or in the darkness, the astonishing light of your own being." If your life was dimmed, as mine was before I wrote this book, I hope you now have some of the tools you need to shine again. There's too much for all of us to do to stay in the darkness.

Acknowledgements

As an author I owe so much in this book to the research and experience of neuroscientists, psychiatrists, psychologists, anthropologists and counsellors. My thanks also go to the people who were willing to share their experience of anhedonia with me to help others out of it.

It's been an intense journey, and I am so grateful that many of the scientists whose research I have cited have also generously agreed to contribute, whether by adding explanatory quotes, or by checking over the science for accuracy.

I am delighted that this included professors at the forefront of neuroscience: Professor Kent Berridge, whose research lab has helped changed the way we think about the role of dopamine in the reward system, and Professor Robert Zatorre who has led the understanding of how music gives us pleasure in the brain. Professor Anna Lembke, who has also highlighted the way dopamine overload is affecting modern life, gave me the green light to quote her at length, while Professors Jennifer Felger and Carmine Pariante also gave guidance on the discoveries on the link between inflammation and mental health. Thanks too to Dr Henning Beck who helped with a clear analogy on how the brain thinks, while Matt Killingsworth clarified the thinking on how we can all get happier.

Here in the UK, Professors Russell Foster, Charles Spence, Francis McGlone and Dr Kat Lederle helped with the sections on the senses.

From the outset, Dr Ferhat Uddin was brilliantly knowledgeable about changing moods in menopause.

Professor Dr Cynthia Bulik and psychologist Deanne Jade helped me appreciate how anhedonia is also a feminist issue. Then there are the many psychotherapists who shared their experience of dealing with anhedonia. They include Lohani Noor, who offered guidance throughout.

My interview with nervous system expert Irene Lyon on how we can all leave behind our childhood to experience more joy was no less than transformational.

Thanks, too, to CBT therapist Navit Schechter of consciousandcalm.com for the invaluable help, and Gabrielle Lichterman who pioneered the understanding of the link between hormones and mood for the general public.

My stalwart has always been psychotherapist Phillip Hodson who has been a guiding light over my years of writing about psychology.

The wonders of Zoom meant I was also thrilled to virtually meet life coach Jackie Kelm, who was specializing in helping emotional flatlining and anhedonia long before most of us had ever heard of it.

I also want to thank my journalist colleagues, the menopause champion Alice Smellie and the inspirational Leah Hardy, who showed me what gratitude really looks like, as well as the *You* editors for commissioning that first piece on anhedonia which got the ball rolling.

Then there's Mars Webb, the best health PR there is, who introduced me to brilliant neuroscientist Professor Hana Burianová, who gave me the big picture from the start. As I wrote this book, I thought a lot about what my father, the late Dr Kim Mukerjee taught me about the link between anthropology and psychology, as early as the 70s. He was ahead of this time.

As a child, he taught me how to think laterally and join the dots. He should have been here to read this.

As always, my thanks always go to my agent Caroline Montgomery whose calm counsel keeps us moving onward. Finally, thanks to my family Anthony, Lily, Clio. I loved everything I have learned when writing this book, but the worst part was that working on it for so many months meant that, ironically, we didn't have as many fun times we as we should have had. I am back ready to bring what I have written in this book into action, so we can all have more joy in our lives. And a final scruffle must go to Honey, who reminds me every day what real joy looks like. I will do my best to repay you with dog treats.

A note on this book

As a writer on health and psychology, I always aim to bring readers the bigger picture by joining the dots on ideas and discoveries that are already out there. The workings of the brain are so complex that I have simplified and sometimes use metaphors to help make it easier to digest. Where I have delved into technical areas, I have asked for the guidance of some of the scientists who did the research to check I am correctly translating their findings. This hasn't been possible in every single case, but my thanks go to anyone whose work has contributed to my understanding of anhedonia.

However, even with checking, when writing a book of this density, it's hard not to make any errors. If there's any research which supersedes the findings I have cited, drop me a line via my website www.tanithcarey. com so future editions of this book can be updated.

Further Reading and Support

Further Reading

Chatter: The Voice in Our Head and How to Harness it, Ethan Kross PhD, Ebury, 2021

Cracking the Menopause While Keeping Yourself Together, Mariella Frostrup, Alice Smellie, Blue Bird books, 2021

Dopamine Nation: Finding Balance in the Age of Indulgence, Dr Anna Lembke, Headline, 2021

Find your flow: The Art of Impossible: A Peak Performance Primer, Steven Kotler, Harper Wave, 2021

How to Break Up With your Phone, Catherine Price, Trapeze, 2018

Joyful: The Surprising Power of Ordinary Things to Create Extraordinary Happiness, Ingrid Fetell Lee, Rider, 2018

Love Bombing: Reset Your Child's Emotional Thermostat, Oliver James, Karnac Books, 2012.

The Cognitive Neuroscience of Music, Isabelle Peretz and Robert J. Zatorre, OUP Oxford, 2003

The Dance Cure: The surprising secret to being smarter, stronger, happier, Dr Peter Lovatt, Short Books, 2020

The Dopaminergic Mind in Human Evolution and History, Professor Fred Previc, Cambridge University Press, 2011

The Emotionally Exhausted Woman: Why You're Feeling Depleted and How to Get What You Need, Nancy Colier, New Harbinger, 2022

Fair Play: Share the mental load, rebalance your relationship and transform your life, Eve Rodsky, Quercus, 2021

Scatterbrain: How the Mind's Mistakes Make Humans Creative, Innovative, and Successful, Henning Beck, Greystone Books, 2019

Sensehacking: How to Use the Power of Your Senses for Happier, Healthier Living, Professor Charles Spence, Penguin, 2021

The Inflamed Mind: A radical new approach to depression, Professor Edward Bullimore, Short Books, 2018

The Molecule of More: How a Single Chemical in Your Brain Drives Love, Sex, and Creativity - And Will Determine the

Fate of the Human Race, Daniel Lieberman, Michael Long, Ben Bella Books, 2018

The Upward Spiral: Using Neuroscience to Reverse the Course of Depression, One Small Change at a Time, Alex Korb PhD, New Harbinger Publications, 2015

The Woman in the Mirror, Cynthia Bulik, Bloomsbury USA, 2012

The XX Brain: The Ground-breaking Science Empowering Women to Prevent Dementia, Dr Lisa Mosconi, Allen & Unwin, 2021

What We Owe the Future: A Million-Year View, William MacAskill, Oneworld Publications, 2022

Your Brain on Porn: Internet Pornography and the Emerging Science of Addiction, Gary Wilson, Commonwealth Publishing, 2014.

28 Days: What Your Cycle Reveals About Your Moods, Health and Potential, Gabrielle Lichterman, Independently published, 2019

Support

- Anhedonia Support: www.anhedoniasupport.com
- Somatic Therapy support: irenelyon.com/blog
- CBT with Navit Schechter: consciousandcalm.com
- Dear Therapists podcast: lorigottlieb.com/podcast
- Dr Rami Nader You Tube Channel: www.youtube.com/c/drraminader
- Eating disorders and anhedonia: www.orri-uk.com
- Menopause Health Support: www.libertyhealthclinics.com
- Microbiome Testing: Omnos: www.omnos.me
- Sleep Issues and SAD: drkatsleep.com

Reference Sources

INTRODUCTION:

New York Times: There's a Name for the Blah You're Feeling: It's Called Languishing The New York Times, April 19, 2021

https://www.nytimes.com/2021/04/19/well/mind/covid-mental-health-languishing.html

Berrios, G.E. et al.1995). The anhedonias: a conceptual history. History of Psychiatry, 6(24), pp.453–470.

Keyes, C.L.M. (2002). The mental health continuum: from languishing to flourishing in life. Journal of Health and Social Behaviour, pp.207–222. Available at: https://pubmed.ncbi.nlm.nih.gov/12096700/.

https://www.ipsos.com/en-us/news-polls/ipsos-us-mental-health-2021-report

https://www.betterup.com/blog/not-ill-not-well-massive-middle

https://www.gallup.com/workplace/284180/factors-driving-record-high-employee-engagement.aspx

https://workplaceinsight.net/more-than-a-third-of-workers-in-the-uk-are-languishing/

Vinckier, F., et al. (2017). Anhedonia predicts poor psychosocial functioning: Results from a large cohort of patients treated for major depressive disorder by general practitioners. European Psychiatry, 44, pp.1–8.

Sansone, R.A., et al. (2010). SSRI-Induced Indifference. Psychiatry, pp.14–18. https://www.ncbi.nlm.nih.gov/pmc/articles/PMC2989833/.

Burns, R.A., et al. The protective effects of wellbeing and flourishing on long-term mental health risk. SSM - Mental Health, 2, p.100052.

Page, G.G., et al. (2016). Sex differences in sleep, anhedonia, and HPA axis activity in a rat model of chronic social defeat. Neurobiology of Stress, 3, pp.105–113.

Estrogen Deprivation Leads to Death Of Dopamine Cells In The Brain. www.sciencedaily.com/releases/2000/12/001204072446.htm

Yang, C., et al. (2019). Key role of gut microbiota in anhedonia-like phenotype in rodents with neuropathic pain. Translational Psychiatry, p.57.

Hagerty, S.L., et al. (2020). THE IMPACT OF COVID-19 ON MENTAL HEALTH: THE INTERACTIVE ROLES OF BRAIN BIOTYPES AND HUMAN CONNECTION. Brain, Behavior, & Immunity - Health, 5, p.100078.

Boldrini, M., et al. (2021) "How COVID-19 affects the brain," JAMA psychiatry pp. 682–683.

El Sayed., et al. (2021) "Post-COVID-19 fatigue and anhedonia: A cross-sectional study and their correlation to post-recovery period," Neuropsychopharmacology reports, 41(1), pp. 50–55.

Lamontagne, S.J., et al. (2021). Post-acute sequelae of COVID-19: Evidence of mood & cognitive impairment. Brain, Behavior, & Immunity - Health, 17, p.100347.

Subramanian, A., et al. (2022). Symptoms and risk factors for long COVID in non-hospitalized adults. Nature Medicine, pp.1706–1714.

Willame, H., et al. (2022). The association between type 2 diabetes and anhedonic subtype of major depression in hypertensive individuals. Journal of Clinical Hypertension, pp.156–166.

Lieberman, M.D., et al. (2007). Putting feelings into words: Affect labelling disrupts amygdala activity in response to affective stimuli. Psychological Science, pp.421–428.

CHAPTER ONE:

Ekers, D.et al. (2014). Behavioural Activation for Depression; An Update of Meta-Analysis of Effectiveness and Sub-Group Analysis. PLoS ONE.

Caldeira, C., et al. (2018). Mobile apps for mood tracking: an analysis of features and user reviews. AMIA Annual Symposium Proceedings, pp.495–504. https://www.ncbi.nlm.nih.gov/pmc/articles/PMC5977660/.

CHAPTER TWO:

One in two million neurons on the brain produce dopamine: The Molecule of More: How a Single Chemical in Your Brain Drives Love, Sex, and Creativity - And Will Determine the Fate of the Human Race, Daniel Lieberman, Michael Long, Ben Bella Books, 2018

https://www.newscientist.com/article/2154343-huge-dose-of-brain-chemical-dopamine-may-have-made-us-smart/

Blum, K., et al. (2018). Our evolved unique pleasure circuit makes humans different from apes: Reconsideration of data derived from animal studies. Journal of Systems and Integrative Neuroscience.

Pearce, E., et al. (2013). New insights into differences in brain organization between Neanderthals and anatomically modern humans. Proceedings of the Royal Society B: Biological Sciences, 280(1758)

Sousa, A.M.M., et al. (2017). Molecular and cellular reorganization of neural circuits in the human lineage. Science, pp.1027–1032.

Limbic capitalism: How Limbic Capitalism Preys on our Addicted Brains, David Courtwright, 31 May, 2019,

https://quillette.com/2019/05/31/how-limbic-capitalism-preys-on-our-addicted-brains/

LaFreniere, L.S.,et al. (2019). Exposing Worry's Deceit: Percentage of Untrue Worries in Generalized Anxiety Disorder Treatment. Behaviour Therapy.

Isovich, E., et al. (2000). Chronic psychosocial stress reduces the density of dopamine transporters. European Journal of Neuroscience, 12(3), pp.1071–1078.

Baik, J.H., (2020). Stress and the dopaminergic reward system. Experimental & Molecular Medicine, 52(12), pp.1879–1890.

Gilbert, P., et al. (2002). Relationship of anhedonia and anxiety to social rank, defeat and entrapment. Journal of Affective Disorders, [online] 71(1-3), pp.141–151.

Brooks, J., Kano, et al. (2021). Divergent effects of oxytocin on eye contact in bonobos and chimpanzees. Psychoneuroendocrinology, 125, p.105119.

Rilling, J.K., et al. (2011). Differences between chimpanzees and bonobos in neural systems supporting social cognition. Social Cognitive and Affective Neuroscience, 7(4), pp.369–379.

REFERENCE SOURCES

Theofanopoulou, C., et al. (2022). Oxytocin and vasotocin receptor variation and the evolution of human prosociality. Comprehensive Psychoneuroendocrinology, p.100139.

Raleigh, M.J., et al, (1991). Serotonergic mechanisms promote dominance acquisition in adult male vervet monkeys. Brain Research, pp.181–190.

Love, T. et al, (2015). Neuroscience of Internet Pornography Addiction: A Review and Update. Behavioral Sciences, [online] 5(3), pp.388–433.

Zimbardo P., et al. How porn is messing with your manhood, (2016)

https://www.skeptic.com/reading_room/how-porn-is-messing-with-your-manhood/

Ito TA., et al. (1998). Negative information weighs more heavily on the brain: The negativity bias in evaluative categorizations. J Pers Soc Psychol. 75(4):887-900.

CHAPTER THREE:

Freudenberger, H., (1980) Burnout: How to Beat the High Cost of Success, Doubleday

Parents get burn-out too: DO-IT-ALL PARENTS ARE SUFFERING FROM BURNOUT, Palm Beach Post, December 19, 1991.

Computer processing power up a trillion times since 1960s: https://www.techspot.com/community/topics/processing-power-has-increased-by-one-trillion-fold-over-the-past-six-decades.213394

Bloomfield, M.A., et al. (2019). The effects of psychosocial stress on dopaminergic function and the acute stress response.

Burnout effects on the Brain; Prof Amy Arnsten:

https://edition.cnn.com/2022/03/10/health/burnout-changing-brain-wellness/index.html

Carbone, J.T. (2020). Allostatic Load and Mental Health: A Latent Class Analysis of Physiological Dysregulation. Stress, pp.1–33.

CHAPTER FOUR:

DePierro., J et al. (2014). Anhedonia in Trauma Related Disorders: The Good, the Bad, and the Shut-Down. Anhedonia: A Comprehensive Handbook Volume II, pp.175–189.

Cohen, J.R., et al. (2020). Childhood Maltreatment and Anhedonic Symptoms: Test of a Dual-risk Model in Emerging Adults. Journal of Interpersonal Violence.

Nawijn L., et al. (2015). Reward functioning in PTSD: A systematic review exploring the mechanisms underlying anhedonia. Neuroscience & Biobehavioral Reviews, 51, 189–204.

Pizzagalli D. A., et al (2014). Depression, stress, and anhedonia: Toward a synthesis and integrated model. Annual Review of Clinical Psychology, 10, 393–423.

Hanson, J.L., et al. (2021). Impact of Early Life Stress on Reward Circuit Function and Regulation. Frontiers in Psychiatry, [online] 12, p.744690.

De Bellis, MD, et al. (2014). The Biological Effects of Childhood Trauma. Child and Adolescent Psychiatric Clinics of North America, [online] 23(2), pp.185–222.

FEAR OF HAPPINESS SCALE: https://www.researchgate.net/publication/308913779_Fear_of_Happiness_Scale/link/59881901aca27266ada37237/download

Joshanloo, M., (2013). The influence of fear of happiness beliefs on responses to the satisfaction with life scale. Personality and Individual Differences, 54(5), 647-651.

Quotes from Dr Susan Overhauser : https://lilipoh.com/product/lilipoh-issue-99-spring-2020/ LILIPOH, March 22, 2020, Vol. 26; No. 99".

Hanson, J.L., et al. (2015). Cumulative stress in childhood associated with blunted reward-related brain activity in adulthood. Social Cognitive and Affective Neuroscience, 11(3), pp.405–412.

CHAPTER FIVE:

Miller, A.H., et al. (2015). The role of inflammation in depression: from evolutionary imperative to modern treatment target. Nature Reviews Immunology, 16(1), pp.22–34.

Lontchi-Yimagou, E, et al. (2013). Diabetes Mellitus and Inflammation. Current Diabetes Reports, pp.435–444.

Dinan, K. et al. (2022). Antibiotics and mental health: The good, the bad and the ugly. Journal of Internal Medicine.

Durso, G.R.O. et al.(2015). Over-the-Counter Relief From Pains and Pleasures Alike: Acetaminophen Blunts Evaluation Sensitivity to Both Negative and Positive Stimuli. Psychological Science, pp.750–758.

Quotes from Lisa Mosconi https://www.npr.org/transcripts/973805003.

https://www.youtube.com/watch?v=JJZ8z_nTCZQ

Cameron E., et al. (2019) The female aging body: A systematic review of female perspectives on aging, health, and body image. Journal Women Aging.):3–17.

Sabik NJ. (2017) Is social engagement linked to body image and depression among aging women? J Women Aging. Sep 3;29(5):405–16.

Jones, H. (2008). Testosterone for the aging male; current evidence and recommended practice. Clinical Interventions in Aging, Volume 3, pp.25–44.

Johnson, J.M., et al. (2013). The Effect of Testosterone Levels on Mood in Men: A Review. Psychosomatics, 54(6), pp.509–514.

Hage, M.P., (2012). The Link between Thyroid Function and Depression. Journal of Thyroid Research, pp.1–8.

Gietka-Czernel, M. (2017) The thyroid gland in postmenopausal women: physiology and diseases. Menopausal Review, 16(2), pp.33–37.

Gilbert, J.A., et al. (2018). Current understanding of the human microbiome. Nature Medicine, pp.392–400.

Felger, J., et al. (2016) Inflammation Effects on Motivation and Motor Activity: Role of Dopamine. Neuropsychopharmacology. 42. 10.1038/npp.2016.143.

Volkow, N.D., et al (2012). Evidence that Sleep Deprivation Downregulates Dopamine D2R in Ventral Striatum in the Human Brain. Journal of Neuroscience, pp.6711–6717.

Martynhak, B.J., et al. (2014). Circadian Fluctuation of Reward Response and Synchronization to Reward. Anhedonia: A Comprehensive Handbook Volume I, pp.51–63.

CHAPTER SIX:

Scientists enjoyed a eureka moment: The Gazette (Montreal, Quebec) December 21, 2002.

Berridge, Kent C., et al. (2015). Pleasure Systems in the Brain. Neuron, 86(3), pp.646–664.

PET: "A machine that reads the human mind". Called positron-emission tomography (PET): Source: Scanning the Human Mind Newsweek, September 29, 1980.

Maas, L.C., et al. (1998). Functional Magnetic Resonance Imaging of Human Brain Activation During Cue-Induced Cocaine Craving. American Journal of Psychiatry, 155(1), pp.124–126.

Da Silva, J.A., et al. (2018). Dopamine neuron activity before action initiation gates and invigorates future movements. Nature, 554(7691), pp.244–248.

Sherdell, L. et al. (2012). Anticipatory pleasure predicts motivation for reward in major depression. Journal of Abnormal Psychology, 121(1), pp.51–60.

Robinson, M.J.F., et al. (2015). Roles of 'Wanting' and 'Liking' in Motivating Behavior: Gambling, Food, and Drug Addictions. Behavioral Neuroscience of Motivation, pp.105–136.

Berridge, K.C., (1996). Food reward: Brain substrates of wanting and liking. Neuroscience & Biobehavioral Reviews, 20(1), pp.1–25.

Berridge, K., et al, (2015). Pleasure Systems in the Brain. Neuron, 86(3), pp.646–664.

Depression and Anhedonia: A failure of the brain's reward circuits may lead to anhedonia, Faith Brynie Ph.D. https://www.psychologytoday.com/us/blog/brain-sense/200912/depression-and-anhedonia

Heller, A.S., et al. (2009). Reduced capacity to sustain positive emotion in major depression reflects diminished maintenance of fronto-striatal brain activation. Proceedings of the National Academy of Sciences, 106(52), pp.22445–22450.

CHAPTER SEVEN:

Ferreri, L., et al. (2019). Dopamine modulates the reward experiences elicited by music. Proceedings of the National Academy of Sciences, [online] 116(9), pp.3793–3798.

Mas-Herrero et al. (2021). Unravelling the Temporal Dynamics of Reward Signals in Music-Induced Pleasure with TMS. Journal of Neuroscience, [online] 41(17), pp.3889–3899. https://www.jneurosci.org/content/41/17/3889.

Belfi, A.M. et al. (2019). Musical anhedonia and rewards of music listening: current advances and a proposed model. Annals of the New York Academy of Sciences, 1464(1), pp.99–114.

Juslin, P.N., et al. (2008). An experience sampling study of emotional reactions to music: Listener, music, and situation. Emotion, 8(5), pp.668–683.

Nusbaum, E.C. et al. (2015). Turn That Racket Down! Physical Anhedonia and Diminished Pleasure from Music. Empirical Studies of the Arts, 33(2), pp.228–243.

Blood A. J. et al. (2001) Intensely pleasurable responses to music correlate with activity in brain regions implicated in reward and emotion. Proceedings of the National Academy of Sciences, USA 98: 11818–11823.

Harvey, A.R. (2020). Links Between the Neurobiology of Oxytocin and Human Musicality. Frontiers in Human Neuroscience.

Salimpoor, V.N., et al. (2011). Anatomically distinct dopamine release during anticipation and experience of peak emotion to music. Nature Neuroscience, 14(2), pp.257–262.

Sachs, M.E., et al. (2016). Brain connectivity reflects human aesthetic responses to music. Social Cognitive and Affective Neuroscience, [online] 11(6), pp.884–891.

Roper, S. D. (2007) Signal transduction and information processing in mammalian taste buds. European Journal of Physiology, 454: 759-776.

Heath, T.P., et al. (2006) Human Taste Thresholds Are Modulated by Serotonin and Noradrenaline. Journal of Neuroscience, 26(49), pp.12664–12671.

Noel, C., et al. (2015). The effect of emotional state on taste perception. Appetite, pp.89–95.

Bedwell, J.S., et al. (2019). The Sweet Taste Test: Relationships with Anhedonia Subtypes, Personality Traits, and Menstrual Cycle Phases. Journal of Psychopathology and Behavioral Assessment, 41(2), pp.235–248.

Pouliot, S., et al. (2008). Increase in Anhedonia Level in Menopausal Women is Accompanied by a Shift in Olfactory Function. Chemosensory Perception, 1(1), pp.43–47.

Bedwell, J.S., et al. (2019). The Sweet Taste Test: Relationships with Anhedonia Subtypes, Personality Traits, and Menstrual Cycle Phases. Journal of Psychopathology and Behavioral Assessment, 41(2), pp.235–248.

Heath, T.P., et al. (2006). Human Taste Thresholds Are Modulated by Serotonin and Noradrenaline. Journal of Neuroscience, 26(49), pp.12664–12671.

Sorokowska, A., et al. (2017). Food-Related Odors Activate Dopaminergic Brain Areas. Frontiers in Human Neuroscience, [online] 11.

Kohli, P., et al. (2016). The Association Between Olfaction and Depression: A Systematic Review. Chemical Senses, 41(6), pp.479–486.

Carruthers, H.R., et al. (2010). The Manchester Color Wheel: development of a novel way of identifying color choice and its validation in healthy, anxious and depressed individuals. BMC Medical Research Methodology, 10(1).

Bubl, E., et al. (2009). Vision in depressive disorder. The World Journal of Biological Psychiatry: The Official Journal of the World Federation of Societies of Biological Psychiatry,) pp.377–384.

McCarthy, M.M. (1995). Estrogen modulation of oxytocin and its relation to behavior. Advances in Experimental Medicine and Biology, 395, pp.235–245. https://pubmed.ncbi.nlm.nih.gov/8713972/ .

Ng, K.K. (2004). Sperm output of older men. Human Reproduction, 19(8), pp.1811–1815.

Tan, M. et al. (2020). Social anhedonia and social functioning: Loneliness as a mediator. PsyCh Journal, 9(2), pp.280–289.

Liu, B. et al. (2019). Humour processing deficits in individuals with social anhedonia. Psychiatry Research, pp.345–350.

Winer, E.S, et al. (2017). Mapping the relationship between anxiety, anhedonia, and depression. Journal of Affective Disorders, 221, pp.289–296.

Hu, H., et al. (2018). Mediation effect of beliefs about pleasure and emotional experience between social anhedonia and prediction of pleasant events. Psychiatry Research, pp.39–45.

REFERENCE SOURCES

CHAPTER EIGHT:

Lucas, R.E. (2007) Adaptation and the Set-Point Model of Subjective Well-Being: Does Happiness Change after Major Life Events? Current Directions in Psychological Science, pp.75–79. Available at: https://www.jstor.org/stable/20183166

Diener, E., et al. (2006). Beyond the hedonic treadmill: Revising the adaptation theory of well-being. American Psychologist, 61(4), pp.305–314.

Feelings of control over happiness: https://www.trackinghappiness.com/controlling-happiness-new-study-results/

Fredrickson, B.L. (2004). The broaden–and–build theory of positive emotions. Philosophical Transactions of the Royal Society of London. Series B: Biological Sciences, 359(1449), pp.1367–1377.

Sheldon K.M., et al. (2019): Revisiting the Sustainable Happiness Model and Pie Chart: Can Happiness Be Successfully Pursued?, The Journal of Positive Psychology.

Klug, H. J. P., et al. (2015). Linking goal progress and subjective well-being: A meta-analysis. Journal of Happiness Studies: an Interdisciplinary Forum on Subjective Well-Being, 16 (1), 37–65

CHAPTER NINE:

Anhedonia is not a character flaw: Dr Rami Nader, https://www.youtube.com/watch?v=IbuIdHW0hPM

Raichle, M.E, et al. (. (2001). A default mode of brain function. Proceedings of the National Academy of Sciences, 98(2), pp.676–682.

Killingsworth, M.A, Gilbert, D.T. (2010). A Wandering Mind Is an Unhappy Mind. Science, pp.932–932.

Berkovich-Ohana, A., et al. ((2015). Repetitive speech elicits widespread deactivation in the human cortex: 'The Mantra Effect?. Brain and Behavior, 5(7).

Try the 90-second rule: Whole Brain Living, The Anatomy of Choice and the Four Characters That Drive Our Life, Dr Jill Bolte Taylor, Hay House, 2021

CHAPTER TEN:

Alexander, R., et al. (2021), The neuroscience of positive emotions and affect: Implications for cultivating happiness and wellbeing, Neuroscience & Biobehavioral Reviews, Volume 121, Pages 220-249,

Watson, R., et al, (2020). A qualitative study exploring adolescents' experience of brief behavioural activation for depression and its impact on the symptom of anhedonia. Psychology and Psychotherapy: Theory, Research and Practice, 94(2).

Starr, L. R., et al. (2017). Depressive symptoms and the anticipation and experience of uplifting events in everyday life. Journal of Clinical Psychology.

Erika Forbes quotes: Maron, D.F. (n.d.). Can Talk Therapy Help People Who Are Unable to Experience Joy? Scientific American. https://www.scientificamerican.com/article/can-talk-therapy-help-people-who-are-unable-to-experience-joy/

Ellen Hendriksen quotes: Quick and Dirty Tips TM. (n.d.). What to Do When Nothing Feels Good. https://www.quickanddirtytips.com/articles/what-to-do-when-nothing-feels-good/

Chen, K., et al. (2021). Virtual Reality Reward Training for Anhedonia: A Pilot Study. Frontiers in Psychology, 11.

Kurtz, J. L., & Lyubomirsky, S. (2013). Happiness promotion: Using mindful photography to increase positive emotion and appreciation. In J. J. Froh & A. C. Parks (Eds.), Activities for teaching positive psychology: A guide for instructors (pp. 133–136). American Psychological Association.

Hazlett, L., et al. (2021) Exploring neural mechanisms of the health benefits of gratitude in women: A randomized controlled trial,Brain, Behavior, and Immunity, Volume 95.

Jackowska, M., et al. (2016). The impact of a brief gratitude intervention on subjective well-being, biology and sleep. Journal of Health Psychology, 21(10), pp.2207–2217.

Emmons RA., et al. (2011) What we know, what we need to know. In: Sheldon KM, Kashdan TB, Steger MF, editors. Designing positive psychology: Taking stock and moving forward. New York, NY: Oxford University Press; pp. 248–262.

Shipon, R. W. (2007). Gratitude: Effect on perspectives and blood pressure of inner-city African-American hypertensive patients. Dissertation Abstracts International: Section B: The Sciences and Engineering.

Kumar, A, et al. (2018). Undervaluing Gratitude: Expressers Misunderstand the Consequences of Showing Appreciation. Psychological Science, pp.1423–1435.

Keeler, J.R., et al. (2015). The neurochemistry and social flow of singing: bonding and oxytocin. Frontiers in Human Neuroscience.

Hunter, M.R., et al. (2019). Urban Nature Experiences Reduce Stress in the Context of Daily Life Based on Salivary Biomarkers. Frontiers in Psychology.

Tsai, H.-Y., et al. (2011). Sunshine-exposure variation of human striatal dopamine D2/D3 receptor availability in healthy volunteers. Progress in Neuro-Psychopharmacology and Biological Psychiatry, 35(1), pp.107–110.

Shinhmar .H., et al.(2021). Weeklong improved colour contrasts sensitivity after single 670 nm exposures associated with enhanced mitochondrial function. Scientific Reports, 11(1), p.22872.

McGlone, F., et al. (2014). Discriminative and Affective Touch: Sensing and Feeling. Neuron, 82(4), pp.737–755.

Walker, S.C., et al. (2017). C-tactile afferents: Cutaneous mediators of oxytocin release during affiliative tactile interactions? Neuropeptides, 64, pp.27–38.

CHAPTER ELEVEN:

Cuevas J, (2019). "Neurotransmitters and Their Life Cycle". Reference Module in Biomedical Sciences. Elsevier

Höflich, A., et al. (2018). Circuit Mechanisms of Reward, Anhedonia, and Depression. International Journal of Neuropsychopharmacology, 22(2), pp.105–118.

Diagnosis of dysregulated dopamine:

https://my.clevelandclinic.org/health/articles/22588-dopamine-deficiency

Blum K., ,et al (2014) . Dopaminergic Neurogenetics of Sleep Disorders in Reward Deficiency Syndrome (RDS). J Sleep Disord Ther. 2014

Graf H, et al. (2019). Serotonergic, Dopaminergic, and Noradrenergic Modulation of Erotic Stimulus Processing in the Male Human Brain. J Clin Med. 2019;8(3):363.

Volkow, Nora D. et al. (2015). The Brain on Drugs: From Reward to Addiction. Cell, 162(4), pp.712–725.

Takano, A., et al. (2004). Estimation of the time-course of dopamine D2 receptor occupancy in living human brain from plasma pharmacokinetics of antipsychotics. The International Journal of Neuropsychopharmacology, pp.19–26.

Nawijn L., et al. (2010) Vacationers Happier, but Most not Happier After a Holiday. Applied Research in Quality of Life.

De Bloom, J., et al. (2012). Vacation (after-) effects on employee health and well-being, and the role of vacation activities, experiences and sleep. Journal of Happiness Studies, 14(2), pp.613–633.

Zald, D.H., (2004). Dopamine Transmission in the Human Striatum during Monetary Reward Tasks. Journal of Neuroscience, [online] 24(17), pp.4105–4112.

MacLeod, A. K., et al. (2008). Increasing well-being through teaching goal setting and planning skills: Results of a brief intervention. Journal of Happiness Studies: An Interdisciplinary Forum on Subjective Well-Being, 9(2), 185–196.

Warren, J. (2021) Goal Setting: How to Programme Your Brain – Psych Liverpool. https://www.psychliverpool.co.uk/student-life/study-resources/goal-setting-how-to-programme-brain/

Sramek, P., et al. (2000). Human physiological responses to immersion into water of different temperatures. European Journal of Applied Physiology, 81(5), pp.436–442.

Huberman, A. (2021). Controlling Your Dopamine For Motivation, Focus & Satisfaction. Huberman Lab. https://hubermanlab.com/controlling-your-dopamine-for-motivation-focus-and-satisfaction/.

Ruhé HG., et al. (2007). Mood is indirectly related to serotonin, norepinephrine, and dopamine levels in humans: a meta-analysis of monoamine depletion studies. Mol Psychiatry 2007; 12: 331- 59.

Young, S.N., (2007). How to increase serotonin in the human brain without drugs. Journal of psychiatry & neuroscience: JPN, 32(6), pp.394–9.

Carabotti, M., et al. (2015). The gut-brain axis: interactions between enteric microbiota, central and enteric nervous systems. Annals of gastroenterology, 28(2), pp.203–209.

Cardoso C., et al (2013) R. Intranasal oxytocin attenuates the cortisol response to physical stress: a dose-response study. Psychoneuroendocrinology.

McQuaid, R.J., et al. (2016). Relations between plasma oxytocin and cortisol: The stress buffering role of social support. Neurobiology of Stress, 3, pp.52–60.

Sumioka, H., et al. (2013). Huggable communication medium decreases cortisol levels. Scientific Reports, 3(1).

Sprecher S., et al. (2013) Taking turns: Reciprocal self-disclosure promotes liking in initial interactions, Journal of Experimental Social Psychology, Volume 49, Issue 5, Pages 860-866,

Spengler, F.B., et al. (2017). Oxytocin facilitates reciprocity in social communication. Social Cognitive and Affective Neuroscience, [online] 12(8), pp.1325–1333.

Martin, RA., et al (1999): "Daily occurrence of laughter: Relationships with age, gender, and Type A personality", vol. 12, no. 4 pp. 355-384.

Manninen, S., et al. (2017). Social Laughter Triggers Endogenous Opioid Release in Humans. The Journal of Neuroscience, [online] 37(25), pp.6125–6131.

Harber, V.J., et al. (1984). Endorphins and exercise. Sports medicine. 1(2), pp.154–71.

Rh, S., et al. (2017). Gender Differences in Depression in Representative National Samples: Meta-analyses of Diagnoses and Symptoms. [online] Psychological bulletin.

Barth, C., et al. (2015). Sex Hormones Affect Neurotransmitters and Shape the Adult Female Brain during Hormonal Transition Periods. Frontiers in Neuroscience, 9(37).

Angold, A. (1998). Puberty and depression: the roles of age, pubertal status and pubertal timing. Psychological Medicine, 28(1), pp.51–61.

Joffe, H. et al. (1998). Estrogen, serotonin, and mood disturbance: where is the therapeutic bridge? Biological Psychiatry, 44(9), pp.798–811.

Gordon, J.L., et al. (2018). Efficacy of Transdermal Estradiol and Micronized Progesterone in the Prevention of Depressive Symptoms in the Menopause Transition. JAMA Psychiatry, 75(2), p.149.

Norton, S., et al. (2014). Cognitive-behavior therapy for menopausal symptoms (hot flushes and night sweats). Menopause, 21(6), pp.574–578.

Johnson, J.M., et al. (2013). The Effect of Testosterone Levels on Mood in Men: A Review. Psychosomatics, 54(6), pp.509–514.

Trumble, B.C., et al. (2013). Age-independent increases in male salivary testosterone during horticultural activity among Tsimane forager-farmers. Evolution and Human Behavior, 34(5), pp.350–357.

CHAPTER TWELVE:

Sin, N.L., Wen, J.H., Klaiber, P., Buxton, O.M. and Almeida, D.M. (2020). Sleep duration and affective reactivity to stressors and positive events in daily life. Health Psychology, [online] 39(12).

Kang, J.-H., et al. (2009). Effects of an irregular bedtime schedule on sleep quality, daytime sleepiness, and fatigue among university students in Taiwan. BMC Public Health, 9(1).

Haghayegh, S., et al. (2019). Before-bedtime passive body heating by warm shower or bath to improve sleep: A systematic review and meta-analysis, Sleep Medicine Reviews, Volume 46, 2019,Pages 124-135.

Mead, M.N., (2008). Benefits of Sunlight: A Bright Spot for Human Health. Environmental Health Perspectives, [online] 116(4).

The science behind why hobbies can improve our mental health. (2021): https://research.reading.ac.uk/research-blog/the-science-behind-why-hobbies-can-improve-our-mental-health/.

Pressman, S.D., et al. (2009). Association of Enjoyable Leisure Activities with Psychological and Physical Well-Being. Psychosomatic Medicine, pp.725–732.

Appleton, J. (2018). The Gut-Brain Axis: Influence of Microbiota on Mood and Mental Health. Integrative Medicine: A Clinician's Journal, pp.28–32.

Cronin, P., et al. (2021). Dietary Fibre Modulates Gut Microbiota. Nutrients, 13(5), p.1655.

Lampariello, L.R., et al. (2012). The Magic Velvet Bean of Mucuna pruriens. Journal of Traditional and Complementary Medicine), pp.331–339. https://www.ncbi.nlm.nih.gov/pmc/articles/PMC3942911/.

Knüppel, A., et al. (2017). Sugar intake from sweet food and beverages, common mental disorder and depression: prospective findings from the Whitehall II study. Scientific Reports.

Muijs, L.T., et al. (2020). Glucose variability and mood in adults with diabetes: A systematic review. Endocrinology, Diabetes & Metabolism.

Wallace, C.W., et al. (2021). Obesity and dietary fat influence dopamine neurotransmission: exploring the convergence of metabolic state, physiological stress, and inflammation on dopaminergic control of food intake. Nutrition Research Reviews, pp.1–16.

Reyes, T.M. (2012). High-fat diet alters the dopamine and opioid systems: effects across development. International Journal of Obesity Supplements, 2(S2), pp. S25–S28.

Hryhorczuk, C., et al. (2016). Dampened Mesolimbic Dopamine Function and Signalling by Saturated but not Monounsaturated Dietary Lipids. Neuropsychopharmacology.

MENOPAUSE AND DIET:

Bedell, S., et al. (2014). The pros and cons of plant estrogens for menopause. The Journal of Steroid Biochemistry and Molecular Biology, 139, pp.225–236.

Barnard, N.D., et al. (2021). The Women's Study for the Alleviation of Vasomotor Symptoms (WAVS): a randomized, controlled trial of a plant-based diet and whole soybeans for postmenopausal women. Menopause (New York, N.Y.).

Messina, M. et al. (2016). Evaluation of the potential antidepressant effects of soybean isoflavones. Menopause, 23(12), pp.1348–1360.

Cheng, P.-F., et al. (2015). Do soy isoflavones improve cognitive function in postmenopausal women? A meta-analysis. Menopause, 22(2), pp.198–206.

Sherwood, A., et al. (2016). Effects of Exercise and Sertraline on Measures of Coronary Heart Disease Risk in Patients with Major Depression: Results From the SMILE-II Randomized Clinical Trial. Psychosomatic medicine, [online] 78(5), pp.602–9.

Craft, L.L, et al. (2004). The Benefits of Exercise for the Clinically Depressed. Primary care companion to the Journal of clinical psychiatry, [online] 6(3), pp.104–111. Available at: https://www.ncbi.nlm.nih.gov/pmc/articles/PMC474733/.

Reid, K.J., et al. (2010). Aerobic exercise improves self-reported sleep and quality of life in older adults with insomnia. Sleep Medicine, [online] 11(9), pp.934–940.

Exercise May Be Just as Effective as Medication For Treating Major Depression." ScienceDaily, Duke University. 27 October 1999. <www.sciencedaily.com/releases/1999/10/991027071931.htm>.

Gordon, B.R., et al. (2018). Association of Efficacy of Resistance Exercise Training with Depressive Symptoms. JAMA Psychiatry, 75(6), p.566.

Liu, P.Z. et al. (2018). Exercise-Mediated Neurogenesis in the Hippocampus via BDNF. Frontiers in Neuroscience.

Tsukiyama, Y., et al. (2017). Effects of exercise training on nitric oxide, blood pressure and antioxidant enzymes. Journal of Clinical Biochemistry and Nutrition, pp.180–186.

Gleeson, M., et al. (2011). The anti-inflammatory effects of exercise: mechanisms and implications for the prevention and treatment of disease. Nature reviews. Immunology, pp.607–15.

Anderson, E. et al. (2013). Effects of Exercise and Physical Activity on Anxiety. Frontiers in Psychiatry.

Keeler, J.R., et al. (2015). The neurochemistry and social flow of singing: bonding and oxytocin. Frontiers in Human Neuroscience.

Stewart, N.A.J. et al. (2016). It's better together: The psychological benefits of singing in a choir. Psychology of Music, 44(6), pp.1240–1254.

Xygalatas, D., et al. (2011). Quantifying collective effervescence: Heart-rate dynamics at a fire-walking ritual. Communicative & Integrative Biology, 4(6), pp.735–738.

Hanna, J.L. (1995). The power of dance: health and healing. Journal of Alternative and Complementary Medicine (New York, N.Y.), [online] 1(4), pp.323–331.

Interview with Professor Howard Markman: News, A.B.C. (n.d.). Married Couples Who Play Together Stay Together. [online] ABC News. Available at: https://abcnews.go.com/Health/Family/story?id=5387217&page=1

Aron, A., et al. (2000). Couples' shared participation in novel and arousing activities and experienced relationship quality. Journal of Personality and Social Psychology, 78(2), 273–284.

Interview with Dr Arthur Aron: Creating love in the lab: The 36 questions that spark intimacy. Berkeley News. Available at: https://news.berkeley.edu/2015/02/12/love-in-the-lab/.

Women's unentitlement: The Female Lead. Women at Work. https://www.thefemalelead.com/women-at-work

Lopez Portillo, B. (2020). Disclosure Reciprocity. Encyclopaedia of Personality and Individual Differences, pp.1137–1139.

Aron, A., et al. (2000). Couples' shared participation in novel and arousing activities and experienced relationship quality. Journal of Personality and Social Psychology, pp.273–284.

Kret, M.E. et al. (2017). Pupil-mimicry conditions trust in partners: moderation by oxytocin and group membership. Proceedings of the Royal Society B: Biological Sciences, 284(1850), p.20162554.

Aune, K.S., et al. (2002). Antecedents and consequences of adult play in romantic relationships. Personal Relationships 9, 279-286.

Stressed parents create stressed kids: Kids Pick Up On Everything – How parental stress is toxic to kids, David Code, Createspace, September 2011.

Vartanian, L. R., et al. (2016). Clutter, Chaos, and Overconsumption. Environment and Behavior, [online] 49(2), pp.215–223.

Windheim, K., et al. (2011). Mirror gazing in body dysmorphic disorder and healthy controls: effects of duration of gazing. Behaviour research and therapy. https://www.semanticscholar.org/paper/Mirror-gazing-in-body-dysmorphic-disorder-and-of-of-Windheim-Veale/43345ce219051f23d41de9e9fbadae20c57eecd2

Boubekri, M., et al. (2014). Impact of Windows and Daylight Exposure on Overall Health and Sleep Quality of Office Workers: A Case-Control Pilot Study. Journal of Clinical Sleep Medicine.

Kobayashi, H., et al. (2019). Combined Effect of Walking and Forest Environment on Salivary Cortisol Concentration. Frontiers in Public Health, 7.

Spence, C. (2022). On the benefits of the blue gym: Multisensory well-being on/by the water. https://tangibleterritory.art/journal/issue-4-content/.

Sturm, V. E., et al. (2022). Big smile, small self: Awe walks promote prosocial positive emotions in older adults. Emotion, 22(5), 1044–1058.

OTHER APPROACHES TO ANHEDONIA:

PsilocybinStudies.org. (n.d.). Studies Archives. [online] Available at: https://www.psilocybinstudies.org/category/studies/#:~:text=Psilocybin%20with%20psychological%20support%20appears%20to%20improve%20processing

Nógo, D., et al (2022). The effect of ketamine on anhedonia: improvements in dimensions of anticipatory, consummatory, and motivation-related reward deficits. Psychopharmacology.

Millón, C., et al. (2019). Role of the galanin N-terminal fragment (1-15) in anhedonia: Involvement of the dopaminergic mesolimbic system. Journal of Psychopharmacology, pp.737–747.

All Accessed December 2022